THE ALGORITHMIC COMPOSER

THE COMPUTER MUSIC AND DIGITAL AUDIO SERIES

■

Volume 16 • The Computer Music and Digital Audio Series

THE ALGORITHMIC COMPOSER

David Cope

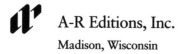

A-R Editions, Inc.

Madison, Wisconsin

Library of Congress Cataloging-in-Publication Data

[CD]

Cope, David
    The algorithmic composer / David Cope
        p. cm. — (The computer music and digital audio series ; v. 16)
    Includes bibliographical references (p.) and index.
    ISBN 0-89579-454-3 (alk. paper)
    1. Computer composition. 2. Alice (Computer file) 3. Composition
(Music)—Computer programs. I. Title II. Series

    MT56 .C668 2000
    781.3'4—dc21   99-059109

    A-R Editions, Inc., Madison, Wisconsin 53717-1903
        © 2000 All rights reserved.
        Printed in the United States of America
        10 9 8 7 6 5 4 3 2 1

Contents

Preface

On page 246 of *Experiments in Musical Intelligence* (Cope 1996), I wrote, "In the first and last chapters of *Computers and Musical Style*, I waxed eloquently, or so I thought, about an EMI workstation. The code presented with this book does not compose on such a workstation, nor does one yet exist. The dream continues of a digital extension of myself that provides music from which I can extract at will. This music would be *in* my style and *of* the nature of my current work." *The Algorithmic Composer* provides an historical perspective and describes a program that resembles such a digital extension.

The Algorithmic Composer is designed to complete a trilogy of books of which *Computers and Musical Style* and *Experiments in Musical Intelligence* constitute the first two volumes. *Computers and Musical Style* presents the foundation for the computational analysis of musical style. *Experiments in Musical Intelligence* extends these analytical concepts and provides code capable of generating new works in the style of music stored in its database. *The Algorithmic Composer* describes in detail the need for, concepts of, and use of computer-assisted composition. *The Algorithmic Composer* includes a CD-ROM containing the Alice (ALgorithmically Integrated Composing Environment) program, a subset of Experiments in Musical Intelligence, along with CD-quality performances of many of the musical examples presented in the book.

The Alice program extends user-composed passages, develops potentials of composer-created germ ideas, and offers new ideas when inspiration temporarily wanes. The program can also compose as much relevant music as desired—from a single note to an entire section in the user's general style as evident in the music in its database and in the style of an in-progress composition. Alice works *with* composers by extending user-composed music rather than *for* composers by creating entire works in a given style. This collaborative approach should interest composers who wish to augment their current composing processes as well as experiment in new directions. Theorists, especially those studying musical style, should find this book useful for their research as well as valuable in the teaching of college-level music theory courses. Musicologists studying musical style and hierarchical structure should also find the book and program useful.

Chapter 1 of *The Algorithmic Composer* presents definitions, history, theory, and descriptions of a few approaches to algorithmic composition. This chapter includes historical examples of some of the ways composers throughout past centuries have implemented algorithms in their composing processes. Chapter 1 further describes how most algorithmic computer composition programs generate new musical ideas from mathematic, connectionist, or pattern-processing algorithms (Rowe 1993) and how these techniques do not offer all the potential that computational means can provide. Many composers seek a program that can track their in-progress compositions and that, by combining found harmonic, motivic, and structural ideas with elements of their style, can produce logical musical continuations.

This background sets the stage for the ensuing discussion of Alice, the program presented in this book and on the accompanying CD-ROM. The discussion of Alice begins with background information on the Experiments in Musical Intelligence program described in numerous sources (see Cope 1990, 1991a, 1991b, 1992a, 1996) and the Simple Analytic Recombinant Algorithm (SARA) program (Cope 1996). These descriptions are followed by an overview of Alice, a program that hierarchically analyzes a work in progress, interactively explores solutions to certain composition problems, and produces alternative routes at musical pivot points.

Chapter 2 introduces three programs found on this book's CD-ROM. These programs successively implement increasing amounts of intelligent-like behavior. The Fun program offers users opportunities to explore simple visual graphics. Déjà vu, on the other hand, incorporates analysis, recognition, and creativity in a drawing environment. The BackTalk program, in contrast, explores language interactively by using association and ultimately adaption. Chapter 2 continues by attempting to define intelligence and concludes with some of the ways Alice benefits from the assets of each of the three programs presented in the chapter.

Chapter 3 presents the basic principles of the Alice inference processes, including grouping techniques and rules inheritance. This chapter further discusses rules inference, that is, the ability of the Alice program to infer voicings and progressions that do not exist explicitly in the database. These inferences range from simple re-voicings of progressions to the creation of new versions. Rules inference is based in part on the notion of heuristics, or the ability of a program to learn or develop principles on its own.

Chapter 4 covers new rules creation, rules abstraction and approximation, non-pitch creativity, and texture. These transformational processes create new music in ways that differ from inheritance and inference. Figures in this chapter provide detailed examples of how Alice extrapolates new rules, in part by separating voice-leading from pitch and applying the basic principles to a variety of new musical circumstances.

Chapter 5 presents the structural coherence techniques used by Alice. Since music resulting from rules inheritance and inference generally wanders without any sense of balance or development, the structural integrity of new music requires formal logic. This chapter shows how, when called on for algorithmic composition, Alice inherits the structure of the music in its database. This inheritance requires a deep hierarchical analysis as well as a specialized search for structural meta-patterns. Important structural patterns called *earmarks* also play a critical role in Alice's ability to analyze and generate logical musical structures. Chapter 5 also shows how earmarks indicate, at least to the experienced listener, important attributes about a listener's temporal position in a work and foreshadow especially important structural events. Earmarks can further contribute to expectations of points of arrival or the end of a movement or work. This chapter also shows how Alice integrates earmarks into their immediate environment.

Chapter 5 then discusses how Alice protects earmarks and musical signatures—patterns derived from pattern matching according to processes described in Cope 1991b and 1996. Such protection ensures that earmarks and signatures survive the rules-composing process and provide more style coherence to resulting output. This chapter further shows how Alice utilizes a special program capable of recognizing pattern similarities at a variety of hierarchical levels. This analysis algorithm operates independently and quite differently from Alice's signature recognition program.

Chapter 6 presents the Alice interface. This presentation includes Alice's notation program, the various analytical windows, and the hierarchical analysis and generation programs. This chapter also describes the `loop` macro and presents examples of using this macro in functions to enhance code readability. The chapter further describes the analysis interface that presents musical data by way of a series of instructive graphs. Chapter 6 then shows how the hierarchical interface presents its analysis. The lower layer in this analysis reveals repetitions or near repetitions of individual phrases. Middleground analysis shows the SPEAC patterning resulting from textural tension and release. The highest level, the one showing an entire work, produces a single SPEAC character from which all others branch.

Chapter 7 outlines many of Alice's implications and the challenges such programs present to composers, performers, audiences, musicologists, and theorists. This chapter also discusses how the differentiation between human- and machine-composed music can become blurred. For example, in an ultimate interactive-composing program, works emerge from an integration of composer and program so complete that even expert analysts cannot identify their origins.

Throughout this book I have incorporated examples of a number of recent works by my Experiments in Musical Intelligence program and works composed interactively with Alice. The CD-ROM includes performances of many of these works and others presented in the figures in the book. The index for *The Algorithmic Composer* is followed by a combined index for this volume plus *Experiments in Musical Intelligence* and *Computers and Musical Style* so that readers of the current volume can locate relevant information in this book and the preceding two volumes of this trilogy.

Readers are expected to be able to read music and have a practical knowledge of the general operation of personal computers. While it would be advantageous to have read the previous volumes of this trilogy and have a rudimentary ability to program in Common LISP, neither is necessary for understanding the fundamental concepts presented in *The Algorithmic Composer*.

The version of Alice on this book's CD-ROM is not the one that I personally use. The Alice described here concentrates on compositional techniques, while the one that I have written for myself incorporates more complicated composition, notation, and performance subprograms that, because of the need for clarity of presentation and the limited scope of this book, could not be included here. Whenever I wish to refer to my own version of Alice, I do so explicitly. Readers should be careful to distinguish between these two versions of Alice so as not to build false expectations of the software on the CD-ROM. Those wishing to extend their version of Alice beyond that presented here can e-mail me at howell@cats.ucsc.edu for examples of these subprograms.

I wish to thank again all those individuals who have contributed so very much to this body of work, especially Douglas Hofstadter, who has spoken in great detail about my work in his numerous lectures and presentations. I also wish to thank Bill Schottstaedt of Stanford University for creating and making available his Common Music Notation, which serves as the output notation module of Alice. Thanks also go to Alexander Repenning for his work on the QuickTime® Musical Instrument interface and the GRAME research team of Lyon, France, who provided MidiShare, the software MIDI interface used in Alice. Jon Hallstrom and Dale Skrien of Colby College in Maine created the Alice MIDI file load and save code. Without the moral support and advice from colleagues such as these, this trilogy could not have been completed.

ONE

Background

■ ALGORITHMIC COMPOSERS

The term *algorithm* originates from the Greek word *arithmós* (number) and the Arabic word *algorism* (number series). Rosen (1988) defines algorithm as a "corruption of . . . algorism which comes from the book *Kitab al jabr w'al-muqabala* (Rules of Restoration and Reduction) written by Abu Ja'far Mohammed ibn Musa al-Khowarizmi in the ninth century. The word *algorism* originally referred only to the rules of performing arithmetic using Arabic numerals" (Rosen 1988, p. 49ff). Today the term *algorithm* is roughly defined as "a set of rules for solving a problem in a finite number of steps" (Webster 1991, p. 35). This definition, applied liberally, includes almost any process that involves rules—which in essence means almost any process.

We use algorithms whenever we reduce an activity to a series of rules or instructions that automate that activity (Ames 1987; Buxton 1978; Cope 1991a; Sedgewick 1983). "Examples of algorithmic methods include travel directions and the rules of algebra. Just as an algebraic equation specifies *relationships* between symbolic objects, an algorithm specifies *actions* on symbolic objects. Most things one does repeatedly with a purpose can be considered algorithmic" (Loy 1989, p. 293). Some algorithms are explicit, such as speech—a complex activity accomplished by a set of mental rules or instructions. Some algorithms are implicit, such as blinking our eyes—an involuntary action necessary for healthy sight.

Obviously then, algorithms do not require computers, even though that association often occurs. Explicit written algorithms that do not use computers are often called *paper* algorithms.

> The analysis of algorithms can be shown to demonstrate not merely clever means to ends, but, more important, it can reveal the value systems—the true aims—of individuals and cultures: because what is formalized into algorithms is always the essence of what is felt to be so central to an enterprise as to warrant such expenditure of effort. For instance, we shall see that the formal elements of a musical style are often its most salient and revealing aspects. (Loy 1989, pp. 296–97)

Algorithms in music are used in a variety of ways, including sound synthesis, sampling, and composing, wherever benefits result from applying a series of rules or instructions. Of these, algorithms for composing music have the most serious philosophical implications since they tend to replace what many feel are activities more rightfully the domain of humans: principally the freedom of choice but including more illusory concepts, such as imagination, soul, inspiration, and intuition. However, as we will soon discover, what some see as choice, others see as routine, easily replaced by a series of instructions.

Many terms have been applied to algorithmic music composition. *Algorithmic composition* itself, for example, seems simply and clearly to differentiate this form of composing from more traditional methods. However, as we will see, most composers employ algorithms when composing. That is, most composers apply rules, steps, or sets of instructions when composing music, especially when composing music in a particular *style*. The terms *computer-assisted composition* or *computer-aided composition* are also often used to refer to algorithmic composition, although I fear their connotations may be somewhat pejorative. Assistance usually implies weakness, a need for help, when in fact many, maybe even most, algorithmic composers actually turn to algorithmic composition out of curiosity and a search for knowledge rather than need. In addition, the terms *computer-assisted* and *computer-aided* restrict the use of algorithms to computers.

Interactive composition, another popular term for algorithmic composition, implies a close-knit collaboration between composer and computer that may not necessarily exist. Many composers use algorithms that do not *interact* at all, they only respond appropriately when prompted by their users. The term *automated music* does not take into account the human contributions in both creating the algorithm and then using it. Both *machine composition* and *computer composing* are also used to represent algorithmic composition, but with less frequency. Both terms suffer the misconception that hardware rather than software actually does the composing. Thus, in general I will use the term *algorithmic composition* since it seems to cover more bases and with less baggage. However, since all these terms, including *algorithmic composition,* are flawed in some way, I will occasionally use the other terms I have mentioned here, especially when one or the other of them seems more appropriate.

Composers have utilized various types of algorithms in composing their music for centuries. Constraints of almost any kind require algorithmic solutions, whether such constraints are dictated by a composer or style. This seems especially true with algorithm defined as "a set of rules for solving a problem in a finite number of steps." Since we assume composers use finite numbers of steps and not infinite numbers of steps and that composing itself can be seen as a problem requiring solving, it seems natural to view the process of composing music as algorithmic, no matter who the composer is. Tonal part-writing, for example, which dictates rules limiting creativity, acts as an algorithm around which composers embroider their own stylistic choices. Fugues and other contrapuntal formalisms represent constraints and often require severely limiting algorithms.

Fourteenth-century isorhythmic compositions represent early and obvious examples of strict algorithmic composition. The practice of composing isorhythmic music in the fourteenth century incorporated a *color* (set of intervals) and a *talea* (rhythmic pattern). The isorhythmic motet, devised in part by Philippe de Vitry (1291–1361) but brought to its zenith by Guillaume de Machaut (1300–1377), consisted of various lengths of color and talea that, once begun, might not coincide again for many repetitions. Figure 1.1 gives a simple example from an isorhythmic motet. The talea is shown in figure 1.1a. This talea consists of twelve notes or entrances, not including the interpolated rests. The color appears in figure 1.1b and lasts for thirty-six notes. Figure 1.1c shows how the two fit together in a work by de Vitry, the tenor line from *Garrit gallus—In nova fert—Neuma* (see Hoppin 1978). Here, the twelve notes of the talea fit neatly three times into the thirty-six-beat color, a coincidence that might more typically, with more irregularly related segments, occur several dozen times further into a work. For example, adding a single note to the talea of figure 1.1a (making it thirteen) would mean that the talea and color would not coincide again until the four-hundred-and-sixty-eighth note. Observe the manner in which, once begun, the two elements proceed inexorably to their conclusion in figure 1.1c. Note as well that at any given point the next notes can be predicted if one knows the color and talea and the process by which the music is constructed. Such rigor exemplifies the isorhythmic algorithm—the simultaneous repeating of unequal-lengthed pitch and duration lists—for composing this kind of music.

Strict adherence to an established musical form constitutes yet another compositional use of musical algorithms. For example,

Figure 1.1   An example from an isorhythmic motet: (a) talea; (b) color; (c) composite from de Vitry's *Garritt gallus—In nova fert—Neuma.*

imagining a song form of the medieval period, a dance form of the baroque, or a sonata allegro form of the classical period of Western music history as symbols in a flowchart—one way to describe an algorithm—does not seem unreasonable. Figure 1.2a shows a flowchart for producing remainders after all possible consecutive halvings of a given number have taken place. Figure 1.2b presents a similar diagram describing a medieval song form called the *virelai*. The virelai here is represented by letters for both text (R equals refrain and L equals line here) and music (A and B) and appears as a musical form and as a flowchart. With the exception of the number of elements in the flowcharts, the two processes appear visually quite similar, although obviously I am not attempting to compare actual mathematical operations with musical operations. Neither process

Figure 1.2 (a) A flowchart for producing the remainder after all halvings of a given number; (b) a simple diagram of a medieval virelai represented by letters for both text and music expressed traditionally (R equals refrain and L equals line here) and as a flowchart.

a.

b.

text:	R1 R2	L1 L2	L3 L4	R1 R2
music:	A	B B	A	A

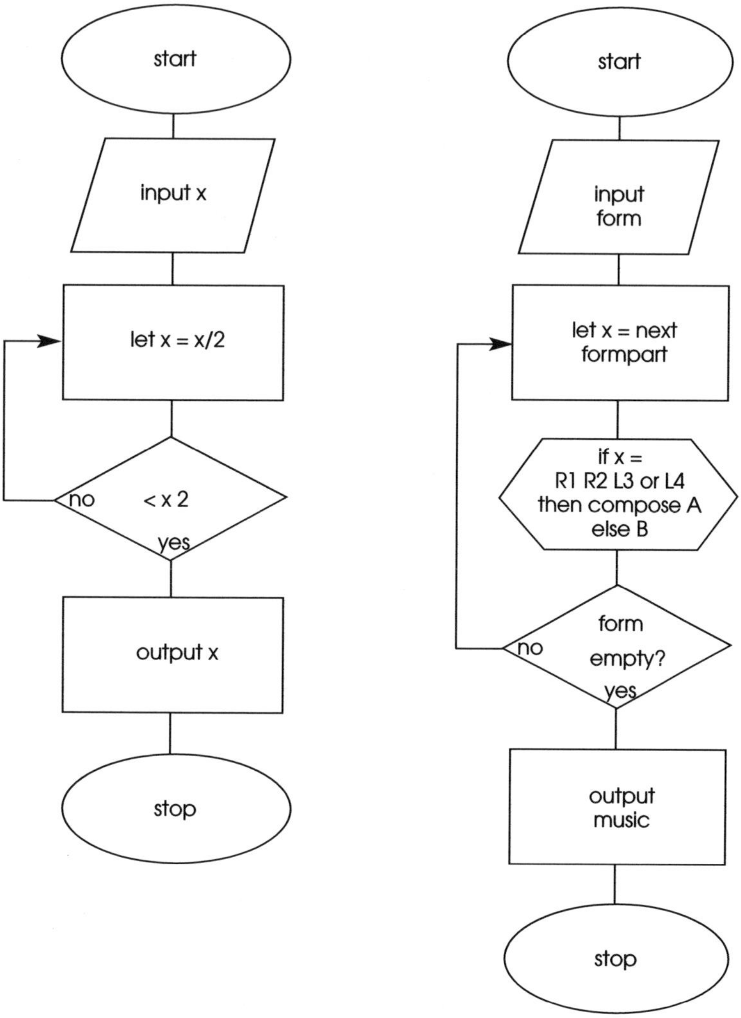

suffers from the flowchart abstraction. Both processes indicate how a particular problem can be solved in a finite number of steps.

Figure 1.3 shows an early example of algorithmic composition from the seventeenth century. This *rota* (wheel) appears in Giovanni Andrea Bontempi's (1624–1705) *New Method of Composing Four Voices, by means of which one thoroughly ignorant of the art of music can begin to compose* (1660; see also Lester 1993). Each tier—aligned inside to outside layer—of this *rota* contains numbers representing scale degrees in mixolydian mode for one of the four voices of a new composition. The music below the *rota* shows a sample phrase derived from consecutive choices in a clockwise direction appearing in F mixolydian. Any order of chords shown here produces correct results. Bontempi further describes how to calculate rhythms and cadences for more pleasing results (not shown). Bontempi's work represents one of the many forerunners of contemporary algorithmic composition. Other such forerunners include the *Musikalisches Würfelspiele,* or musical dice games, of the seventeenth century composed by Mozart, Haydn, C.P.E. Bach, and Johann Philipp Kirnberger, among others (see Cope 1996).

Johann Joseph Fux established another algorithmic-like process by describing many of the basic contrapuntal techniques of tonal music (1725). Although Fux was not the first to codify such rules, he was certainly the most notable and widely read. Griesinger (1810) notes, "Haydn took infinite pains to assimilate the theory of Fux; he went through the whole work laboriously, writing out the exercises, then laying them aside for a few weeks, to look them over again later and polish them until he was satisfied he had done everything exactly right." Expressed simply but eloquently, Fux's rules encompass the following:

> First rule: From one perfect consonance to another perfect consonance one must proceed in contrary or oblique motion.
>
> Second rule: From a perfect consonance to an imperfect consonance one may proceed in any of the three motions.
>
> Third rule: From an imperfect consonance to a perfect consonance one must proceed in contrary or oblique motion.
>
> Fourth rule: From one imperfect consonance to another imperfect consonance one may proceed in any of the three motions. (Fux 1943)

Many notable composers, including Bach (Spitta 1899), Mozart (1822), Beethoven (Nottebohm 1873), Cherubini (1837), and Hindemith (1942), referenced Fux in their letters, writings, or various diaries. Most tonal composers of the common-practice period generally

Figure 1.3   From Giovanni Andrea Bontempi's (1624–1705) *New Method of Composing Four Voices, by means of which one thoroughly ignorant of the art of music can begin to compose* (1660).

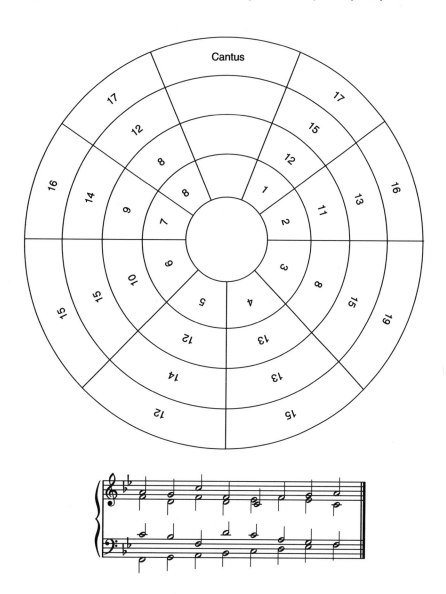

adhered to Fux's basic rules. Present-day theory books dealing with the common-practice period incorporate versions of these rules in their approach to analysis and imitative composition.

The rules listed here merely scratch the surface of those required to produce correct common-practice voice leading. For example, an emphasis on stepwise motion and leaps followed by stepwise contrary motion often increases the complexity of composing music in this general style. Figure 1.4 shows a partially complete example of one-against-one two-voice first-species counterpoint. Note how the unfinished line has little choice but to move to the note shown in parentheses, as those that precede it seem to inevitably progress to their following notes.

In figure 1.5a we see how Fux's rules create a simple contrary motion scale-like passage in two-voice second (2:1) species counterpoint. This example is followed by three of the many similar examples found in Bach that follow these rules with slight variations (figure 1.5b–d). In figure 1.5b the upper voice is embellished by rocking thirds in the final beat of the first measure. However, the basic configuration remains the same as in the example by Fux in figure 1.5a. In figure 1.5c the intervals are changed to match the key, and in figure 1.5d the voices are inverted. However, these variations do little to mask the basic predictability here. Once we have observed the model, the examples seem logical extrapolations.

Composers of the common-practice period also utilized melodic rules or templates. Most melodic lines, for example, move stepwise with leaps followed by either contrary direction steps or continued leaps outlining triads. To gauge the predictability of these and other traits, I coded a very small program in LISP that, when given the first three notes of a melodic line, predicts the next note. When correct, the program continues to predict on the basis of its answer. When wrong, the program retracts the incorrect note, accepts the correct note, and then predicts the next note and so on.

This *Melody Predictor* program found on this book's CD-ROM has three basic rules in its algorithm:

1. If the preceding three notes represent a scale, continue the scale in the same direction.

2. If the preceding interval leaps, either continue leaping in the same direction following triadic formation or fall back a scale step in the opposite direction (decision based on note motion previous to the leap).

Figure 1.4   Fux-like one-against-one first-species counterpoint.

Figure 1.5   (a) Fux (1943, p. 48); (b) Bach *Invention* No. 1, mm. 9–10; (c) Bach *Goldberg Variations* No. 12, m. 11; (d) Bach *Well-Tempered Clavier*, Fugue No. 15, m. 5.

3. If the preceding three notes represent the continuance of a pattern, continue the pattern (including repeated notes).

Melody Predictor uses the scale of the piece under analysis and does not predict chromatic notes.

Figures 1.6a and c show two melodies given to the predictor, the initial themes of Mozart's piano sonatas K. 279 and K. 533. Figures

Figure 1.6   (a) Mozart *Sonata* K. 279, mvt. 1, mm. 1–3; (b) results of the Melody Predictor; (c) Mozart *Sonata* K. 533, mvt. 1, mm. 1–4; (d) results of the Melody Predictor.

1.6b and d show the results of the program's attempts to predict the notes Mozart chose. Sixty-four and 71 percent of its guesses correctly match. These percentages are quite high when compared to the percentages earned by the program when attempting to match randomly created tonal melodies, which ranged between 0 and 12 percent on balance. While strikingly accurate in the case of the Mozart examples, especially given the simplicity of the program, this does not prove either that Mozart was a predictable composer or that with a little revision such a program could compete with Mozart's melodic composing skills. However, the Melody Predictor's results do show, and quite convincingly, that Mozart used rather straightforward rules to compose some of his melodies and that his note choices were often based, at least in part, on the rules listed previously. While we might rather imagine that each note of Mozart's music was an inspired original, the fact remains that a great deal of his music, like most of his contemporaries of the classical period, follows algorithms and that these algorithms produce relatively predictable results. The extraordinary nature of Mozart's musical genius arises from those occasions when he avoids the pedestrian choices.

Heinrich Schenker's (1933) method of describing middle and background motions in his definitions of the *Urlinie,* or fundamental line, suggests that tonal music almost inevitably falls scalewise from the third, fifth, or eighth scale degree of a diatonic scale down to the ultimate tonic note. While such a description oversimplifies his process of revealing fundamental structure, it suggests that tonal music follows a rather strict algorithm. While neither Schenker nor most other analysts would assert that tonal composers composed by fleshing out these simple downward scales, the fact that these background scales can be found without too much difficulty in a significant number of common-practice tonal works makes them logical candidates for algorithmic creation. Figure 1.7a–c provides examples of Schenker's reductive process, which culminates in the previously mentioned downward scale, here from the fifth degree of the C-major scale. Of course, Schenker's approach to analysis deserves a far more in-depth discussion than it receives here (Schenker 1933). However, this brief presentation demonstrates, I hope, the basic algorithmic nature of the approach.

More recently, contemporary twelve-tone or serial composition follows even stricter algorithms. The ensuing description provides a succinct overview of serial techniques:

> The following postulates, then, must be understood to refer only to the set on which a given work, or section of a work, may be based.
>
> 1. The set comprises all twelve notes of the semitonal scale, arranged in a specific linear order.
>
> 2. No note appears more than once within the set.
>
> 3. The set is stable in any of its linear aspects: prime, inversion, retrograde, and retrograde-inversion.
>
> 4. The set in each of its four transformations (that is, linear aspects) is stable upon any degree of the semitonal scale. (Perle 1962, pp. 2–3)

These postulates relate interestingly both in number and in general flexibility to those of Fux. They also have affinity with those of de Vitry in terms of fixed sets of notes in particular orders. As with de Vitry and Fux, serial procedures have had significant impact on many contemporary composers, even those using quite different approaches. Boulez has noted, "I have found that if you have not gone through this experience of twelve-tone writing, and tried to enlarge upon it and go forward, you can fall into these traps of chance and the parascientific. These latter are mythologies, ways of escaping the real center" (Cope and Wilson 1969).

Figure 1.7   A foreground, middleground, and background of Mozart's melody shown in figure 1.6a.

Figure 1.8 shows a serial passage by Ernst Krenek in which the row appears only in its original form. Note how once the ear has been exposed to the row and a new repetition begun, each new pitch (in name, not necessarily octave) can be predicted. The serial algorithm, once begun, allows composers few choices.

Algorithmic processes can sometimes occur quite subtly. In fact, the rules that we follow may be subconsciously self-imposed when we face arbitrary obstacles while composing. For example, music notation itself has constraints that often require algorithmic solutions. Plotting clef changes in many instrumental parts requires complex strategizing to avoid using excessive ledger lines. The interplay between composer and notation can be a dynamic one. In effect, notation limits what composers compose. Such problems are especially noticeable with computer notation programs in which some ideas translate easily from the imagination to the visual correlate, and other ideas do not.

Familiarity with instruments can also lead composers to create algorithms for composing idiomatic music for them. Classical music includes many examples of works that demonstrate how their composers write well for certain instruments and not for others. Chopin's and Liszt's orchestrations, for example, represent relatively poor examples of instrumental writing. Factoring in the complications posed by performance spaces, idiosyncrasies of performers, imposed deadlines, and so on makes for a quite impressive list of constraints that inhibit composer freedom and argue for algorithmic solutions.

Performance algorithms offer further demonstration of both significant obstacles to, and wellsprings of, inspiration.

Figure 1.8   The beginning of Ernst Krenek's *Suite for Violoncello Solo.*

Keyboard instruments of the old and new styles .   .   . have proved to be more than mere tools assisting the composer in the process of sketching. Some composers were also great performers on the organ or clavier, masterful executants who spent inspired hours with their favorite instruments. To them the keyboard served often as a springboard for their tonal imagination. Bach and Handel, César Franck and Bruckner on the organ bench, Haydn, Mozart and Couperin on the harpsichord, Beethoven, Schumann, Brahms, Chopin and Liszt on the modern piano were all famous for their extemporaneous playing and composing. And many of their compositions originated in this impromptu style, improvised in productive hours of instrumental performance. Later some of these fantasies were set into script from memory. (Dorian 1947, p. 130)

The literature is resplendent with examples of great composers using algorithms to help them realize their ideas.

Bach's first attempts at composition were, like all first attempts, defective. Without any instruction to lead him from step to step, he was obliged, like all those who enter on such a career without a guide, to do at first as well as he could. To run or leap up and down the instrument, to take both hands as full as all the five fingers will allow, and to proceed in this wild manner till they by chance find a resting place .   .   . (Forkel 1802)

Frederick Dorian speaks of the rigors of craft, and indirectly of algorithms, in his book *The Musical Workshop* in a chapter titled "The Bondage of Theory."

All knowledge springs from the craft of composition. Rules and skill guide the musician along the creative path. The point of procedure was given frequently on the basis of an already existing music. The composer borrowed, adopted or copied. Melodic loans were made from anywhere and everywhere. To borrow the music of another artist seemed natural. .   .   . Such procedure had no odor of plagiarism, but was the generally accepted state of affairs. (Dorian 1947, p. 150)

Given the context of this current book, it seems only fitting that Dorian should pair borrowing and rules.

> It may appear baffling to the modern mind that the invention of melodies was not considered a criterion for the greatness of the composer. Is it not the discovery of original and beautiful ideas that differentiates the true artist from the mere amateur? And is not that astonishing talent to create beautiful melodies the chief characteristic of the great composer? No, not according to the evaluation of this era. The high esteem of sheer inventiveness in music is a relatively recent trend. It is strongly conditioned by the romantic ideology of an inspirational art where the emphasis falls upon the creator's subjective experience rather than upon the objective architecture of the art work itself. (Dorian 1947, p. 153)

Dorian refers here to the pre-Beethovian classical period. In Dorian's view great music of this period survived the rigors of performance algorithms.

There are many other examples of composers who stretched their compositional craft through performance. In fact, with few exceptions, composers throughout history have devoted much of their time to composing on instruments. Even many of the exceptions who were not so performance adept worked at ancillary crafts such as conducting (e.g., Berlioz and Mahler). It is possible then to discover, at least in part, a composer's algorithm by studying the constraints imposed by the instruments on which they composed as well as the constraint-context of the period in which they lived.

In essence, deciding any aspect of a composition prior to its actual creation invites algorithmic composition. Defining the instrumentation, work length, vocal texts, and so on all involve implied constraints that by nature require some type of algorithmic solution. Even indeterminacy, by its prescriptive nature, requires algorithms for realization. As indeterminacy's greatest proponent John Cage points out,

> Those involved with the composition of experimental music find ways and means to remove themselves from the activities of the sounds they make. Some employ chance operations, derived from sources as ancient as the Chinese *Book of Changes,* or as modern as the tables of random numbers used also by physicists in research. Or, analogous to the Rorschach tests of psychology, the interpretation of imperfections in the paper upon which one is writing may provide a music free from one's memory and imagination. Geometrical means employing spatial superimpositions at variance with the ultimate performance in time may be used. The total field of possibilities may be roughly divided and the actual sounds within these divisions may be indicated as to number but left to the performer or to the splicer to choose. (Cage 1973, p. 9)

The rigor with which Cage applied indeterminate rules to divest himself from the "activities of the sounds" represents a classic algorithm.

Ultimately, then, algorithmic approaches are endemic to creativity in general and to music composition in particular. Composers throughout history have relied on the techniques, processes, and rules provided not only by their own inspiration but by the period or school to which they belonged. In fact, I believe that we demean composers when we ascribe to them creative powers that they have not used. Most composers have spent their lifetimes learning craft, techniques, and processes and deserve proper credit for their perspiration as well as their inspiration.

Defining all composers as algorithmic also helps diffuse the usually destructive segregation between composers who do not explicitly use algorithms for composing and those who explicitly do use algorithms for composing. Once all composers, to one degree or another, can be viewed as algorithmic, then programs such as the one described here will have integral relevance to all rather than the few who currently identify themselves as algorithmic.

It does not require such a supreme leap of faith, then, to imagine that in the future, possibly even in the near future, many if not most composers will have need for, or at least could make use of, algorithmic composing programs. It is also likely that with the almost ubiquitous use of computers in the First World at the turn of the millennium, such programs will generally be implemented on computers, especially personal computers.

■ ALGORITHMIC COMPOSING PROGRAMS

There are virtually hundreds of currently available compositionally-related computer music programs. Synthesis programs, for example, offer composers opportunities to create and modify timbres and sonic space (Loy 1989). Sequencer and notation programs provide visual and aural control over orders and playback of note sequences (Puckette 1991; Yavelow 1992). Computer analysis programs often reveal harmonic functions, pitch relationships, and so on (Castine et al. 1990). Computer composition programs typically generate quasi-random music using genetic algorithms, Markov chains, fractal and chaotic algorithms, and various mathematic, connectionist, or pattern-matching algorithms (Buxton 1978; Rowe 1993; Winsor 1987). However, important as each of these types of programs can be to composers, they do not offer all the potential that computational means can provide.

Common Music, Patchwork, and Symbolic Composer represent three of the more popular composition programs currently available. Each of these programs composes interactively with users. All three, interestingly, are written in Common LISP, which allows LISP-savvy users opportunities to extend the programs. The first two programs (Common Music and Patchwork) are, as of this writing, freely available in one form or another, and the third (Symbolic Composer) is a commercial program.

Common Music (Common Music 1998), a multi-platform music composition tool, was created at, and continues to be supported by, the Center for Computer Research in Music and Acoustics (CCRMA) at Stanford University. Common Music is an object-oriented music composition environment. This program treats composition as an experimental process, allowing broad descriptions of sound and their higher-order structural relationships. Common Music provides what its creators call an extensive compositional toolbox through a public interface with which composers can modify and extend the system (Taube 1991).

Common Music breaks the composing process into three distinct categories: composition, sound rendering, and performance. As previously mentioned, composers can interact with the system through its functional interface using LISP code. However, a more efficient way to interact with Common Music involves its interpreter. Called Stella, this interpreter translates textual commands into appropriate actions. Common Music also has a graphic interface called Capella. At one level, then, composers develop musical ideas and express structural relationships between sounds. On another level, composers realize these ideas. Although compositional structure and realization are conceptually intertwined, Common Music's modularization provides distinct advantages, not the least of which is using the modules independently.

Patchwork (Patchwork 1998), in contrast to Common Music, uses a graphic interface exclusively for computer-assisted composition. Patchwork helps composers represent, generate, and manipulate musical materials. Like Common Music, Patchwork has an extendible environment that can be adapted to suit quite different user needs. Patchwork was originally designed to generate compositional material for instrumental music and thus offers a flexible environment for testing compositional material. Patchwork also allows composers to add personalized functions specifically adapted to their compositional needs.

A patch in Patchwork is a graphically programmed procedure represented on-screen by inter-connectable objects having visual inputs and outputs. The path traced by user-drawn lines between objects defines a behavior relating to the creation, transformation, or editing of musical data. This software imitation of hardware patchcord connections between electronic components follows a similar one used in MAX (Puckette 1991).

The creators of Symbolic Composer (often called S-Com) claim that "it's time to break through the prison of historical music notation. Times are changing and composition modeling experts are working in music laboratories and private MIDI studios to discover the secrets of Mozart, Beethoven, Vivaldi, Bach, Schönberg, Messiaen, and other masters. In the path toward deeper understanding of musical processes Symbolic Composer plays an increasingly important role. Someday composers will be able to use these tools as fluently as they can now play with sequencers" (Symbolic Composer 1997). While admirable as a goal, Symbolic Composer falls somewhat short of delivering on this claim. Many composers, however, have found the program useful.

Symbolic Composer uses two different grammars to define what the program delineates as sections and instruments. Sections refer to formal structures of a work that consist of any number of instruments. Instruments define the timbres to be used. Each instrument inherits musical properties called classes. The main classes include symbols, lengths, tonalities, zones, and velocities. Motives are controlled by methods (see Cope 1996, chap. 4) and may be nested within motives creating complex tree-like structures. The program also includes modules with names such as neurons, tonalities, processors, and generators. Processors include filters, shifters, transposers, mixers, and morphing tools. Generators, on the other hand, generate fractal and chaos-based music, programmable neurons, Fibonacci series, autocatalysis, Fourier analysis/synthesis, and recursive structures. "The easiest way to learn to use Symbolic Composer is to have an open mind and adopt a surfing attitude, pick up a function here another there from the almost unlimited resources, and listen to what comes out" (Symbolic Composer 1997). The creator of S-Com claims that it is a "style-independent solution for composing and composition modeling. All musical styles will likely find their representation within this framework. You need clear thinking to be able to use it. If this state of mind is achieved, Symbolic Composer does not make restrictions on styles" (Symbolic Composer 1997). Unfortunately, all programs restrict style to some degree, and S-Com is no exception. However, more to the point, style in S-Com results from processes having little in common with most of what we traditionally construe as "all musical styles."

Each of these programs, Common Music, Patchwork, and Symbolic Composer, offers composers a rich range of different compositional tools and resources. In some cases, especially Patchwork and Symbolic Composer, these opportunities create mazes through which composers must negotiate rather than providing true opportunities. The likelihood of new material generated agreeing in style with the style of already composed music is also negligible.

Many composers prefer programs that provide cohesion and continuity for their music as well as those that create novelty. As Stravinsky so eloquently states,

> Variety surrounds me on every hand. So I need not fear that I shall be lacking in it, for I am constantly confronted by it. Contrast is everywhere. One has only to take note of it. Similarity is hidden; it must be sought out, and it is found only after the most exhaustive efforts. When variety tempts me, I am uneasy about the facile solutions it offers me. Similarity, on the other hand, poses more difficult problems, but also offers results that are more solid and hence more valuable to me. (Stravinsky 1960, p. 34)

Such similarity requires programs that extend creativity and imitate the processes used by their human counterparts, explicitly or implicitly, rather than imposing formulae. While such formulae may be extraordinary in their inventiveness, they typically lack the ability to develop the already conceived foundations of new works.

There exist few style creation or imitation programs that have potential. Of those that do, Music Is the Message (Yavelow 1997) and the Bol Processor (Bel 1998) seem most intriguing. Music Is the Message (MIM, created by Christopher Yavelow) generates film and video soundtracks in three generic styles by adapting its internal compositional models according to feedback from its users. MIM is based on the YAV Music Engine, a modular expert system. The Bol Processor (created by Bernard Bel) composes music using a set of rules or grammar supplied by users. Once a grammar has been established and perfected, the program can create innumerable examples of music in a given style. The Bol Processor deals with music as hierarchical sound objects or musical gestures. Successful examples of music in the style of, for example, Steve Reich have been created. However, neither MIM nor the Bol Processor analyzes a style of music and then produces output in that style.

Songworks II (Songworks 1998), a commercial application released by Ars Nova, incorporates a full-scale notation program along with what its designers call "idea generators." These generators, while relatively simple, suggest harmonies, melody continuations, and/or both simultaneously whenever users request them. The generators are rule-based and imitate only certain popular music styles.

Limited as the program may be, especially in terms of available pre-programmed styles, Songworks does provide algorithmic processes for a certain segment of the music population and aligns these processes with a relatively sophisticated notation program.

Composing programs that offer true style replication are rare, and often their poor ratio of success to failure greatly diminishes their usefulness. With this in mind, I created the Experiments in Musical Intelligence program and its subset, SARA, the Simple Analytic Recombinancy Algorithm (Cope 1991b, 1996), which was released on CD-ROM with my 1996 book. Both of these programs attempt to replicate works in the style of the music supplied in their databases.

■ EXPERIMENTS IN MUSICAL INTELLIGENCE AND SARA

Experiments in Musical Intelligence, described in numerous sources (see Cope 1990, 1991a, 1991b, 1992a, 1996), has composed examples of music arguably in styles as varied as Bach, Mozart, Chopin, Joplin, and Gershwin. The program uses analysis of music in databases, pattern matching for signatures, and recombination techniques as basic tools for composition. Written in Common LISP and using the Common LISP Object System (CLOS), Experiments in Musical Intelligence offers composers a process for creating stylistically-sensitive algorithmic composition. Because the program I discuss later in this book is based in part on the Experiments in Musical Intelligence program, it will be useful to briefly review that program's composing algorithm.

When I first began Experiments in Musical Intelligence, my idea was to code the rules of basic part-writing as I understood them. After much trial and error, my program produced a kind of styleless common-practice music that basically adhered to these rules. After further improvements, I was able to generalize these rules so that this program could create a variety of different instrumental textures. This was the kind of rule-based material to which the program added patterns, called signatures, derived from pattern-matching music in databases. Signatures occur in many works of a given composer and reveal some aspects of musical style, as demonstrated in *Computers and Musical Style* (Cope 1991b).

While some of the music composed using this approach proved successful, much of its output was uninteresting and unsatisfying. Having an intermediary (myself) form abstract sets of rules for composition seemed artificial and unnecessarily premeditative. In addition, having to code new sets of rules for each new style encountered proved daunting. Thus, I revised the program to derive new music from the music coded in its database rather than having me code rules for each new style.

My idea was that every work of music contains a set of instructions for creating different but highly related replications of itself. These instructions, interpreted correctly, can lead to important discoveries about structure and possibly style. At the least, these instructions should not be ignored.

My process to discover such instructions was based, in part, on the concept of recombinancy. Recombinancy can be defined simply as a method for producing new music by recombining extant music into new logical successions. I describe this process in detail in my book *Experiments in Musical Intelligence* (1996). I argue that recombinancy appears everywhere as a natural evolutionary and creative process. All the great books in the English language, for example, are constructed from recombinations of the twenty-six letters of the alphabet. Similarly, most of the great works of Western art music exist by recombination of the twelve pitches of the equal-tempered scale and their octave equivalents. The secret is not in the invention of new letters or notes but in the subtlety and elegance of their recombination.

I then created a new program to separate Bach chorales (Bach 1941) into beats and save these beats as objects (see Cope 1996, chap. 4). Along with each beat I had this program store the pitch to which each voice moved in the subsequent beat—one of that work's innate instructions. I further had the program collect these beats in various groups called lexicons delineated by the pitch and register of their entering voices (i.e., C1-G1-C2-C3). To compose, then, the program simply chooses the first beat of any chorale in its database and examines this beat's destination notes. The program then selects one of the stored beats with those same first notes, assuming enough chorales have been stored to make more than one choice possible. New choices then create the potential for different offbeat motions and different following chords while maintaining the integrity of Bach's original voice-leading rules. In this manner this simple program created interesting new chorales, all absolutely correct in terms of chord-to-chord voice-leading but without the program having to initiate any user-supplied rules.

Applying this basic concept to a number of different styles, including my own, produced similarly correct results, although varied in terms of quality. The music, a product of very simple syntactic networking, in effect inherits the voice-leading rules of the works on which it bases its replications. Figure 1.9a shows a simple chorale phrase composed in this manner with sources given above

Figure 1.9 (a) A Bach-like chorale phrase composed by a simple recombinant composing algorithm with sources shown above each beat by chorale number, measure number, and beat number; (b) Bach *Chorale 5* beginning, the chorale whose first beat provided the beginning of figure 1.9a.

a.

b.

each beat by chorale number, measure number, and beat number, with P representing pickup. The absence of a chorale number signifies a continuation of the previous chorale number given. Figure 1.9b shows how the original Bach chorale phrase continues after its initial chord for comparison to the newly composed chorale phrase in figure 1.9a.

However, the problems with this approach are many. First and foremost, the music often meanders with very unbalanced and uncharacteristic phrase lengths. There is no real musical logic present beyond the chord-to-chord syntax. Further, phrases simply string together randomly, without any large-scale structure, usually in a single key, and without any sense of the kinds of repetition and development necessary for intelligent music composition (see the *compose* program on this book's CD-ROM).

To provide some sense of this larger order, and again wanting to avoid the urge to simply program some of my own basic knowledge of musical form, I rewrote the program to inherit more of the structural aspects of the music in its database. This involved coding an analysis module so that the program could store other information with each beat along with its destination notes. For example, I had the program analyze the harmonic function (see Cope 1996) of each beat and then store not only this function name but the function names of neighboring beats as well. Making three-chord groupings of functions conform to their original order during composition helped achieve more satisfactory results.

Having the program also store references pertaining to general temporal location of cadences helped produce effective phrase and section endings. Ultimately, I added fairly elaborate analysis subprograms for generating the hierarchical structure of small works. Retaining too much information with each beat caused the program to simply reiterate one of the chorales in its database, so I took great care to ensure that, whenever possible, the program chose new possibilities rather than old connections. Providing very large databases also helped guarantee that more than one possible correct measure existed at each recombinant junction.

This nascent version of the Experiments in Musical Intelligence program was capable of producing more interesting, even occasionally satisfying music. Unfortunately, it produced fairly awkward results as well. For example, no matter how carefully I chose works for the database, almost anything besides Bach chorales created incongruities between individual beats—combining music with one type of musical character with music of a completely different character. Thus, my next addition to the program was to have it store representations of the musical character of each beat so that continuity could be maintained. The program first analyzes such continuities in the original music before it breaks the music into beat-size segments to ensure that changes of continuity take place at reasonable locations in new works.

Storing attributes of musical character with each segment of original music has significant advantages. Using information about an originating work's beat-to-beat character, for example, allows the program to produce works that have unifying elements. If, for example, the program were not able to access such information, one can imagine that each beat of a resulting piece could have different types of internal patterns, thus jarring listeners from one musical context to another (see figure 5.3 as an example). This lack of unity would most likely be uncharacteristic of either the style or the intent of the original works. With its stored character attribute, the program produced works having more logic and continuity.

To accomplish this structure and character analysis, I had the program use a musical version of an augmented transition network (ATN). ATNs, formulated by researchers in natural-language processing (NLP), offer excellent opportunities for analysis and generation of natural-language sentences (Bates 1978). ATNs also can provide the logic required for the assembly of beats of music from different works by the same composer. In brief this means that only those beats with compatible textures and keys are chosen from the available choices of beats with identical initial notes. This is accomplished both by storing abstractions of each beat's texture and by comparing these abstractions to a texture map of one of the original compositions in the database. In short, ATNs add context sensitivity to otherwise syntax-driven programs. Adding a pattern matcher further ensures that signatures remain intact and retain their location (see Cope 1991b, 1996).

With this basic core set of subprograms in place, I added fairly elaborate code capable of combinatorially reorganizing music by voice as well as by beat. Called MATN, for micro ATN, such reorganization may take place between the various voices of a single beat or between voices of different beats that have the same function and identical entering notes. Figure 1.10 shows how various recombinations succeed in transforming groups of beats of Bach chorales into new music.

Figure 1.10a shows a number of musical examples that present possibilities for voice interchange. Here the various chorales (measure numbers shown in parentheses in the figure caption) have identical initial notes. In addition, the secondary beat in each pair is identical or nearly identical, making voice interchange possible. In effect, any voice may be exchanged with its matching voice (tenor with tenor and so on) to produce new music. Figure 1.10b shows vertical voice interchange. Here the voices of the same beats (the beginning of Bach Chorale 102) are interchanged, effectively producing new music. Figure 1.10c shows how voices from various chorales can be combined to produce new music while preserving much of the style of the original chorales. This and the previous form of recombination pose more risk for the program in that some of the voices now have new beginning and ending notes.

Figure 1.10   Various recombinations of voices of beats of Bach chorales: (a) 124(1), 128(9), 29(9), 67(9), 248(3), and 128(2); chorale passages with identical onset notes; (b) passage from *Chorale 102* with voices of the same beats interchanged; (c) various chorale voice combinations: m. 1: 128, 138, 128, 128; m. 2: 131, 128, 131, 128; m. 3: 136, 131, 136, 128; m. 4: 131, 128, 293, 148.

a.

b.

c.

I then employed a pattern matcher to discover the previously-mentioned signatures. Signatures, defined as patterns that recur in different compositions, here represent patterns longer than a measure that, if broken during recombinancy, will lose important aspects of style. The program protects such signatures during composition so that these fundamental elements of style will remain intact.

Recombinancy, ATN, and pattern matching as described in both *Computers and Musical Style* (Cope 1991b) and *Experiments in Musical Intelligence* (Cope 1996) constitute the basic principles of algorithmic composition practiced in the Experiments in Musical Intelligence program and SARA. Of course, the recombinancy, ATN, and pattern matching of these programs are much more elaborate than the descriptions presented here.

The Experiments in Musical Intelligence program produces generally quite simple but often startlingly effective compositions. The program models itself so thoroughly around the compositions it attempts to emulate that some, including myself, contend that part of the original message seems to be captured in the newly-composed music. The program's Rachmaninoff *Suite* for two pianos, for example, composed in much the same manner as presented here, is so convincing that, for me at least, I mistook its first MIDI performance for one of the actual Rachmaninoff works in the program's database. This particular work is reproduced in part in Cope (1996).

As a further example, in the winter of 1987, I had the Experiments in Musical Intelligence program compose more than one hundred mazurkas in the style of Frédéric Chopin. I selected one of these for performance, recording, and publication in the first book in this series, *Computers and Musical Style* (Cope 1991b, pp. 198–204). My choice was made quickly because of time constraints and was based almost entirely on ease of performance, clarity of material derivation, and structural simplicity. In recent years I have revisited this set of mazurkas and have been amazed by the overall quality of the music, general authenticity of style, and the appearance of inspired creativity.

The mazurka style consists generally of a triple-meter three-part form, with, at least in Chopin's incarnations, an emphasis on dotted rhythms and triplets. The um-pah-pah left hand and monophonic right-hand melody, while not obligatory, often further characterize the mazurka style. Some of Chopin's mazurkas remain fixed diatonically to the initial key while others are highly modulatory. Thus, because they are based on various combinations of Chopin's original mazurkas, the mazurkas by the Experiments in Musical Intelligence program are not simply reiterations of one another but separate and distinct compositions.

The Experiments in Musical Intelligence program's mazurkas are also not mere compilations of patterns or simply out-of-order regurgitations of Chopin's mazurkas. In fact, comparing the harmonic progressions, the melodic contours, and the chromaticism of the Experiments in Musical Intelligence mazurka shown in part in figure 1.11 to those by Chopin proves this mazurka's originality. Showing derivations is as difficult as it would be when comparing Chopin's mazurkas with one another. The Experiments in Musical Intelligence mazurka resembles the mazurkas by Chopin stylistically. Thus, I maintain that even though there is no single paradigm that would characterize human algorithmic processes, the processes used by the Experiments in Musical Intelligence program described here resemble some human composing processes and generally make innate musical sense.

As another example, Experiments in Musical Intelligence composed over a thousand nocturnes in the style of Chopin in less than one month. Chopin, on the other hand, composed nineteen nocturnes over a period of sixteen years (1830–1846). Shown in part in figure 1.12, one of the machine-composed nocturnes uses Chopin's Op. 72, No. 1, as a model for its initial material and general form. The beginning of this model nocturne appears in figure 1.13. Note how the composing program's version in figure 1.12 varies the main thematic idea by extending it downward an octave and then continuing in a different manner than the original in figure 1.13. The theme of the B section, beginning in measure 30 of the machine-composed Chopin, seems derived from the middle theme of Chopin's Nocturne Op. 48, No. 2, beginning in measure 57, as shown in figure 1.14. A Chopin signature (see figure 1.15) occurs frequently in various guises in the machine-composed nocturne (mm. 8, 12, 15, and so on) forming part of the basis of the second theme in measure 30.

The chromaticism that appears on beat 4 in measure 3 of the machine-composed Chopin imitation in figure 1.12 between the right and left hands is quite interesting (G-sharp against G-natural). In this guise it seems unlike Chopin. However, as is often the case with the Experiments in Musical Intelligence program's replications, careful examination of Chopin's music reveals a number of cases in which he approximates what we find here. For example, figure 1.16a from Op. 72, No. 1, shows an E-natural occurring against an E-sharp on beat 4 in measure 21. In addition, measure 37 of this same nocturne has F-sharp sounding against F-natural during beat 4 as shown in figure 1.16b. Both of these examples use chromaticism in passing scalewise formations just as in the machine-composed example in figure 1.12.

Figure 1.17 shows the beginning of a computer-composed rag called *Another Rag* (1988), in the style of Scott Joplin. The rhythms,

Figure 1.11   The beginning of an Experiments in Musical Intelligence Chopin mazurka.

Figure 1.12   The beginning of a machine-composed nocturne in the style of Chopin.

Figure 1.12 Continued.

Figure 1.13   The beginning of Chopin's *Nocturne* Op. 72, No. 1 (1827).

Figure 1.14   Measure 57 from Chopin's *Nocturne* Op. 48, No. 2 (1841).

harmonic progressions, and melodic configurations, so reminiscent of Joplin, are derived from pattern matching a number of rags to extract signatures. Most Joplin rags begin with octaves and include syncopation with tied sixteenth notes both across and within beats. The main body of the rag then typically contains an um-pah left-hand figuration in eighth notes. The Experiments in Musical Intelligence program took these elements, especially the ones that occur in more than one of the Joplin rags, and counted them as signatures, helping create a more convincing new rag.

Note how in figure 1.17 the program has held introductory (mm. 1–4) material together even though this material often has the same initiating number of notes as material in the main theme appearing in measure 5. For example, the rag begins with three simultaneous notes, the same number that begins measure 5. Measure 2 begins with two notes, the same number that begins measure 11. Yet none of this contextual material gets mixed together. The introductory material is consistent, as is the main theme. This process results from the previously mentioned texture mapping stored with the objects in the database.

Figure 1.18 provides an example of the imitative style of inventions and demonstrates how the Experiments in Musical Intelligence program

Figure 1.15   Various forms of a signature found in Chopin mazurkas: (a) Op. 6, No. 1 (1830), m. 1; (b) Op. 6, No. 4 (1830), mm. 9–10; (c) Op. 7, No. 2 (1830–1831), m. 3; (d) Op. 17, No. 4 (1832–1833), m. 13; (e) Op. 17, No. 4 (1832–1833), m. 15; (f) Op. 17, No. 4 (1832–1833), m. 29; (g) Op. 50, No. 1 (1841–1842), m. 18.

Figure 1.16   From Chopin's Nocturne Op. 72, No. 1 (1827): (a) m. 21; (b) m. 37.

uses an interlocking approach to inheritance from databases and special rules for creating new works in given styles. Clearly this work is derived from the Bach inventions. However, the special invention rules in the program circumvent exact inheritance by requiring immediate imitation in the lower-voice counterpoint, an imitation not found so exactly in Bach's inventions. The variations appearing in figure 1.18 are welcome aberrations that infuse output with a kind of non-imitative vigor similar to the kind that seems endemic to the invention form. This computer-composed invention belongs to a set of fifteen (like Bach's) composed by the Experiments in Musical Intelligence program, of which five were recorded on the CD *Bach by Design* (Cope 1994) and three later released on *Classical Music Composed by Computer* (Cope 1997b).

These Chopin, Joplin, and Bach replications, while certainly not as convincing as the original works on which they are based, nonetheless can challenge previous concepts about music, human versus machine creativity, how we listen to music, and so on. Such challenges, it seems to me, are healthy and useful. For example, I often understand the originals better when I have machine imitations for comparison. The program also produces more examples of music in the approximate style of dead composers, and on occasion I truly appreciate this. Research with the Experiments in Musical Intelligence program also extends my understanding of the importance of style, voice leading, hierarchy, and other compositional implications of the composer's original music.

Figure 1.17 The beginning of an Experiments in Musical Intelligence Joplin rag.

Figure 1.18   The beginning of an Experiments in Musical Intelligence Bach invention.

However, even the program's best efforts often achieve less than satisfactory results. The majority of its works—which generally go unheard by anyone but myself—fall much further from acceptability than those shown here. In addition, the Experiments in Musical Intelligence program is not interactive but rather creates works of whole-cloth that cannot smoothly connect to surrounding human-composed music. This whole-composition creation results in large part from the fact that the program models its compositions on music and structures found in its database. With the exception of manipulating variables associated with pattern matching for stylistic signatures, users of the Experiments in Musical Intelligence program merely load databases and wait for the program to produce new compositions.

■ NEED FOR A NEW PROGRAM

There is, then, a need for an interactive program that can track a composition in progress and combine found harmonic, motivic, and structural elements with more generic elements of a composer's style to create situationally relevant music—a note, measure, phrase, and so on—within the current work's and the composer's overall style. This new music should be available at any point during composition and be logical and relevant to the user-created music surrounding it. In short, the program must be highly interactive.

I should note that all computer programs are interactive to some degree. The Experiments in Musical Intelligence program, for example, while it produces complete compositions on its own, requires human assistance on several levels, not the least of which is its initialization (i.e., its reason for composing in the first place). The program also depends on the inputting and selection of databases, user setting of controllers in pattern matching, and occasionally the choice of musical form for output. Any one of these elements would make Experiments in Musical Intelligence a program dependent on the user: together they make it an interactive one. However, as we will see, this kind of interactivity does not allow for much contribution by the user.

Creating a program that truly collaborates requires a composing algorithm as good, if not better, than the current offerings. This program would need to keep a running tabulation of the melodic, harmonic, motivic, and structural content of a current work as well as maintaining an accurate sense of a composer's overall ongoing style. No small feat this, but an enviable goal, one that I feel would constitute a true composer's assistant. Users composing with this program could request algorithmically-composed music to present possible solutions to certain compositional problems, indicate alternative routes at musical pivot points, extend passages experimentally, develop the potentials of composer-created germ ideas, and offer new ideas when inspiration temporarily wanes.

With these requirements in mind, I created Alice (ALgorithmically Integrated Composing Environment). Alice can compose as much relevant music as desired—from a single note to an entire piece—in a composer's general style as evidenced in previously-composed music provided in its database and in the style of a work currently being composed. Alice composes this music as either connective material or extensions that maintain the stylistic continuity and appropriate formal logic of the music already present. The program also has the analytical tools that I and others have found useful while composing.

As with the Experiments in Musical Intelligence program and SARA, Alice relies on its databases for its creative abilities. These databases determine the basic rules of composition, the form of the works in the output, and the general style of music produced. Composers can greatly influence the ultimate content produced by Alice by carefully selecting the databases used for composition. For example, the output from a single phrase used as a database will be a phrase or set of phrases almost identical to the input phrase. In contrast, using a thousand different phrases as a database will produce unpredictable results. Using diatonic input phrases will create diatonic output. In contrast, using chromatic phrases will produce chromatic output and so on.

Beyond its need for a coherent database, Alice offers many user-controllable settings, input parameters, and a wide range of analysis tools that are discussed in later chapters. Users also have opportunities to extend the program using LISP just as they do with Common Music, Patchwork, and Symbolic Composer.

Most composers using algorithmic composing programs in the twenty-first century will not be programmers. They will not have the ability to create their own programs or to revise such programs to fit their precise needs. On the other hand, programs such as Alice offer many opportunities for users to individualize their interfaces and, at least to a certain extent, control the output without programming experience. As just discussed, one of the principal ways to do this in Alice involves sculpting databases. Another way to individualize Alice, as will be described in the next three chapters, involves the fundamental nature of the program itself—Alice has elements of intelligent-like behavior and attempts to actively respond to user preferences.

TWO

Fundamentals

■ **MARKOV CHAINS**

Most of the programs I created previous to Alice (ALgorithmically Integrated Composing Environment), while sometimes producing interesting output, have not behaved very intelligently or creatively. However, with Alice I have attempted to initiate strategies that, while most likely not having legitimate intelligence (see Turing 1950), use processes that I believe parallel some of those that lead to intelligence. To understand my approach to building programs that demonstrate such intelligent-like behavior, I will first establish some relevant background and then proceed to more important concepts.

Many of the simplest forms of program behavior can be expressed in terms of orders of Markov chains (Ames 1989). Describing programs in terms of their Markov orders can sometimes provide a convenient method of determining the complexity of their constraint mechanisms and to some extent legitimize or contradict any claim they may have to being intelligent. For example, a *zeroth-order* Markov chain relies completely on random decisions. On the other hand, a *first-order* Markov chain makes decisions on the basis of relationships between the current possibilities and the last choice made. A *fifth-order* Markov chain constrains the current choice by conditions prescribed by the previous five decisions.

As an example, let's imagine that a simple melody-composing program chooses each new note by virtue of the interval it creates with a previously-composed note. If only major seconds and thirds were allowed between consecutive notes, such a first-order Markov chain would produce simple noodling melodies controlled only at their immediate point of composition. A more elegant program might have a new choice dependent not only on a note's preceding interval but also on the resultant note's preceding interval. For example, if the previous interval choice were a third, then new choices might be limited to seconds in contrary motion. This second-order Markov chain would be considerably more elegant than the first-order one. The Melody Predictor program on this book's CD-ROM and discussed in the previous chapter represents just such a second-order Markov chain.

As has and will be seen, Experiments in Musical Intelligence, SARA (Simple Analytic Recombinant Alogrithm), and Alice all represent nth-order Markov chains, where n represents the number of previous determinants. A first-order Markov equivalent in these programs consists of simple inheritance from the database as discussed in Cope (1996, chap. 5). Augmented transition networking provides an approximate second-order Markov equivalent (Cope 1996, chap. 5). The hierarchical pattern-matching program and structural analysis process (to be discussed in chaps. 4 and 5) provide several more Markovian orders. In effect, few decisions in Experiments in Musical Intelligence and SARA are actually random. Truly random choices occur only when two or more correct possibilities exist with equal probability for selection.

Describing algorithmic programs according to Markov probabilities can be useful as a comparison tool, not just in terms of sophistication but in terms of complexity, hierarchy, and integration. For example, it can be enlightening to know that a work was produced relatively randomly by a first-order Markov chain as opposed to one produced more determinately by a sixth-order Markov chain. The first example results from moment-to-moment processes, while the latter from much deeper considerations. As will be seen, Alice represents a multidimensional Markov chain in that intersecting constraints contribute to a kind of three-dimensional hierarchy with one set of choices relying on other sets of choices (orders).

RANDOMNESS AND RECOGNITION

To a degree at least, randomness and recognition are dependent on the observer or listener as much as they are on the state of the observed or heard.

Having heard all the musical events in the piece up to a certain point, we await the next event—the next pitch or chord, with its attendant dyna-

mic level, orchestration, and duration (or perhaps the event is a silence).
. . . Some of these the listener feels to be more likely than others, that
is some have higher probability. . . . How the probabilities are
assigned to the various possible sonic events depends in part on general
psychological laws, and in part on how much exposure the listener has
had to works in the same or a similar style. The second of these influences is hardly a one-way transaction, however, since it is precisely the
retroactive reconsideration of relative likelihoods, in view of what actually happened, that helps the listener to learn a style. In fact, the very
meaning of "style," at least of "aurally detectable style," is tied up in the
felt probabilities of sonic events. (Cooper 1978, p. S-1)

To help demonstrate these aspects of detectable style compared
with randomness, I will describe three simple applications. I have
chosen visual and language models instead of musical ones in order
to focus on aspects of machine recognition and to avoid often com-
plicating musical factors. Each of the applications discussed here
has been designed to concentrate on aspects of machine intelligence, or lack of intelligence, in hopes that in so doing a clear definition will become apparent.

Fun is a simple application that, it is hoped, provides its users
with a realization of its name. Fun—found on this book's CD-ROM—
possesses no intelligence or recognition abilities. Fun consists of
straightforward code that produces, in league with the intelligence
of those who use it, a colorful palette of visual images. Like most
applications, Fun provides its users with a vehicle for achieving a
desired end. Since Fun does not demonstrate intelligence in any
way, the program may appear trivial. However, Fun belongs to a category of applications that includes word processors, spreadsheets,
graphics programs, and others that act as tools for accomplishing
particular goals. Thus, most applications are not intelligent, whatever their importance may otherwise be to us.

Fun is also a small and fairly self-explanatory program. To run
Fun, simply select one of its menu choices and then draw on the
Canvas—Fun menu item—with the mouse. To create non-random
drawings with more than one figure type, select the type using the
associated number macro, and then place the selected object as
desired. Random and algorithmic menu choices also produce quite
interesting results. Fun demonstrates simple zero-order Markov
chaining.

The Fun program also offers somewhat synchronized QuickTime®
sound accompaniment, although this should not be confused with
actual music composition anymore than Fun's visual images should
be confused with actual art. While providing diversion and an occasionally elegant visual treat, Fun, like most applications, possesses

no intelligence or creativity beyond what the user provides either by design or by interpreting the images.

On the other hand, the *déjà vu* program—found on the CD-ROM—can analyze and recognize images drawn in its input window. This program can also associate images and recognize them by name when they have enough characteristics in common. Thus, déjà vu has some elements of what I call intelligence. Part of déjà vu's intelligent-like behavior results from its programming. Concomitantly, however, neither déjà vu nor I as its programmer has any advance knowledge of the kind of images users will draw. To a degree, then, the program must adapt itself to any image, however complex it may be. As will be seen, I believe that this adaption also resembles intelligent-like behavior.

Users draw shapes using the computer's mouse. Déjà vu then analyzes and stores these figures in memory with a random name. When subsequent images resemble an image already stored in memory, the program identifies this original image by name. Once one or more different images have been stored in memory, déjà vu can create new images that have aspects of the originals recombined in what the program determines as logical sequences. Although much less complex, this recombinance is not unlike the recombinance of the Experiments in Musical Intelligence program and SARA.

Thus, while extremely simple, déjà vu has some attributes of intelligence. These include analysis, association, and adaption. The uses of these attributes in déjà vu as it attempts to match figures that resemble but do not duplicate those in its memory can be quite interesting. Triangles, for example, will match one another regardless of the order of the lines drawn (i.e., left to right, top to bottom, and so on). However, déjà vu does far more than simply map points on the screen. Thus, many triangle-like images will not match a triangle image already in memory. Certainly three-pointed figures that do not connect triangularly will not match triangles. At the same time, some roughly drawn figures that barely resemble their archetypes can match and not produce new names or additions to memory. Only careful comparisons will reveal the reasons behind successful matches.

Déjà vu's creativity, while also primitive, depends on the analysis stored in its memory to create new images. These analyses can produce quite interesting images whose origins may sometimes be unclear. The rules governing déjà vu's decisions are based on complex negotiations between the objects in its memory that store weightings on the basis of frequency of figure types. In essence, each object stores matched variations of its initially-created image that are then used to create specialized varieties of their design on the basis of these weightings. Déjà vu's creative strategies then rely on these weightings.

Interestingly, many of the music programs I have created have subprograms that parallel those of déjà vu. For example, Experiments in Musical Intelligence and SARA both have analysis subprograms as well as pattern matchers that compare different versions of various musical motives.

The objects of déjà vu require some explanation. All the matched drawings of a single type are stored in the same object. This allows such objects to become specialists in a particular shape. When these objects are called on for drawing, they use combinations of these versions to produce subtle variants of the original figures. This combinatorial approach to creating new drawings offers important advantages over techniques typically used by non-object-oriented programs. Imagine, for example, that a non-object-oriented database had twenty or more different figure types in its single database along with several versions of each type. Collecting and comparing like-structured images from the numerous variations present to create a new version of those variants would be extremely time consuming. Clearly, storing these variants in a well-organized and thus easily-accessed object-oriented database makes such creation several magnitudes faster and easier (for more information on object orientation, see Cope 1996, chap. 4).

Another advantage offered by using object-oriented strategies involves combining related but different drawing types to create dynamic new versions. These new versions result from having two or more objects negotiate with one another such that new figures result from logical rather than random procedures. This negotiation takes place using the weightings stored in each object. These weightings result from computations based on the average size of drawings they store. This makes some sense because size can be a measure of the apparent confidence of the user. The weightings increase with the number of variants stored. This follows the assumption that more variations indicate the user's attraction to a particular drawing type. When users ask déjà vu to create combinatorial drawings, the various relevant drawing types compete with one another with their individual weightings figured into every decision.

Thus, déjà vu assumes that creation does not exist in a vacuum—that creative decisions are based on a variety of factors, especially the weighting of preferences based on known types of relevant activity. This aspect of déjà vu makes its creativity more elegant than Fun, at least in terms of the acknowledgment by the program of the user's taste—granted that the particular factors determining weighting here represent just two of many such possibilities.

Déjà vu uses other principles that I feel help create intelligent-like programs. First, the program is small and relies on user-input data rather than pre-coded rules. Most of the code for the program is dedicated to its interface, object system, menus, and so on. The actual code for analyzing and creating new figures represents only a small fraction—possibly 10 percent—of the overall code. Second, déjà vu contains no data. The program uses only a few techniques for analyzing and recombining data input by users. Thus, déjà vu is not predisposed toward one figure type over another. Déjà vu also recognizes objects of similar type regardless of variances in their appearance. While humans take such recognition of similarity for granted, it remains one of the more difficult things for computers to accomplish. As previously mentioned but worth repeating, déjà vu's method of creation is not random but rather uses preferences exhibited by users. These preferences represent the focus of negotiations between the objects in déjà vu's database. These negotiations produce interactivity both between users and the program and between the objects within the program itself.

Déjà vu's Imagine menu item provides more interesting results than the Create menu item. However, using Create allows users to view the sometimes subtle interplay of déjà vu's interpretation of user preferences in creating new images. I call this reliance *resonance*. While subtle, this resonance reflects an interactivity that may not at first be evident. On the other hand, the Imagine menu item uses the figures as seeds for developing often radical departures from the drawings on which it bases its new images. The function of the Imagine menu item resembles that of the Create menu item except that all available images and their variants contribute to new images rather than just the variations of chosen images.

Folding the results of either Create or Imagine back into the database—by using Analyze—produces a kind of generational effect with inherited attributes alongside attributes developed through algorithmic means. Thus, déjà vu's architecture allows generations of shapes to occur. These generations show subtle growth over time, and this can prove quite interesting, especially in how the user's preferences combine with the program's algorithmic negotiations. As we will see, Alice also has this option.

There are many ways to experiment with déjà vu. For example, drawing a simple geometric shape and then, with subsequent drawings, attempting to fool the program can provide insights into how déjà vu's recognition process operates. For example, drawing triangles of different types (i.e., isosceles, right, and so on) and sizes, beginning at different locations, plotting them backward and forward, and even making the lines separately from an assortment of directions produces an intriguing mix of matches and non-matches. Drawing two or more variations of different figures using Create to produce a new figure type and then using only the offspring of the original drawings can produce quite interesting results as well.

Another useful experiment with déjà vu involves drawing two different figures, one an original with several variations and the other a single figure of approximately the same size. Using Create then demonstrates how the program biases its new images toward the one with variations. This bias also occurs with two figures of quite different sizes that have an equal number of variations.

I do not want to overstate the importance of these processes. Certainly déjà vu does not exhibit true intelligence or even true creativity. At the same time, I do believe that the principles stated here, when applied in larger and more elegant projects (such as the Alice program) can produce sophisticated results. To that end, then, the following figures should provide useful examples.

Figure 2.1 shows a set of three similar drawings all recognized by déjà vu as belonging to the same family of rectangles. Figure 2.2 then shows a group of three drawings created by déjà vu using the Create menu item based on the sets of human-created drawings shown in figure 2.1. The first of the program's creations, shown in figure 2.2a, is a simple variant of the original. However, figure 2.2b seems curiously twisted into three dimensions. The last program-created drawing in figure 2.2c appears more like the original and yet has characteristics different than any one of the original drawings of figure 2.1.

Figure 2.1   Three drawings recognized by déjà vu as being basically the same.

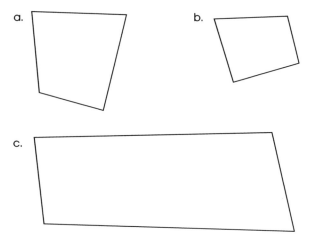

Figure 2.2   Three new drawings created by déjà vu using the model of the figures in figure 2.1.

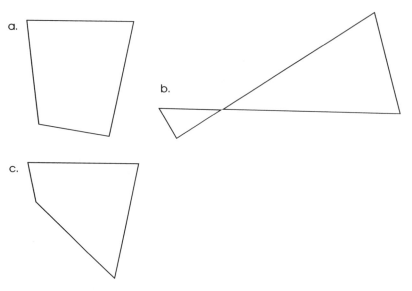

a.

b.

c.

Figure 2.3a shows the memory of an IJDE—a random name created by the program—object, similar to the rectangle figures shown in figure 2.1. Figure 2.3b shows three variants of a triangular figure in the memory of a JSP object. The program-created drawings presented in figure 2.3c then show three variations of IJDE and JSP resulting from déjà vu's negotiations between these two objects. The first drawing in figure 2.3c is a subtle variant of the JSP figure using the four sides of IJDE. The second drawing in figure 2.3c shows a four-sided figure that has elements of the JSP triangles in its right half. The final example of figure 2.3c represents an even more subtle variant of the combination of the IJDE and JSP figures, demonstrating, possibly even more than the other two, how effective the negotiating approach can be when using déjà vu.

The level of detail presented for this discussion of déjà vu will hopefully serve readers well when musical decisions result from similar negotiations that take place in Alice. In fact, the core code for déjà vu resembles that of Alice, although the two programs have vastly different interfaces and data structures.

Figure 2.4 shows the function `create-by-negotiation`. This function is written in the computer language LISP (for more details, see Cope 1991b, chap. 3). Function definitions in LISP (short for "list processing") begin with a parenthesis followed by `defun` (for "define function"), followed by a list of variables that will ultimately

Figure 2.3 Examples of déjà vu's creativity: (a) memory of an object named IJDE; (b) memory of an object named JSP; (c) new objects derived from IJDE and JSP objects.

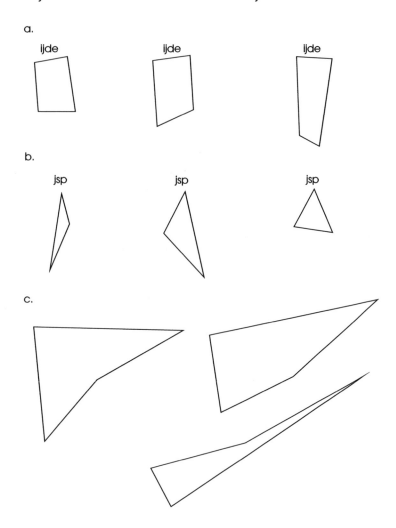

a.

ijde   ijde   ijde

b.

jsp   jsp   jsp

c.

represent data, followed in turn by the body of the function itself as shown in figure 2.4. To run functions in LISP, function names must appear after left parentheses with arguments (data) followed by right parentheses. Thus, the function in figure 2.4 might appear as "(create-by-negotiation '(xsej toi))." The single quote that appears before the list of objects "(xsej toi)" indicates that these objects should not be evaluated independently by the LISP evaluator. It should be noted that the word *function* here is an operator that

Figure 2.4   The function `create-by-negotiation`.

```
1. (defun create-by-negotiation (names)
2.   (let ((initial-weighting (get-initial-weighting names)))
3.     (assemble initial-weighting
4.               (negotiate-the-weightings names)
5.               (if (closure (negotiate names)
6.                            initial-weighting)
7.                   (list initial-weighting)))))
```

alters data in ways described by the function's definition and does not mean the same thing as function in music.

Wherever possible in this book, I have named LISP functions according to what they do. Thus, the intent of the code "(create-by-negotiation '(xsej toi))" should be clear: "create a new object by negotiating with the two objects XSEJ and TOI." I have also attempted to name the variables present appropriate to what these variables represent. Thus, `names` and `initial-weighting` in figure 2.4 stand for a list of names, in this case the names of shapes, and an initial weighting derived from the variable `initial-weighting`. Because arguments containing calls to other functions must be evaluated before a function can act on them, `assemble` in line 3 must wait for both `negotiate-the-weightings` and `closure` to act on their arguments before it can return the various parts of a new drawing. The function `negotiate-the-weightings` (line 4) creates the basic form of the shape. The function `closure` (line 5) determines whether the shape should be closed, and if so, the initial point becomes the last point in the resultant drawing. To understand more fully how each of these processes works, one needs to look up the code for `get-initial-weighting`, `closure`, `negotiate-the-weightings`, and any déjà vu functions that they themselves may call. However, figure 2.4 demonstrates the basic logic of the process and should be fairly transparent to even a first-time observer of LISP.

The following examples provide a sample session using déjà vu. Figure 2.5 shows a user-created reversed sigma-like drawing that in figure 2.6 déjà vu names KSB. Figure 2.7 shows another user-created drawing of a reversed sigma-like figure but with extended limbs and angles. Déjà vu still identifies this drawing as KSB (see figure 2.8). Figure 2.9 shows an even greater exaggeration of the reversed sigma-like figure with lengths and angles so distorted as to make the relationship with the original quite tenuous. However, déjà vu still identifies this drawing with the original drawing in figure 2.5 and calls it KSB, as shown in figure 2.10.

Figure 2.5   A user-created reversed sigma-like drawing.

Figure 2.6   The user-created sigma-like drawing named KSB by déjà vu.

ksb

Figure 2.7   Another user-created reversed sigma-like drawing.

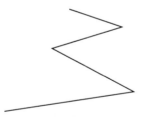

Figure 2.8   The sigma-like drawing of figure 2.7 also identified as KSB by déjà vu.

ksb

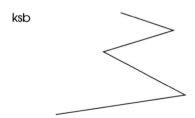

Figure 2.9   An exaggerated user-created sigma-like drawing.

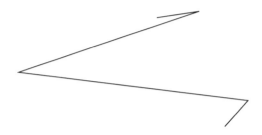

Figure 2.10   Once again, this new drawing identified as KSB by déjà vu.

ksb

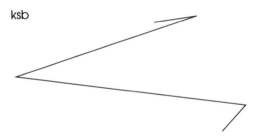

Figure 2.11 shows another reversed sigma-like drawing. However, this figure has another, fifth line attached to its lower extremity. This variation proves too difficult for the matching program to identify as a KSB-type figure, and déjà vu identifies the figure as a new drawing called JAH, as shown in figure 2.12. Figure 2.13 now shows the two basic figure types as members of déjà vu's memory. Figure 2.14 then shows a new user-created drawing similar to figure 2.11 but with different angles and line lengths. Nonetheless, déjà vu correctly identifies this drawing as of the type JAH, as shown in figure 2.15.

Figure 2.16 shows an original drawing by déjà vu using Create based on the two present in its memory. Close inspection of this drawing reveals the origins of each line in the original two drawing types in memory. Figure 2.17 shows the memory of déjà vu after subsequent drawings by both the user and the program.

Figure 2.11   An extended sigma-like drawing.

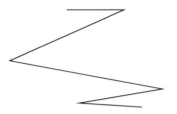

Figure 2.12   This drawing identified by déjà vu as JAH.

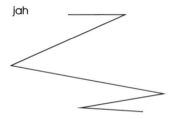

Figure 2.13   Memory of the two previous figure types in déjà vu.

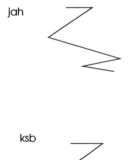

Figure 2.14   A new drawing for identification by déjà vu.

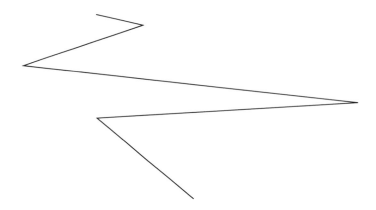

Figure 2.15   This drawing identified by déjà vu as JAH.

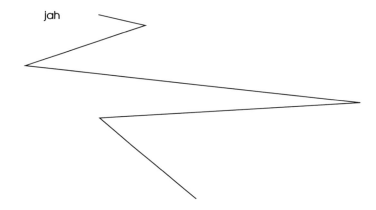

Figure 2.16   An original drawing by déjà vu identified as the new object CMH.

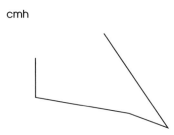

Figure 2.17   Memory of déjà vu after many new drawings.

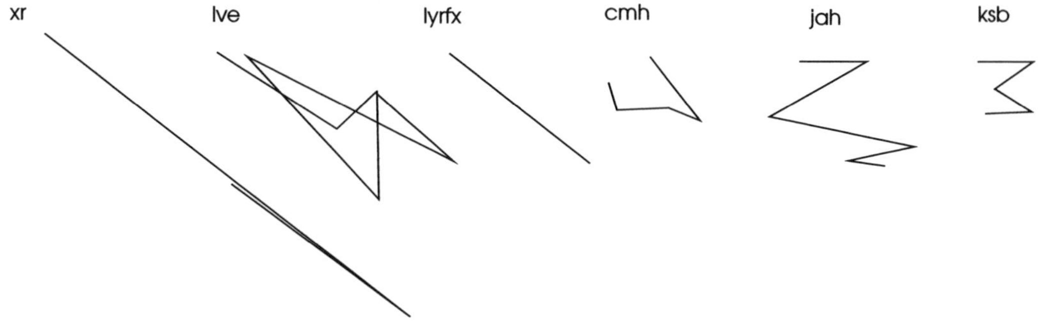

xr   lve   lyrfx   cmh   jah   ksb

■ ASSOCIATION NETS

While déjà vu provides a quantum leap toward the kind of analysis and creative-like behavior one typically associates with intelligence, neither Fun nor déjà vu could actually fool users into believing that they really do have intelligence. However, by adding more subtle degrees of association and adaptability to the analysis displayed by déjà vu, programs can make significant gains toward achieving intelligent-like behavior (Fodor 1983; Haugeland 1981; Newell 1990).

One of the ways to achieve adaptability involves connectivity. Connectivity can deepen association and increase opportunities for adaption. Herbert Dreyfus speaks to this point.

> Anybody who has children must be struck by the number of years they can spend playing around with sand, even just playing around with water, just splashing it around, sopping it up, pouring it, splashing it. It seems endlessly fascinating to children. And one might wonder what are they doing? Why aren't they getting bored? How does this have any value? Well, I could say, they're acquiring the 50,000 water sloshing cases that they need for pouring and drinking and spilling and carrying water. And they've got their 50,000 cases of how solids bump in, scrape, stack on, fall off. Common sense knowledge would, in this story, I believe, consist in this huge number of special cases which aren't remembered as a bunch of cases, but which have tuned the neurons, so that, when something similar to one of those cases comes in, an appropriate action or expectation comes out. And that's what underlies common-sense knowledge. (Dreyfus 1992, p. xi)

Interestingly, Dreyfus tries to make the case that this kind of experimentation argues convincingly against computers being able to acquire the same knowledge, or intelligence, that humans acquire.

On the other hand, I think his case provides even more compelling evidence that computers can demonstrate, at the least, intelligent-like behavior. After all, while 50,000 experimental cases for humans seems extraordinary, for computers this number is routine. Likewise, storing special cases and applying them to new situations, a feat not that far removed from what déjà vu accomplishes in its limited way, hardly extends our vision of what computers can do beyond reason. With these thoughts in mind, I have included a program called *BackTalk* on this book's CD-ROM. BackTalk uses language—any language, including artificial languages—as its interface.

Since I believe that association plays a major role in developing intelligent-like behavior (Anderson 1973, 1983; Fodor 1983; Kohonen 1984; MacKay 1970; Mackintosh 1983), I have developed an approach called an "association net" and used it as the heart of BackTalk. Figure 2.18 shows an example of an association net. The U's on the left refer to input by the user, and the C's represent BackTalk's responses. Time flows from the top of the diagram to the bottom. The association net cannot respond until both a question and statement—defined by the use of question and exclamation marks—have been entered: thus the two initial inputs by the user with no response from the program.

The interconnecting lines between words represent paths of influence with each line having a separate weight as will be discussed shortly. This example uses English as choice of language, though any language may be used including artificial ones. The program possesses no knowledge of any language. The user designates a word for No with an asterisk. Each time this word appears the program weakens the connections between the words in the previous two sentences. As will be seen, the net adapts and could, with extended conversation and a liberal use of the No word, be said to learn.

Association nets rely on the ability of a program to store data in objects. Thus, object-oriented programs such as C++, Smalltalk, and the Common LISP Object System (CLOS—the language used for the association net described here; see Keene 1989) work best for implementing these types of programs. Each entered and newly generated word instance is an object that has stored attributes such as its place in its sentence, the words that precede and follow it, its weighting, and so on. Each entered and newly generated word instance also has the ability to connect—associate—with all of the other words in a conversation as will be seen.

Figure 2.18   An association net.

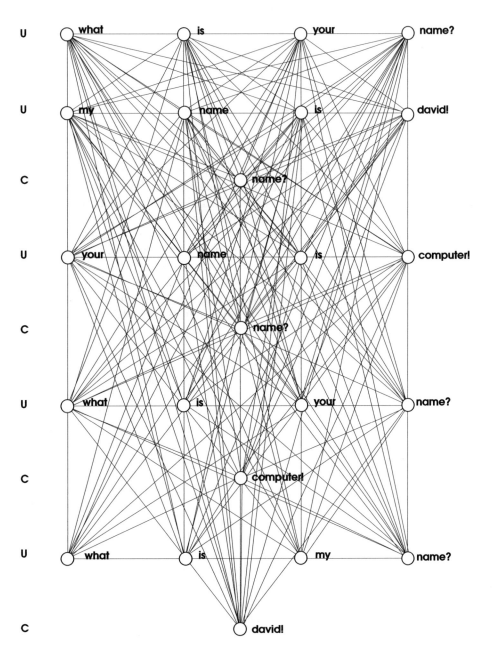

The lines between the words or nodes in figure 2.18 indicate important two-way connections for association nets. Lines connect every word to every other word. However, each connection has a different weighting. For example, first and last words of sentences rate higher than other words. Preceding and following words of a given word also rate highly. Words that duplicate relate strongly no matter what the temporal distance separating them as do words of similar spelling. Each word in a sentence also relates significantly to the longest word—in terms of number of letters—in that sentence. This rather simple notion relies on the premise that common words of short length such as prepositions and pronouns do not hold as much meaning as more complex, polysyllabic words—certainly not true in all or possibly most languages but a useful compromise for this simple association net. In sentences with two or more equally-long words, the later-occurring of such words stands as the longest. This designation follows the premise that later words tend to be more important as in last words of prepositional phrases and the fact that adjectives usually come before more important nouns—at least in many languages.

Since weighting can be affected by relationships in any direction in an association net, the word "name" in sentence 5 has access to the word "name" in any one of the previous sentences, and vice versa. The only requirement for these processes to work properly, obviously, is that words have to occur before they can associate. Since the word "name" has been associated with both David and Computer by line 5, the program's correct choices in its responses here result directly from the weighting of the words Your and My in relation to Name. This is born out by the weightings as shown in figure 2.19. Note that every word expressed thus far is listed on the left of this chart in boldface and that all other words and their respective weightings (in relation to the word on their left) are listed slightly below and to the right of that word.

Patterns can also serve as important associative interrelations. Figure 2.20 shows—using boxes around appropriately-grouped words—how found patterns relate in the conversation of figure 2.18. Identifying important patterns can, for example, ensure that colloquialisms such as "cold day in hell" remain intact and not become "cold day in October," "cold day in 1995," or "cold day tomorrow," none of which has the meaning and intent of the original "cold day in hell." Pattern association requires sensitive application, however, since a severe approach would produce mimicking of word order, something undesired in a program such as this.

The power of association nets can be seen in figure 2.21a. Here the word "name" has been extracted from figure 2.18 with its highly

Figure 2.19   Weightings for words in conversation of figure 2.18.

```
((what
   ((name? 7.61)  (is 3.7)  (computer! 1.72)  (david! 1.72)  (name 1.0)  (my 1.0)  (your 1.4)))
(is
   ((name? 7.43)  (my 1.7)  (computer! 3.17)  (david! 3.27)  (name 1.2)  (your 2.5)  (what 1.6)))
(your
   ((name? 6.9)  (computer! 2.57)  (david! 1.72)  (name 1.5)  (my 1.0)  (is 2.1)  (what 1.3)))
(name?
   ((computer! 1.72)  (david! 1.72)  (name 1.0)  (my 1.0)  (your 1.2)  (is 2.0)  (what 1.2)))
(my
   ((name? 4.69)  (computer! 1.62)  (david! 2.57)  (name 1.4)  (your 1.0)  (is 1.8)  (what 1.0)))
(name
   ((computer! 2.47)  (is 2.7)  (david! 2.19)  (my 0.9)  (name? 3.24)  (your 1.0)  (what 1.0)))
(david!
   ((name 0.6)  (my 0.6)  (name? 3.14)  (your 0.9)  (is 1.4)  (what 0.9)  (computer! 1.52)))
(computer!
   ((david! 0.1)  (name 0.2)  (my 0.5)  (name? 3.14)  (your 0.6)  (is 1.0)  (what 0.9))))
```

Figure 2.20   Pattern relationships in conversation of figure 2.18.

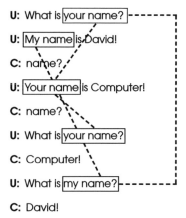

weighted and important lesser weighted connections shown as derived from figure 2.19. The words My, Your, David, and Computer also appear in figure 2.21a with their respective important associations. This kind of connectivity contributes to the program's attempts to define words. Tracing the connections in this figure back to those in figure 2.18 demonstrates how the significant associations derive

Figure 2.21   (a) Complex interassociations to the word Name in figure 2.18;
(b) an extension of the conversation in figure 2.18.

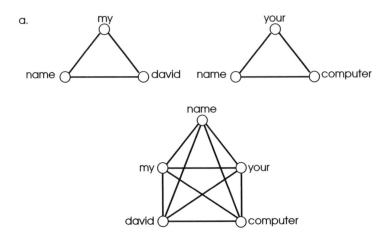

b.

U: What is your name?

U: My name is David!

C: name?

U: Your name is Computer!

C: name?

U: What is your name?

C: Computer!

U: What is my name?

C: David!

U: No*

U: What is my name?

C: is Computer!

from the shown sentences. However, the association net focuses associations so that the program's attempts at individual word meanings become heightened. Many other potential meanings and word uses also benefit from associations. Generating interesting new sentences improves as words gain more concrete generalized meanings.

Using negative stimulus by responding with a No word (designated with a *) causes the program to unlearn its name and acquire the next name available. The dialog extension shown in figure 2.21b indicates that the program can adapt as well as analyze and associate.

Note that because of the large number of initially equal weightings given each node, there are many different directions in which this conversation could have proceeded. Some of these directions would not be so immediately productive. The conversation in figure 2.18 resulted from using the software on this book's CD-ROM.

Association nets resemble neural networks in some respects. The term "neural network" refers to a program that associates output to input through interconnected units whose patterns of connectivity are modified by a learning rule (Loy and Todd 1991). Neural networks consist of layers of input, output, and hidden units. Hidden units form between the input and output and typically are not seen by the user. A neural net operates through a series of back propagations wherein output is compared to input and internal nodal values are altered until the comparison seems favorable, sometimes called "learning."

There are a number of critically important differences between association nets and neural networks. First, neural nets are generally fixed in terms of their nodal content, while association nets can have an indefinite number of interconnected nodes. The hard-wiring of neural nets seems to be based on its attempted imitation of the apparently hard-wired human brain. However, with so much of our brains unused, one can easily envision these neurons as equivalent to an arbitrarily deep association net. In other words, our brains are "softwired" with each bit of new information forging a completely new set of neuronic pathways (Jackendoff 1992).

While association nets can chain backward as well as forward, they do not back propagate as do neural nets. Thus, association nets do not require the same kind of training. Finally, and possibly most important, association nets do not have hidden units. The nodes in association nets can be accessed at any time and will reveal all their immediate associations and make available all their implicit associations. Association nets, as I have described them here, also differ significantly from variations and extensions of neural networks, such as associative neural networks, distributed associative memory, inference networks, and associative memory networks (Anderson 1983; Fodor 1983; Kohonen 1984; MacKay 1970).

As we will see, Alice uses an association net as its composing engine. Thus, a more detailed explanation of BackTalk will help clarify many of the ways in which Alice processes its *n*th-order Markovian musical decisions.

■ BACKTALK

As previously mentioned, BackTalk has no advance knowledge of what natural or artificial language users will choose. BackTalk assigns nodes, analyzes, associates, and adapts by using its initially small association net. As users interact with BackTalk, the program grows to accommodate the associations it derives from new information. BackTalk's ability to analyze, associate, and adapt makes it more advanced than either Fun or déjà vu and allows it to occasionally produce intelligent-like behavior.

BackTalk's association net exists as a natural outgrowth of the slots (see Cope 1996, chap. 4) present in each of its word objects. Examining these slots shows how connection and access continues to expand as a conversation progresses. In addition, since word objects in BackTalk are a subclass of sentence objects, word objects inherit the sentence object's slots. Thus, the nodes shown in figure 2.18 have access to a great deal more information than shown. For example, each word object has direct links to the length and content of each preceding sentence. This information can provide important contextualization of the various instances of associated words and lead to further implied word meanings, parsing representations—of which I have said little, leaving it to readers to explore further—and other critical processes for determining logical responses to user input.

The objects that BackTalk uses to store sentences have slots for the sentence name, sentence type (question or statement), the sentence itself, the length of sentence in number of words, a parsing using SPEAC representations (see Cope 1991b, 1996), and its origin (position), as shown in figure 2.22a. SPEAC is an acronym for *statement* (S), *preparation* (P), *extension* (E), *antecedent* (A), and *consequent* (C), each term roughly following its standard dictionary definition (for more detailed information, see the section "SPEAC" in chapter 5).

Word objects in BackTalk have slots for preceding words, following words, longest words in the sentences (key words), word type (question or statement), position in sentence, associations, and usage. Word representations get stored in many different places, depending on their position in reference to various words and in their repetitions in different sentences.

The function put-sentence-into-database in figure 2.22b enters sentences and words into their respective objects. These lexicons are then assessed during the program's replies. Words are assigned weights depending on their positions in sentences in which they occur and whether they qualify as key words. These

Figure 2.22 (a) BackTalk object definitions; (b) the function `put-sentence-into-database`; (c) the function `reply`.

a.
```
(defclass sentence nil
  ((name :initarg :name :initform nil :accessor name)
   (sentence-type . . .
   (sentence . . .
   (length-of-sentence . . .
   (parse . . .
   (origin . . .)))

(defclass word (sentence)
  ((predecessors :initarg :predecessors :initform nil
      :accessor predecessors)
   (successors . . .
   (keywords . . .
   (word-type . . .
   (positions-in-sentence . . .
   (usage . . .)))
```

b.
```
1.  (defun put-sentence-into-database (sentence)
2.    (establish-keywords sentence)
3.    (let ((sentence-type (get-sentence-type sentence))
4.          (name (make-new-name sentence)))
5.      (make-sentence-object sentence sentence-type name)
6.      (make-word-objects sentence sentence-type name)
7.      (parse-sentence sentence name)
8.      (define-incipients sentence sentence-type)
9.      (define-cadences sentence sentence-type)
10.     (find-associations)
11.     (setq *response* (replay sentence-type sentence))
12.     (if *play* (play (make-notes-into-events *response*)))
13.     (display *response*)))
```

c.
```
1.  (defun reply (type sentence)
2.    (if (recognize-no sentence)
3.      (progn (reduce-weighting (first *sentences*)(second *sentences*))
4.             (list '*))
5.      (let ((incipients (if (equal type '?)(my-remove '(no*)
6.          (incipients *answer-incipient-lexicon*))
7.                            (incipients *question-incipient-lexicon*)))
8.              (choices (compound-associations
9.                         (apply #'append
10.                                (loop for word in sentence
11.                                   collect (associations (eval word)))))))
12.         . . .
13.         new-sentence)))))))
```

weights are continually updated and re-evaluated on the basis of repetitions (incremented) and negative responses (decremented).

Using these processes, BackTalk achieves considerably more than what Hofstadter (1985) calls the renormalization effect, "in which any letter [of the alphabet in this case] . . . acquires a large set of virtual acquaintances despite having only two true acquaintances—its predecessor and successor" (p. 572). In Hofstadter's examples, each letter of the alphabet "has an effective connection to every other letter of the alphabet, although the strength decays rapidly with distance, since it has to be mediated by all the intervening letters, and each extra link weakens the chain by some constant factor" (p. 572). In BackTalk, these strengths between nodes—words in the case of BackTalk—do not decay with distance (time).

The function `reply` in figure 2.22c responds to user input. This function recognizes the word designated as *no* through the use of the symbol "*" and subtracts values from its previous output as a result (see lines 3–4). This function builds replies from two different sources. The first source, one that takes precedence early in collaborations, bases its replies on succession orders derived from user input. This process involves consulting the previously-described association net and building new sentences by retracing succession orders that it finds in the database (see also Cope 1996, chap. 3). The second source, one that occurs after a collaboration has developed significant interchange, bases its replies on the parsing slot in sentence objects. Initially, this slot contains monothematic SPEAC identifiers (see Cope 1991b, 1996) since words used early in conversations have not yet established their SPEAC meanings. As parsing becomes more defined through the use of the `find-associations` function (see figure 2.22b, line 10), the program begins to create its own sentences in response to user input. This approach provides more diversity than simply mimicking previous word orders.

BackTalk is a small program and thus, even with extensive use, does not create deep meanings for the words it uses, nor does it have any sense of the greater meanings of the combinations of words in its vocabulary. However, BackTalk can produce some striking dialogue. Unlike ELIZA (Weizenbaum 1976), an early interactive program, BackTalk does not contain any pre-programmed replies. Thus, the occasionally meaningful responses result from complicated networking between words and sentences and not from my programming.

BackTalk attempts to achieve all three of the previously mentioned criteria for intelligent-like behavior: analysis, association, and adaption. The program responds to any language, learns from negative stimuli provided by its user, and, possibly most important, develops conceptual configurations that can occasionally approach generalized meanings. BackTalk also develops parsing and generating mechanisms without explicit instructions from users.

Adding a pattern-matching component to BackTalk allows the program to find and reuse repeated subphrases, a process similar to locating and regenerating signatures in music (Cope 1991b). Successfully matched patterns tend to strengthen and solidify possible definitions of words by increasing word weightings. Using a non-linear pattern matcher, which attempts to recognize non-contiguous patterns within and between sentences, also discovers links between words that otherwise relate only through intricate combinatorial nodal connections—usually too complex for BackTalk to fully incorporate. Unfortunately, I have only just begun using such processes with BackTalk and cannot at present verify their full potential.

BackTalk listens to MIDI input as well as to ASCII text. While this form of the program remains limited and primitive, it can provide interesting, amusing, and occasionally educational repartee with users who typically improvise on MIDI keyboards. Because grouping pitches into word-like segments represents an imperfect science at best, BackTalk substitutes notes for words. Thus, this version of the program remains monophonic. Each note claims a node in the Back-Talk association net and acquires its relevance through proximity weighting and succession rules, as do words when using language with BackTalk. Musical conversations take more mysterious forms than their language counterparts, with imitations seemingly less problematic simply because exact or close duplication in music is commonplace rather than exceptional.

Interestingly, BackTalk is only one of many of my programs that began with language and ended with music. For example, the Experiments in Musical Intelligence program has its origin in a simple Haiku-generating algorithm. In fact, my gravitation toward using certain elements of linguistics and natural-language processing such as augmented transition networks (ATNs) can be traced directly to early work with language prototypes. My reasoning has been simple: I believe that music is fundamentally a language with its roots deeply formed in self-expression. While some of my papers (e.g., Cope 1988) comparing these two areas of study have occasionally met with controversy, I find that many colleagues secretly agree with this comparison, even though lucid and empirical explanations may yet be many years away.

I believe that music composition programs can benefit from the processes presented in Fun, déjà vu, and BackTalk. Alice has elements of each of these programs. For example, Alice's notation interface requires little more intelligence than that of Fun. The Alice analysis program resembles déjà vu's drawing program and has the ability to recognize thematic processes and associate formal elements. Alice's composing program utilizes an association network very similar to that of BackTalk with many identical slot names.

It is with this latter relationship that Alice develops what I call *character* (not to be confused with "musical character" discussed on p. 22) for it is Alice's association net that decides what choice to make when more than one right choice presents itself or when the variations I discuss in chapter 4 should be employed. Alice's character depends on three principal elements. First, Alice attempts to please users by augmenting and diminishing weights in its rule objects as users accept and reject music respectively. Second, Alice's association net attempts to communicate to its users through the music it composes, just as BackTalk does with language. While many might find this a rather prosaic and limited form of communication, I believe that it nonetheless represents communication. Finally, Alice stores the current increments of its variables and various other data in a preferences file so that certain aspects of its character continue to develop from one session to another.

By virtue of the complexity of its nodal interconnections, users of Alice cannot possibly know how the program will react to their input. Because of this, and because each user will have different reactions to Alice's output, each version of Alice develops its own individual character, beginning immediately after users enter their first note into the program's notational component. These unique personal implementations of Alice have their advantages and disadvantages, as we will see.

Whenever I need to express Alice's ability to non-randomly select one or another approach to composition, I will refer to its character. While to some these references may appear mysterious, it is the only way in which I can adequately express what to me represents one of Alice's more important features: its ability to act on its own without the need for random operations.

With its abilities to analyze, associate, and adapt, BackTalk (and Alice) gives the appearance of intelligent-like behavior. Their attributes, combined with character, lay what I hope are cornerstones for the next chapter's discussion of inference and creativity. However, make no mistake: I do not consider any of these programs truly intelligent.

Webster (1991) defines intelligence as "a capacity for learning, reasoning, and understanding." Throughout this chapter I have used similar words in my description of intelligent-like behavior: analysis, association, and adaption. Analysis incorporates the ability to disassemble or deconstruct an object or experience. Association relates these analyses to other objects or experiences with which they may have one or more elements in common. Adaption involves the changes necessary to incorporate the newfound information and associations in future behavior. I have repeated these three words often—analysis, association, and adaption—so that readers can understand their relevance throughout the rest of this book and, it is hoped, better relate to the context that their use evokes. Of course, I have not mentioned self-awareness, consciousness, free will, humor, love, correlation of speech and senses, originality, and so on—all further possible contributors to intelligence. At the same time, programs such as BackTalk and Alice must necessarily be limited in scope and not attempt to encompass too much in their first incarnations. Thus, my definition of intelligence here is simple and it represents just that: *my* definition. I do not suggest that this definition has any greater viability than that of providing consistency within the body of the research presented here.

There are many mitigating factors in making such a definition. Alan Turing writes,

> The extent to which we regard something as behaving in an intelligent manner is determined as much by our own state of mind and training as by the properties of the object under consideration. If we are able to explain and predict its behavior or if there seems to be little underlying plan, we have little temptation to imagine intelligence. With the same object therefore it is possible that one man would consider it as intelligent and another would not; the second man would have found out the rules of its behavior. (Ince 1992, p. 127)

Turing, the often-credited father of artificial intelligence, created a well-known test for determining the possibility of machine intelligence. Turing's test involves three people—a man, a woman (A and B), and an interrogator who seeks to discover the genders of the other two unseen people using only a series of questions. The man and woman answer in writing, and either or both may lie. Turing comments, "We now ask the questions, 'What will happen when a machine takes the part of A in this game?' Will the interrogator decide wrongly as often when the game is played like this as he does when the game is played between a man and a woman?" (Ince 1992, p. 134).

Turing provides a sample question-and-answer session that includes the following:

Q: Please write me a sonnet on the subject of the Forth Bridge [a bridge in Scotland].

A: Count me out on this one, I never could write poetry.

Q: Add 34957 to 70764.

A: (Pause about 30 seconds and then give as answer) 105621.

Q: Do you play chess?

A: Yes.

Q: I have K at my K1, and no other pieces. You have only K at K6 and R at R1. It is your move. What do you play?

A: (After a pause of 15 seconds) R-R8 mate. (Ince 1992, pp. 134–35)

As Hofstadter (1979, p. 596) points out, not only are the pauses typical of humans, but the addition is incorrect and should be 105721. Unfortunately for our interrogator, the machine may have been programmed to respond as a human might. For example, it might lie, and thus the distinctions between human and machine responses blur. Not being able to see one's respondent interferes significantly with the questioner's ability to use all their human perceptions to determine the source of the answers. Turing replies that it is important to draw

> a fairly sharp line between the physical and the intellectual capacities of a man. . . . We do not wish to penalize the machine for its inability to shine in beauty competitions, nor to penalize a man for losing in a race against an airplane. (Turing 1950, p. 435)

On the other hand, Turing notes that his

> game may perhaps be criticized on the ground that the odds are weighted too heavily against the machine. If the man were to try to pretend to be the machine he would clearly make a very poor showing. He would be given away at once by slowness and inaccuracy in arithmetic. May not machines carry out something which ought to be described as thinking but which is very different from what a man does? This objection is a very strong one, but at least we can say that if, nevertheless, a machine can be constructed to play the imitation game satisfactorily, we need not be troubled by this objection. (Turing 1950, p. 435)

Turing's research continued to explore this process and especially the possible arguments one might make against the notion that machines can think. Of these, one seems most apropos (the italics are mine):

> Not until a machine can write a sonnet or *compose a concerto* because of thoughts and emotions felt, and not by the chance fall of symbols, could we agree that machine equals brain—that is, not only write it but know that it had written it. No mechanism could feel (and not merely artificially signal, an easy contrivance) pleasure at its successes, grief when its valves fuse, be warmed by flattery, be made miserable by its mistakes,

be charmed by sex, be angry or depressed when it cannot get what it wants. (Turing 1950, pp. 445–46, quoted from Jefferson 1949)

Hofstadter adds yet further complications to Turing's reservations:

Pat: You could have a range of Turing Tests—one-minute versions, five-minute versions, hour-long versions, and so forth. Wouldn't it be interesting if some official organization sponsored a periodic competition, like the annual computer-chess championships, for programs to try to pass the Turing Test?

Chris: The program that lasted the longest against some panel of distinguished judges would be the winner. Perhaps there could be a big prize for the first program that fools a famous judge for, say, ten minutes.

Pat: A prize for the *program,* or for its *author?*

Chris: For the program, of course!

Pat: That's ridiculous! What would a program do with a prize?

Chris: Come now, Pat! If a program's human enough to fool the judges, don't you think it's human enough to enjoy the prize? That's precisely the threshold where it, rather than its creators, deserves the credit, and the regards. (Hofstadter 1985, p. 510)

Thus, Hofstadter adds a second hurdle to Turing's test (a test that I discuss in more detail in chapter 7). In Hofstadter's model, the computer must not only fool the participant taking the test into believing that it has intelligence equivalent to humans but also be capable of reaping the rewards of its success. Alice may succeed in occasionally passing the spirit if not the letter of Turing's test, but it has not, to my knowledge, enjoyed a prize.

THREE

Inference

■ INFERENCE

For the purposes of this book, the term *inference* indicates an ability to extrapolate basic principles from examples (Anderson 1964; Charniak and McDermott 1985; McCorduck 1979). Inference is a subset of intelligence, part analysis and part association. Inference does not require intelligence. Intelligence, on the other hand, requires inference. For example, I have a cat that, when my garage's front door opens, leaps a fence from my backyard and rushes around to enter the garage. Once there, it heads for the garage's side door and waits to be let into the backyard. This is the same backyard from which it initially came. If let out, the cat will repeat this hopeless and hapless cycle until the main garage door is closed. I believe that the cat thinks that there are an infinite number of backyards; although they seem similar, it wants to explore them all. While I can respect my cat's apparent creativity, trying to bring diversity to its possibly boring life, I doubt its ability to infer the circularity of its path and the fact that there is but one backyard.

This chapter and the next attempt to show my strategy for developing a kind of musical inference process. Ultimately, I hope to show how this inference process in Alice (ALgorithmically Integrated Composing Environment) presents a potential for intelligent-like behavior. Inference provides Alice with an ability to analyze at a more sophisticated level of abstraction than Fun, déjà vu, or Back-Talk. Inference also helps focus Alice's *character*.

The initial version of Alice used recombinancy, a relatively inference-free technique, as described in Cope (1997a) and in chapter 1 of this book. However, this recombinant version of the program often produced new music with recognizable fragments. In general, recombinancy creates new instances of music in a recognizable style that satisfies many who are not extremely familiar with the replicated composer's works. However, Alice, by its very nature, must compose music for the world's authority on the style of music it creates. The intimacy between the composer using the program and Alice is such that no amount of ATN (augmented transition network) can mask the method of composition from the user. Thus, I created a new version of Alice that extracts rules from input music and uses only those rules to compose its new music. This process has proven more successful than recombinancy in surprising me with its output, and, while style consistency occasionally suffers, the trade-offs seem more than worthwhile.

My constraints in creating this new version of Alice have been, and continue to be, to avoid programming explicit rules for composing works in a given style. Thus, Alice's inference program derives rules from the music provided to the program. These rules are relatively easy to acquire, to augment, and, most important, to implement. Like the Experiments in Musical Intelligence program and SARA (Simple Analytic Recombinant Algorithm), Alice emulates the style of music provided in its database. However, unlike Experiments in Musical Intelligence and SARA, Alice composes new music by inferring principles from its database rather than simply recombining groupings from that database.

Deriving rules from music provides many important benefits. First and foremost, rules separate composing from actual data and thus allow programs such as Alice to manipulate and vary these rules in logical and musical ways. Second, users and others have access to these rules. They can view them, in part or in whole, and thus can analyze and interpret them, compare them to rules derived from other databases, and so on. Third, users can change these rules, extend them, and even use them with different scales, providing a completely new level of user interaction than with other of my programs. While accessing rules requires some experience with multiparenthetical LISP notation and knowledge of the rules data type, as will be seen, it does not require any special mathematical or computational expertise.

Since there are many subtle gradations between analysis and inference, and because many of these gradations can be quite useful, I will present my work with inference as a step-by-step hybrid process between the two approaches. I begin with the area that overlaps analysis and inference the most: the databases. Database analysis requires grouping musical events in logical ways (for further information, see Cope 1996, chap. 2). Grouping becomes especially important when attempting to analyze musical function. However, logical grouping poses significant problems for computer analysis programs. Even grouping triads from Bach chorales, an apparently simple process, can create problems when computer programs are faced with separating harmonic from non-harmonic tones. This problem increases almost exponentially when programs must determine the best groupings for non-tonal music. Add to these problems the often contradictory determination of which group of many the composer might have intended and those that the listener might hear as groups, and the problem grows almost impossibly complex.

Determining group *size* in Alice, as with Experiments in Musical Intelligence and SARA, presents the first obstacle. Very small group sizes, while contributing to highly original composition with little resemblance to the database, require large amounts of computation time and memory and risk eroding style recognizability. Very large grouping sizes tend to produce high levels of style recognition and use less computation time but risk generating music that resembles music in the database. The best grouping size is one that allows new music to inherit the style of the composer but not so exactly that output produces recognition of the original music. The Experiments in Musical Intelligence program generally presumes a beat-by-beat grouping size. SARA, as described in Cope (1996), typically presumes measure-by-measure boundaries. For the reasons that now follow, Alice uses a variable grouping size based on event entries and exits.

Atonal music requires pitch groupings based on logical and consistent criteria (Babbitt 1961; Forte 1973; Lester 1989). In some music, this grouping falls naturally and even conveniently within certain boundaries (Crumb 1969; Webern 1928). Figure 3.1a shows an example in which groups tend to separate easily. For example, the first six pairs of sevenths, the group of thirty-second notes, the eighth-note triplet, and the last chord all seem to be logical groupings. In figure 3.1b the contrapuntal nature of the music suggests that, at the least, groups could be formed by following the melodic lines rather than the resultant harmonies. Figure 3.1c presents a more complex example where a variety of groupings could produce successful analysis. Regardless of the process, grouping should follow a consistent, meaningful, and audible logic.

However, for the purposes of Alice, I have avoided these problems by using a simple vertical simultaneity process that collects new groups at the inception or termination of any event. Ignoring the complexities of grouping should not be misunderstood as a refusal to confront the problem but merely as a desire to deal with one problem at a time.

Figure 3.1   Three examples presenting grouping problems.

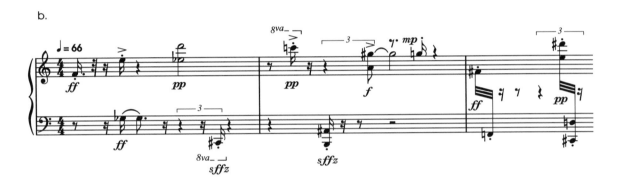

Figure 3.2a shows a simple example of a score in which the various voices enter and exit unevenly and occasionally without predictable regard for the metric beat. Figures 3.2b–g then demonstrate how Alice determines grouping size on the basis of the timings of entries (in this case) or exits and how the resultant groups accordingly vary in texture and length. This approach tends to produce

Figure 3.2   Grouping by entrance: (a) original music; (b) first group; (c) second group; (d) third group; (e) fourth group; (f) fifth group; (g) sixth group.

a.

b.

c.

Figure 3.2 Continued.

Figure 3.2   Continued.

g.

more original music than larger or regularly occurring grouping sizes. The use of signatures, structural patterns, meta-patterns, ear-marks, and unifications (all discussed in chapter 5) help reduce the concomitant risk of style loss when using this process.

■ TONAL INFERENCE

To clearly show the various inference processes at work, I will begin with a tonal example. While the material, the process, and the results seem extremely simple, the idea, once understood, can produce quite powerful and original output, as will be seen. The approach to inference in Alice centers on the analysis of chord groupings and voice leading. While voice leading may not be an important attribute of all types of music, even in the most free style

it can be at least occasionally important, and thus I have made it an essential component of Alice.

One of the ways that a program can infer rules from a musical database involves extracting voice leadings and using them to create music that does not explicitly exist in that database. A particularly good process to accomplish this involves using pitch-class (pc) equivalency, which disregards the octave in which a pitch appears. Assuming that the simple examples shown in figure 3.3a and b exist in a database, inferring voice-leading principles produces the chord motion shown in figure 3.4. Here, the chord of figure 3.3a moves to the resolution chord of figure 3.3b, with one of the notes transposed by octave such that each pitch class of the original chord moves in exactly the same direction as in the original of figure 3.3b: E–F, G–G, and C–B. This new motion retains the voice-leading correctness of the database but is not explicitly present in the database. Thus, the program can be said to infer this new motion.

One could simply view the upper voice of figure 3.3b as transposing down one octave to produce the new voicing of figure 3.4. This approach would resemble the voice exchanging of MATN (micro ATN) in SARA's recombinancy (see Cope 1996, chap. 5). However, compositionally speaking, viewing this as a new motion from the first chord of figure 3.3a based on the abstracted motions present in figure 3.3b provides us with a significantly more fruitful set of resources, as will be seen when we apply these techniques to more complicated tonal and non-tonal examples.

With a large database, the number of possible inferences in tonal music increases significantly. In fact, new voice leadings can be created, as shown in figure 3.5. None of the explicit chord connections in figure 3.5e exist in the database of figure 3.5a–d. All were inferred by using pitch classes instead of actual pitches. Chords 1 to 2 of figure 3.5e come from figure 3.5a, chords 2 to 3 of figure 3.5e come from figure 3.5b, and so on. It would be hard to imagine creating the pro-

Figure 3.3   Two simple examples from a database.

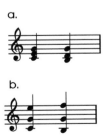

a.

b.

Figure 3.4   A new voicing inferred from figure 3.3.

Figure 3.5   Inferring a new progression (e) from database (a–d) voice leading.

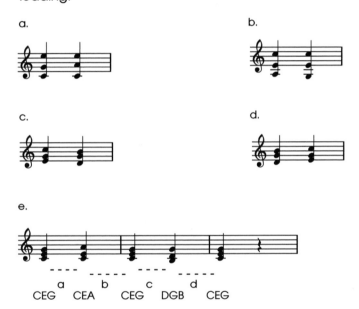

gression of figure 3.5e from successive applications of octave transpositions or MATN. However, using pitch classes, as shown following figure 3.5a–d, makes the derivations appear quite simple. The pitch classes are listed in C-major scale order.

Many of the chords here change inversion. In some cases, such inversions can violate specific rules of a given style. A good example is the second-inversion triad, or $^6_4$ chord in common-practice music. In figure 3.6, the chords of figure 3.6b use the pitch-class voice leadings of figure 3.6a, creating a possibly weak use of the second-inversion triad. However, since the voice leading relies completely on its origins, even these instances typically follow the constraints of specific use, producing, in this case, a passing or neighboring $^6_4$ chord. Other possible poor inferences include the inversion of parallel fourths

Figure 3.6 (a) Progression; (b) inversions resulting from inherited voice leading.

a.

b.

producing parallel fifths. Since we are counting on the program itself to be context free (i.e., free of actual data), some of these problems simply must be risked for the sake of the inferential and, it is hoped, intelligent-like behavior we are trying to emulate. As will be seen in chapter 6, use of style-illegal motion can also be weeded out by Alice's interaction with users' negative responses to output.

It can be advantageous to have basic triad types equate to one another by using reduced pitch classes instead of actual pitches. For example, transposing all major triads to a single major triad produces a substantial increase in inferential potential. For example, all motions to and from all tonic, subdominant, and dominant chords in major keys can be interchanged. An example of this appears in figure 3.7. Here, the pitches have been converted to numbers (C = 0, D-flat = 1, and so on) and the numbers reduced so that each set begins on 0. Such reduction of chords can be very useful and leads to yet further inferred motions and new versions of chords. Figure 3.8 shows how. Figure 3.8c results from the voice leading of figure 3.8b applied to the initial pitches of figure 3.8a. While figure 3.8c can be viewed as a simple transposition of figure 3.8b, calculating the music as pitch classes lays the foundation for far more interesting manipulations that cannot be calculated as transpositions.

Since tonal music relies on scale degrees of a particular diatonic configuration, reducing pitch classes to pure interval content can cause serious problems, as shown in figure 3.9. When the voice leading of figure 3.9b joins with the pitches of the first chord of figure 3.9a, as in figure 3.9c, the B-flat that results from the exact intervallic transposition no longer belongs in the original key of C major. One way to circumvent this problem involves accounting for scale degrees. Figure 3.10 shows an example of how this process works.

Figure 3.7 Conversion to reduced pitch-class numbers.

(0,4,7)   (0,4,7)

Figure 3.8 Inferred motions and new version of chords based on pitch-class equivalency.

a.

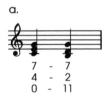

7 - 7
4 - 2
0 - 11

b.

7 - 9
4 - 4
0 - 0

c.

7 - 9
4 - 4
0 - 0

Scale degrees in this example parenthetically follow each pitch class in numerical notation. The inferred example, figure 3.10c, begins with the first example's notes but uses the second example's voice leading. However, the motion moves from scale degree to scale degree rather than by exact interval. This scale degree motion corrects for the interval chromaticism in figure 3.9. The only deterrents to using this approach are the accuracy of the key equivalents in the database and the computation time necessary to figure each variant.

Figure 3.9   Tonal problems with pitch-class transposition in tonality.

a.

```
7  -  7
4  -  4
0  - 11
```

b.

```
7  -  7
4  -  2
0  - 10
```

c.

```
7  -  7
4  -  2
0  - 10
```

As used here, a scale can be derived from any work in which the number of occurrences of some notes severely outnumbers other notes. The term *scale,* which some mistakenly link only with tonality, thus refers to any pitch system that has diatonic members (scale degrees) and chromatic members (non-scale degrees). This simple clarification is very important in that it does not differentiate, for example, between modality and tonality or between music written in various octatonic, whole-tone, or other non-tonal scales. For music in which all pitches have roughly equivalent importance, scale degrees are figured as continuous half steps—a chromatic scale. With this broad approach to scale degree definition, tonal, non-tonal, and atonal music may share the same system of analysis.

The tonal inference process just described utilizes two basic principles: (1) that horizontal voice leading must conform to an original model and (2) that chord order and type must appear in the database. If these two principles are consistent in new music, this new music will follow the basic constraints of its models. The idea is simple, but its execution is not. To further complicate the situation, using inference in atonal examples can be far more intricate than its tonal counterpart, even though most non-tonal music does not require so many scale

Figure 3.10   Using scale degrees to solve the problem of figure 3.9.

a.

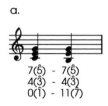

7(5̂) - 7(5̂)
4(3̂) - 4(3̂)
0(1̂) - 11(7̂)

b.

7(2̂) - 7(2̂)
4(7̂) - 2(6̂)
0(5̂) - 10(4̂)

c.

7(5̂) - 7(5̂)
4(3̂) - 2(2̂)
0(1̂) - 11(7̂)

degree corrections. However, using the following processes, inference can produce significant variations of music in the database while maintaining the coherence of the rules found there.

■ PC-SET INFERENCE

Many composers have employed pitch-class sets (pc sets) as a compositional resource (Crumb 1969; Morris 1987; Straus 1990). Pitch-class sets are contiguous pitch groupings (melodic, harmonic, or a combination of both) that can be related to one another regardless of their order or transposition.

Playing the music in figure 3.11 demonstrates the similarities between otherwise (apparently) dissimilar sets. The musical examples appear different but sound roughly similar. As will be shown, they reduce to the same pc set. Analyzing a pc set involves removing all redundant notes in found groups and treating the results as pitch classes. These sets are then converted to numbers and placed in ascending order. Thus, in the first example shown in figure 3.11, the group of notes F, E-flat, F-sharp, and A becomes the set [3,5,6,9]

Figure 3.11   Two dissimilar but equivalent pitch-class sets.

(E-flat = 3, F = 5, F-sharp = 6, and A = 9, in ascending order). Sets should then be transposed so that they begin with 0. Thus, the [3,5,6,9] set transposes to [0,2,3,6] by subtracting the first number in turn from each number of the set. Applying the same basic processes to the second chord in figure 3.11 produces the following: F = 5, D = 2, A-flat = 8, and E = 4 or [2,4,5,8], in ascending order. This set also reduces to [0,2,3,6] with the first number subtracted from the rest so that the set begins with 0.

Not all sets match so easily. Many reduced pc sets require further reduction to reach their prime form. Prime forms ensure that sets occur in their narrowest configuration of pitch classes (least distance between elements of the set). This process resembles the placing of inverted triads into root position, where the distance between notes is smallest.

Figure 3.12 shows another group of notes. Reducing these notes following the previously described process involves removing redundancies from the selected group of notes (B, C-sharp, G-sharp, and B-flat), converting these to numbers [11,1,8,10], placing the set in ascending order [1,8,10,11], and subtracting the first number from each number of the set so that it begins with 0 [0,7,9,10]. Note that this set contains some very high numbers. Thus, it might not be in prime form. Further reduction according to the following processes may yield a more likely prime version.

One of the easiest methods for finding the prime form of such sets involves creating a circle in the form of a clockface with twelve equally spaced notches representing the twelve pitch classes. Figure 3.13a shows such a clockface with numbers beginning at zero to relate to the previously discussed numerical pitch-class notation. To find the prime form of a pitch-class set requires identifying its numbers on the clockface. Sets need not begin on zero for the process to work effectively.

Once a set has been transferred to the clockface, the prime form of the set has the shortest distance between its outer members. If

Figure 3.12   A group of pitches more difficult to reduce.

two sets have equidistant outer members, as is the case when reversing direction on the same set (clockwise to counter-clockwise or vice versa), the set with the closest inner members to the originating pitch class succeeds since the smaller distance between lower adjacent members takes precedence.

Transferring the set [0,7,9,10] to the clockface produces the counter-clockwise set beginning on 0 as the smallest set, as shown in figure 3.13b. This results from the fact that the clockwise difference between the outer members of 0 to 10 (10) is larger than the difference between the counter-clockwise outer numbers of 0 to 7 (5). This new set then equates to set [0,2,3,5] when beginning with 0 [0], going two to the left [2], one further left [3], and yet two further to the left [5]. Interestingly, set [0,2,3,5] occurs whether read counterclockwise from 0 or clockwise from 7—in other words, this particular pc set is symmetrical.

Even very difficult sets, such as that shown in figure 3.14a, reduce to their prime versions rather easily using this method. Here, the notes, without redundancies, are F-sharp, C, A, E-flat, and F-natural. Converting these notes to numbers [6,0,9,3,5] and placing the set in ascending order (without the need for subtraction since the set already contains a C or 0) produces [0,3,5,6,9]. This set does not appear to be a prime form because of the high internal numbers. Circling the appropriate notches in figure 3.14b shows that the smallest version begins on pitch class 6 and proceeds in counter-clockwise direction. This produces the set [0,1,3,6,9] as the prime version.

As previously mentioned, this reduction process is not unlike that of finding inversions in tonal music. Figure 3.15 shows a C-major triad and its inversions. Both inversions reduce to the root position when using this process. Root position chords have the smallest distance between outer members. Interestingly, however, the major triad here reduces further to [0,3,7] when figured in counter-clockwise motion from pitch class 7. However, this interesting feature

Figure 3.13   A shortcut for figuring the prime form of sets: (a) the clockface tablature for figuring prime sets (shortest distance between outer notes, 1–2 notes, and so on); (b) set [0,7,9,10] transferred to the clockface producing the prime form [0,2,3,5].

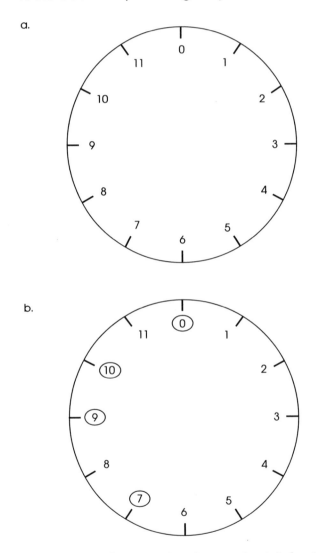

of reduction—that no prime form major triad exists—has no effect on triad inference in Alice since motions will be described with tonal scale degrees.

A list of the most commonly used 208 unique prime form pc sets can be found in many sources (Cope 1997c; Forte 1973). Viewing the

Figure 3.14   (a) A more difficult to reduce set; (b) the clockface
representation used to find the prime form [0,1,3,6,9].

a.

b.

reduction process in reverse from any prime form and transposing
the results to any register generates an extraordinary number of different pitch groupings. Yet, as apparently different as many of these
new sets may appear, they share their prime form pitch-class set
and thus sound similar. Figure 3.16 provides an example of the use
of a single pc set [0,1,3,5,6,8,10] to generate music. Note that the
generated sets group distinctly and clearly. Again, grouping can be
more ambiguous than this. Some of these machinations can thus be
lost to the ear.

Figure 3.17 shows a passage in which three sets are used in a simple palindrome. Here, the first and last groups were generated from
the same set, as were the second and fifth and the third and fourth
groups. In this example, the sets group harmonically so that the
retrograde can be heard even though the pitch content and registers of the groups generated from the same prime sets differ.

Figure 3.15   (a) Two inversions of the C-major triad; (b) reduced to the same triad using the pc clockface.

a.

[0,4,7]   [0,4,7]   [0,4,7]

b.

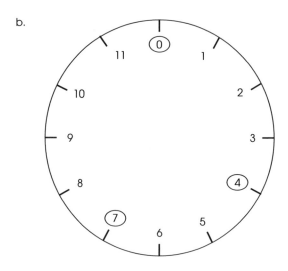

Figure 3.16   Composing with set [0,1,3,5,6,8,10].

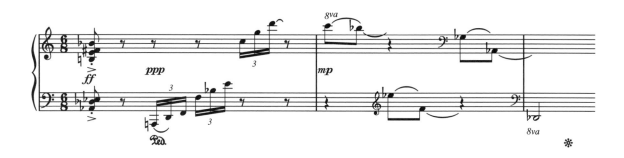

Figure 3.17   Palindromic use of sets.

The atonal inference process reduces a group of pitches to its prime form pc set, analyzes the voice leading between this prime form pc set and the prime form of its destination pc set, and then applies this voice leading to another but equivalent unreduced pc set to produce an apparently new but related-by-prime-form progression. The resultant progression inherits both its voice leading and its destination pc set from the original pc set but produces new logical motions and chord inversions. To fully understand how this atonal inference works, it will be necessary to describe the process in greater detail.

Figure 3.18a gives an example of music stored in a database. Figure 3.18b then presents music derived from figure 3.18a using atonal inference. As can be seen, the variant of figure 3.18b begins with the first two vertical groupings of figure 3.18a before branching into variants. Each of the variants then follows correct succession rules. In other words, no two-set order occurs in the variant that does not occur somewhere in the original (figure 3.18a). For example, take groupings 2 and 3 of figure 3.18b—[0,2,4,7] to [0,2,5,7]—and compare them to groupings 2 and 3 of the original progression in figure 3.18a—[0,2,4,7] to [0,2,6,8]. These two pairs of groupings do not match. However, the progression [0,2,4,7] to [0,2,5,7] does occur between chords 4 and 5 of figure 3.18a, making it an allowable movement. Voice-leading derivation is more difficult to discover. To follow voice leading, we must find the corresponding pairs of pc sets in the original (figure 3.18a), reduce both the original and the variant sets to their prime forms, and correlate the corresponding set member's voice motions.

As an example of this type of voice-leading derivation, I will use chords 2 and 3 of figure 3.18b. As discussed previously, this motion does not correspond to the original music of figure 3.18a. Again, chords 2 and 3 of figure 3.18b do correspond directly to chords 4 and 5 of figure 3.18a in terms of pc set motion with both sets reducing to [0,2,4,7] and [0,2,5,7] respectively. The set members of both

Figure 3.18   (a) Input music; and (b) output music from the Alice program.

a.

[0,2,5,8] [0,2,4,7] [0,2,6,8] [0,2,4,7] [0,2,5,7] [0,2,4,6] [0,2,5,7] [0,2,3,5] [0,2,5,7] [0,2,3,7]

b.

[0,2,5,8] [0,2,4,7] [0,2,5,7] [0,2,3,5] [0,2,5,7] [0,2,4,6] [0,2,5,7]

pairs of chords, the original and the variant, move identically in this instance with the two progressions being simple transpositions of one another as shown in figure 3.19a. As such, this new progression only begins to show the potential of using voice leading as a source for composing using pc sets.

The next two chords of the new generation (chords three and four of figure 3.18b) provide a more powerful example. To follow voice leading we must not only find the corresponding pairs of pc sets in the original (figure 3.18a), but also reduce both the original and the variant sets to their prime forms and correlate the corresponding set member's voice motions. Figure 3.19b shows this progression and the progression which it uses as a model: measures seven and eight of figure 3.18a. Here we see the sets occurring in different inversions and the voice leading has changed channels. The new music thus appears very different than its origins while the prime forms of the sets and the voice leading remain essentially the same.

The remaining pairs of sets in these two examples demonstrate that the music of the variant, however different in note content it may be from the original, follows the order and motions of the originals. However, this new music appears in different orders, transpositions, and inversions, producing an imaginatively new inferred progression.

Figure 3.19   (a.) A simple transposition using voice leading (sets 4 and 5 of figure 3.18a and sets 2 and 3 of figure 3.18b); (b.) a more powerful example in which sets occur in different inversions and the voice leading has changed channels (sets 7 and 8 of figure 3.18a and sets 3 and 4 of figure 3.18b).

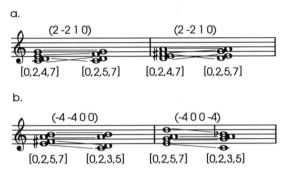

DERIVING RULES

The inference process described thus far differs from the methods used by other implementations of Experiments in Musical Intelligence. Both Experiments in Musical Intelligence and SARA use MATN (see Cope 1996, chap. 5), a subset of what I call transformational composition. In both inference and MATN, database music is transformed into new, often quite different music. Such transformation imitates, in my opinion, some of the techniques human composers use when composing, whether by conscious intent or by intuition. Applying voice-leading rules to different circumstances tends to be a standard procedure for many composers regardless of their style.

MATN switches logically interchangeable voices in larger groupings, such as beats and measures. Such transformations achieve the same goal as inference: different arrangements of notes. However, with MATN pitches remain as events with all of their original durations, channels, and dynamics often masking the pc set variations present. For example, counting the number of repeated chord types—the only easy computation available—would not tell users how many of the chord motions were duplicated (if any) or which ones progressed to the same chord types and so on. In Alice, as we will see, abstracting these progressions into rules allows for powerful processes of combination and comparison as well as determination of frequency of occurrence, which can then be reflected in the output for a truer stylistic replication. More important, Experiments in Musical Intelligence and SARA use MATN as a separate technique applied *after* recombinance takes place, while Alice uses inference as its principal composing process. In effect, inference represents the foundation of Alice's transformational composition techniques.

Thus, Alice, to implement its inference approach to composition, employs a significant new feature that separates it from its data-dependent predecessors. Alice's composing code uses rules rather than data to compose. This means that, unlike most other forms of Experiments in Musical Intelligence, Alice does not have direct access to musical events, only to stored rules derived from these events. These rules pertain to pc sets and voice leading. Obviously, many other types of rules may be generated from the music in a database, especially rules pertaining to dynamics, durations, precise on-times, and so on. However, for ease of explanation and clarity, I will limit the discussion, for the moment at least, to pc sets and voice leading only.

Alice creates rules by first grouping the music appropriately, converting the results to pc sets, and then deriving the individual rules. A rule in Alice takes the following form:

$$(((0\ 0)\ 2\ 1)((3\ 3)2\ 2)((5\ 1)-2\ 3)((8\ 5)-1\ 4))$$

Each rule part (i.e., ((0 0) 2 1)) consists of a head sub-list followed by two numbers. The numbers in the head sub-list represent the origin and destination pc set numbers. The number immediately following the head sub-list indicates the direction and amount of scale-degree motion between the two pc set numbers in the sub-list with negative numbers indicating downward motion. The final number in the rule part represents the channel to which the rule part applies. Thus, the rule part ((0 0) 2 1) indicates the motion of a major second (using a scale measured in half steps) between set member 0 in the chord of origin and set member 0 in the chord of destination in channel 1.

Origin and destination notes appear as pitch classes, and motion is measured in scale degrees according to the current scale. Thus, the 2 in rule part ((0 0) 2 1) indicates a major second upwards only with a scale measured in half steps. Using a current scale measured in whole steps, this 2 equates to a major third. Figure 3.20 shows the previous rule as it would appear in music notation with scale degrees measured in half steps.

Voice motion in rule notation must be flexible enough to represent more than scale degrees. This notation must also be able to represent chromaticism when using scales other than the chromatic scale. For our purposes, each half step above a scale degree that is

Figure 3.20   The rule (((0 0) 2 1) ((3 3) 2 2)((5 1) −2 3)((8 5) −1 4)) in music
notation.

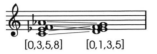

[0,3,5,8]   [0,1,3,5]

not itself a scale degree will receive a superscript caret, one per half
step. Thus, the raising of a minor second from the second degree of
the pentatonic scale of C–D–F–G–A would be {2ˆ} for D-sharp, and
the double raising of the second degree would be notated as a {2ˆˆ}
for E. In Alice, all chromatic notes are figured as raised scale
degrees. Thus, no lowered form of notation need exist. This chromatic notation allows for every possible motion between members
of any scale, and its inclusivity is greatly beneficial to our discussion
about Alice, which requires immense flexibility so that it can adapt
to any conceivable style of music representable in the equal-
tempered tuning system.

Creating new groupings of the appropriate set type and approached with proper voice leading requires a complicated set of
interlaced functions. As with creating new chord versions using
recombinancy and MATN, this process uses a matrix of properly
ordered data. In essence, an appropriately analyzed and named set
is matched to a lexicon of such sets in the database. An alternate
but identically named set is then substituted. For new composition
to take place, this process of substituting similarly named sets
should produce a new ordering of the original chord based on a
matching of the two sets, new voice motions from the originally
ordered set, a new destination set, or some combination of these.
For example, the start notes of a database set [0,2,4,7] could be
rearranged to match a newly created set's [4,7,2,0] note order. This
ensures that the database rule motion will be applied properly. The
database rule then replaces the newly created set's rule. To make
this process even clearer—and this point is not trivial—observe the
two distinct motions shown in figures 3.21a–c.

Figure 3.21a shows the original motion of two groupings in the
database. Figure 3.21b shows the rule formed by this motion with
the scale measured in half steps. Note that the order of the rule follows the sets from lowest to highest note. Figure 3.21c shows a second motion whose first chord reduces to the same set as in figure
3.21a. However, this equivalent set moves to a different destination

Figure 3.21   Extending voice-leading rules.

a.

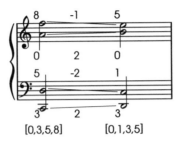

[0,3,5,8]   [0,1,3,5]

b. (((3 3) 2 1)((5 1) −2 2)((0 0) 2 3)((8 5) −1 4))

c.

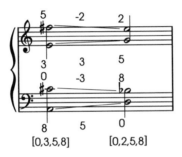

[0,3,5,8]   [0,2,5,8]

d. (((8 0) 5 1)((0 8) −3 2)((3 5) 3 3)((5 2) −2 4))

e.

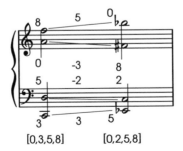

[0,3,5,8]   [0,2,5,8]

f. (((3 5) 3 1)((5 2) −2 2)((0 8) −3 3)((8 0) 5 4))

set with this movement shown in the rule of figure 3.21d. Alice then substitutes the first chord of figure 3.21a for the first chord of figure 3.21c and uses the voice leading of figure 3.21c to create a different—but correct—motion to the second set of figure 3.21c. To link the elements of the first chords together logically, it is necessary to exchange them so that their equivalent elements connect (i.e., so that the first chord connects logically with the appropriate rule). Thus, the first chord of figure 3.21c must be made to have the set-member order of the first chord of figure 3.21a. However, once accomplished, the actual motion from the first chord of figure 3.21a using the rule of figures 3.21c and d follows channels rather than set numbers. The results of this process appear in figure 3.21e. The rule derived from figure 3.21e, shown in figure 3.21f, demonstrates how the elements of 3.21d have been rearranged with different channel settings.

■ PROGRAM EXAMPLE

This book's CD-ROM contains a program called *Inference Creativity*, which creates examples such as that found in figure 3.18. Reviewing this code will help explain the inference process more fully. The data for this program is stored in objects (for more information, see Cope 1996, chap. 5) in a database. To create this database, the program first groups events appropriately. In *Inference Creativity* this follows the previously described technique of collecting vertical simultaneities on the basis of entrances and exits of pitches. Once music is broken into proper-sized groupings, the program converts each grouping to its prime form pc set. The program then stores this information in an appropriate lexicon (see Cope, 1996, chap. 5).

The events in *Inference Creativity* have been attached to their pc numbers in this version of rules composing so that users can, by tracing the various generic functions associated with the objects, observe how the program operates. Since this small program does not reference scales used by the music in the database, two separate top-level functions exist: one for tonal music, called `inference-tonal`, and another for atonal music, called `inference-pc`. Both of these programs are described in some detail at the beginning of their respective files in the *Inference Creativity* folder on this book's CD-ROM. The two databases that accompany the *Inference Creativity* program duplicate the music of figure 3.18a, and running `compose-pc` as described in the *inference-pc* file in the *Inference Creativity* folder produces output similar to that shown in figure 3.18b.

Alice has a much more complex object hierarchy than does *Inference Creativity*. The following paragraphs describe my version of Alice, though the CD-ROM version operates similarly. Figure 3.22 shows the four basic lexicon types and the pc rules grouping objects in Alice. The database lexicon represents the top-level object in Alice. The database lexicon has only one instance, which is stored in the variable *database*. This lexicon stores a list of the various works in the database. The database lexicon also stores the channel ranges, helping ensure that newly created lines stay within the boundaries of the current ranges as defined by the channels of the music in the database.

One work lexicon exists for each work stored in the database, with each such lexicon containing slots for the work name, the timing lexicons, the form of the work, texture and dynamic maps (discussed later), meter and tempo (useful for performing), the previously mentioned ranges, and a list of sets for each work. The position of timing lexicons in the hierarchy of Alice objects indicates their relative importance as opposed to set types and set objects. Beat proximity, at least in Alice, outweighs the importance of other parameters, such as set type, which I ascribe to a more secondary role. This is not to say that succession of set types is haphazard. On the contrary, Alice approaches succession rules as exactly as the user requires. However, sets of the same type are segregated according to their entrance times in relation to beat.

This approach of storing by entrance relation to beat presumes the existence of a large database containing numerous examples of musical groupings with the same on-times in relation to beats. When this is not the case, the order of sets in Alice's musical output will be identical to that of the order of sets in the music in the database. For music with infinitesimal differences between on-times or in which the user has no particular reason to differentiate between certain close-proximity on-times, Alice allows quantization to the nearest setting of the *quantize* variable. Thus, with *beat* size set to 1000 and *quantize* set to 100, all times relate to the nearest one-tenth of a beat, and variances of less than one-tenth of a beat will match and be stored in the same timing lexicon. Setting *quantize* to 1000 nullifies the timing index altogether, and all sets of a work will be stored in the same timing lexicon.

Timing lexicons contain their name, a list of set lexicons they contain, and their timing type. Timing lexicon names are suffixed and stored according to their relationship to on-beats. Thus, a suffix of -600 means that the lexicon contains lists of objects all of which begin .6, or 600/1000, off the beat. This means that during composition, when currently positioned at .6 off the beat, the program will choose

Figure 3.22   A map of the principal objects in Alice.

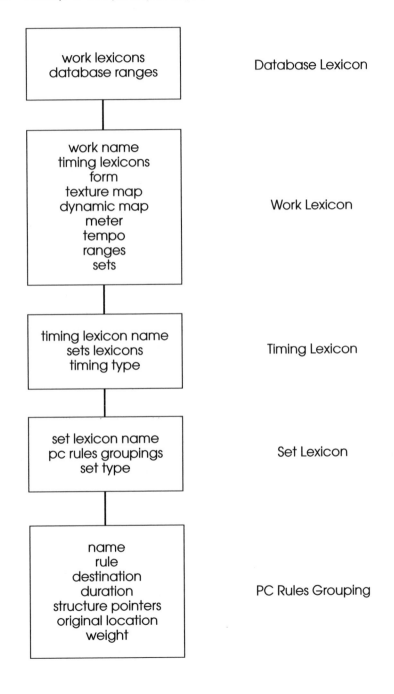

from only those sets that match this criterion. Again, setting the
quantize variable to 1000 defeats this aspect of Alice and stores
all a work's objects in a 0-suffixed timing lexicon. This can be very
helpful when using small rhythmically-complicated databases in
which possibly only one set would be stored in each lexicon almost
ensuring a high degree of similarity between output and input.

Set lexicons contain slots for their name, a list of pc rules groupings they contain, and their type. The pc rules groupings are the
lowest level objects in the hierarchy and have slots that contain
their name, rule, destination set, and duration along with structural
pointers to which they refer (e.g., cadences), their original location,
and weight. This weight slot will change on the basis of preferences
users indicate when saving or discarding algorithmic compositions
produced by Alice.

The weight slot in each pc rules grouping holds the current prior-
ity weighting of that grouping. This weight is initially set to levels
consistent with the number of repetitions of the rule occurring in
the database. Thus, Alice reflects stylistic preferences in its creation
of databases. As weights diminish in value because of rejection,
their chance for ensuing selection also diminishes and vice versa.
Thus, Alice uses the negotiating techniques of déjà vu and the nodal
weighting processes of BackTalk. As pointed out previously in
regard to the slots located in each Alice object, Alice also sets
weights in respect to connections with all other objects in the database, thus taking the form of an association net as used in BackTalk.

This rather primitive form of imprinting user preference in Alice's
objects enhances or reduces the weighting of an object and *any* possible neighboring object. I incorporate a more sophisticated approach
in my more extensive version of Alice by having the weightings spec-
ify the particular context of a decision. The weight slots in this more
extensive version occur as lists of possible following chords along
with their weightings. Thus, a weight slot of "((cope-music-a-24
.78)(cope-music-a-79 .23)..." indicates that the current object
will have significantly greater chance of being followed by cope-
music-a-24 than cope-music-a-79. This contextual approach
provides a more accurate representation of musical taste than does a
single rating, which arbitrarily reduces a chord's chances of occurring
in any situation. Unfortunately, the process of registering and consult-
ing extensive lists of such weightings causes considerable delays in
composition—my main reason for eliminating them from the version
of Alice that appears on this book's CD-ROM.

It may not seem necessary to have all the information in the various slots available. However, inheritance (see Cope 1996, chap. 4)

makes storing these attributes minimal, and creating attributes (slots) for as many characteristics as can be foreseen as useful avoids the need to rewrite code at a later time when enhancements to the program require new aspects of the data. However, as will be seen, even this abbreviated form of Alice uses most of the slots described here at one time or another.

Since all this information is available from any pc rules grouping in Alice, the Alice composing process, as will be seen, resembles that of BackTalk, the language program described in chapter 2 (see figures 2.18 and 2.19). Whatever intelligent-like behavior BackTalk has can thus be ascribed to Alice. The principal difference between Alice's and BackTalk's association nets resides in Alice's ability to transform data and Alice's more elaborate and thus possibly more elegant data types. Alice processes musical events rather than words, analyzes those events, and in particular seeks deep hierarchical information about those events as will be seen.

In Alice, lexicon names begin with SPEAC symbols (see Cope 1991b, 1996). This symbol is followed by the pc type associated with that SPEAC symbol (discussed shortly), the number of pitch classes present, and the number of voices in the source music. Thus, s-10-3-4 represents the tenth S (statement) lexicon of three pitch classes, which appears in a texture of four voices. Note that the last two numbers of the lexicon name need not match since the texture number includes octave duplications. The texture number is quite important for the program in looking up appropriate voicings. For example, if a sought-after set can have any number of voices, then voice leading becomes muddled, and the process will no longer be viable. All lexicon names and types can be found in the sets variable in the file called *reference* in the Alice *compose* folder. Set instances have the same names as their associated lexicons with the addition of the instance number of the grouping, as in s-10-3-4-1, the first member of the s-10-3-4 lexicon.

The initial choice of SPEAC symbol is context free; in other words, the SPEAC designation has been assigned prior to acquiring a context within a piece of music. These SPEAC symbol assignments result from their composite tension as they appear in the raw, so to speak, with antecedents having the most tension and consequents the least tension and so on. Context and assignments of SPEAC symbols occur during the structural portion of the composing process, as described in chapters 5 and 6. Comparing non-contextual and contextual assignments of SPEAC symbols can produce interesting revelations about style, a subject covered in chapter 6.

Figure 3.23 presents the results from calling the function ask after using Alice to extend—by four groupings—the music of the

Figure 3.23   The results of calling the function `ask`: a cross section of Alice's object system.

Database:
work-lexicons: (cope-a-1-notation-events-work)
database-ranges: ((1 (86 76)) (2 (74 63)) (3 (57 49)))

work-name: cope-a-1-notation-events-work
timing-lexicons: (cope-a-1-notation-events-work-0)
form: nil
texture-map: (1 1 1 1 2 2 2 2 1 1 1 1 1 2 2 3 2 3 2 2 1 1 1)
dynamic-map: (127 127 127 127 127 127 . . .)
beats: 4
tactus: 4
tempo: 60
ranges: ((1 (86 76)) (2 (74 63)) (3 (57 49)))
sets: (cope-a-1-notation-events-work-0-s-1-1-1-23 cope-a-1-notation-events-work-0-s-1-1-1-22
    cope-a-1-notation-events-work-0-s-1-1-1-21 cope-a-1-notation-events-work-0-s-5-2-2-20 . . .)
voice-motions: ((y) (-6) (4) (y -6) (0 1) (y -6 0) (0 x 0) (0 y 0) (0 x 0) (0 y x) (0 x)
    (-4)(6) (-9) (2) (0 y) (0 4) (0 -6) (0 4) (0 x) (-3) (6) (-4))

timing-lexicon-name: cope-a-1-notation-events-work-0
sets-lexicons: (cope-a-1-notation-events-work-0-s-4-2-2 cope-a-1-notation-events-work-
    0-c-5-3-3 cope-a-1-notation-events-work-0-c-7-3-3 cope-a-1-notation-events-work-
    0-s-5-2-2 . . .)
timing-type: 0

set-lexicon-name: cope-a-1-notation-events-work-0-s-4-2-2
pc-rules-groupings: (cope-a-1-notation-events-work-0-s-4-2-2-19)
set-type: (s-4-2 (0 3))

object-name: cope-a-1-notation-events-work-0-s-4-2-2-19
rule: (((0 0) 0 -2) ((3 4) 1 3))
destination: (s-5-2 (0 4))
destination-channels: (2 3)
duration: 250
structure-pointers: nil
original-location: 8000
weight: 1

cope database in the folder *work*. Here we see the previously mentioned objects with each of their contents spelled out clearly. Alice's standard nomenclature for new music is `notation-events`, thus the title associated with all of the objects. The database ranges appear by channel number with the ranges given in MIDI pitch equivalents. The variable `*quantize*`, having been set to 1000 here, produces a single *timing-lexicon* with a suffix-0, as previously explained. The form slot's *nil* value results from a lack of presence of other databases in this instance. The *texture-map* helps Alice sculpt passages and determine how one passage can logically extend another. The all-equal *dynamic map* here has little use; however, with more dynamically variable music, this map helps guide newly composed music toward logical use of dynamics. Meter here appears as a combination of the two entries *beats* and *tactus.*

Calling the function `ask` also produces some interesting data not actually present in the objects themselves, such as a catalog of voice motions. This particular catalog can be very useful when Alice attempts to create rule variations, as will be seen in the next two chapters.

The listing for voice motions here includes the symbols y (for voice exits) and x (for voice entrances), which will be explained shortly. The single object cope-a-1-notation-events-work-0-s-4-2-2-19 stores the rule, destination, original location, and weight, among other slots. The *nil* value for the structure-pointers slot relates back to the lack of form mentioned earlier.

Figure 3.24 presents traces of three Alice functions—compose-rules, run-pc-rules, and connect-pc-rules—along with the contents of the variable *history*, which gives users an opportunity to see the order of objects used to create the algorithmic music's *score*, *quantize*, *scale*, and *scale-projection*. Each of these variables plays an important role in the composing process and can reveal a significant amount of detail regarding Alice's use of the rules that it uses to compose. Carefully comparing the code, the values of the variables, and the output music will provide a fairly straightforward sense of Alice's basic composing process.

The top-level function compose-rules, a slightly different version of which appears in the file *compose* in the Alice source code on this book's CD-ROM, initiates the algorithmic composing process. This function takes as arguments the database work names, desired length of extension, the last note or notes composed in the current example, and a list of the related channels, those in use at the moment of initiation. If the main database object does not already exist, then compose-rules creates the database as shown in lines 4–5 in figure 3.25a. The program then accumulates all of the various set types and attaches them to the variable *available-sets* for later use (lines 6–7 in figure 3.25a). In line 8, compose-rules calls Alice's main composing function run-pc-rules which takes the same basic arguments as compose-rules. The remainder of compose-rules (not shown here) calls various cosmetic functions on the completed extension which, as a result of run-pc-rules, now resides in the variable *work*.

The function run-pc-rules, a slightly different version of which appears in the file *compose* in the Alice source code on this book's CD-ROM, first sets the *work* to nil, a mere formality but

Figure 3.24   Sample traces of the functions `compose-rules`, `run-pc-rules`, `connect-pc-rules`, and the contents of some important Alice variables.

```
Calling (compose-rules cope-a-1-notation-events) 4 (49) (3))
  Calling (run-pc-rules cope-a-1-notation-events-work) 4 (49) (3))
  Calling (connect-pc-rules
    4
      cope-a-1-notation-events-work-0-s-1-1-1-23
      cope-a-1-notation-events-work-0-s-1-1-1-22
      cope-a-1-notation-events-work-0-s-1-1-1-21
      cope-a-1-notation-events-work-0-s-1-1-1-13
      cope-a-1-notation-events-work-0-s-1-1-1-12
      cope-a-1-notation-events-work-0-s-1-1-1-11
      cope-a-1-notation-events-work-0-s-1-1-1-10
      cope-a-1-notation-events-work-0-s-1-1-1-9
      cope-a-1-notation-events-work-0-s-1-1-1-4
      cope-a-1-notation-events-work-0-s-1-1-1-3
      cope-a-1-notation-events-work-0-s-1-1-1-2
      cope-a-1-notation-events-work-0-s-1-1-1-1)
    (49)
    (3))
connect-pc-rules returned ((((0 55 250 3 nil)) ((250 49 250 3 nil))
        ((500 61 500 -3 nil) (500 67 500 2 nil))
        ((1000 60 500 -3 nil) (1000 67 500 -2 nil))
        (1000 53 500 3 nil)))
run-pc-rules returned ((((0 55 250 3 nil)) ((250 49 250 3 nil))
        ((500 61 500 -3 nil) (500 67 500 2 nil))
        ((1000 60 500 -3 nil) (1000 67 500 -2 nil))
        (1000 53 500 3 nil)))
compose-rules returned (((0 55 250 3 127) (250 49 250 3 127) (500 61 500 3 127)
        (500 67 500 2 127) (1000 60 500 3 127)
        (1000 67 500 2 127) (1000 53 500 3 127)))
? *history*
(cope-a-1-notation-events-work-0-s-3-2-2-6 cope-a-1-notation-events-work-0-s-7-2-2-14
 cope-a-1-notation-events-work-0-s-1-1-1-13 cope-a-1-notation-events-work-0-s-1-1-1-2
 cope-a-1-notation-events-work-0-s-1-1-1-2)
? *score*
*new-notation-events*
? *quantize*
1000
? *scale*
(60 61 62 63 64 65 66 67 68 69 70 71)
? *scale-projection*
(0 1 2 3 4 5 6 7 8 9 10 11 12 13 14 15 16 17 18 19 20 21 22 23 24 25 26 27 28 29 30 31
32 33 34 35 36 37 38 39 40 41 42 43 44 45 46 47 48 49 50 51 52 53 54 55 56 57 58 59
60 61 62 63 64 65 66 67 68 69 70 71 72 73 74 75 76 77 78 79 80 81 82 83 84 85 86 87
88 89 90 91 92 93 94 95 96 97 98 99 100 101 102 103 104 105 106 107 108 109 110 111 112 113 114
115 116 117 118 119 120 121 122 123 124 125 126 127 128 129 130 131 132)
```

useful for program clarity, and then establishes the `start-set-lexicon` (lines 3–4 in figure 3.25b), the lexicon most closely associated with the last chord composed by the user. The function `test-`

`for-end-notes-in-database` makes sure that the contents of the variable `end-notes` reside as a set in the database, something which when functioning automatically—as opposed to when testing—is guaranteed since these `end-notes` represent the last group entered into the database. The results of `test-for-end-notes-in-database` are stored in the variable `start-set-lexicon`. Lines 5–7 in figure 3.25b provide useful feedback to the user should the program find a discrepancy between the `end-notes` and the database. Line 8 in `run-pc-rules` calls the work-horse function of the compose sequence, `connect-pc-rules`. This latter function's second argument is a list of appropriate rules objects created by calling the generic function `pc-rules-groupings` on the aforementioned `start-set-lexicon`.

The function `connect-pc-rules`, partly shown in figure 3.25c with a slightly different version found in the file *compose* in the Alice source code on this book's CD-ROM, recursively creates the groupings which extend the music currently being composed. This function first checks to see whether the work is complete and, if it is, adds rests to the new composition and sets its timings appropriately (lines 2–8). If the work has not been completed, `connect-pc-rules` sets the local variable `new-grouping` in line 9 to the new chord instance, which is selected from a list of appropriate groupings. Line 10 declares useful internal variables. Newly selected chords are stored in the `*history*` variable, shown in line 11, which allows users to view the rule choices made during algorithmic composition. Line 13 sets the rule variable to the rule of the newly chosen chord. Lines 15 through 22 then check for doubling problems and will recurse without the newly chosen chord if it does not conform to the doubling requirement of the music. This doubling requirement exists for music in which a rule contains more channel movements than the set it represents. This outnumbering occurs when the original music, for example, consists of four voices but, because of doubling, its set contains less than four notes.

The remainder of `connect-pc-rules`, beginning with `progn` in line 28, continues the composing process. Lines 29 to 34 set the variable `new-rule-motion` to the results of the function `create-a-new-rule-motion`. This latter function, which will be discussed shortly, figures out the complicated rule structure of the newly chosen chord and produces actual events for storing in the `*work*` variable. The function `create-new-rule` in line 34 makes allowable variations of the current rule. The remainder of `connect-pc-rules` (not shown) recurses with much the same code that originally called the function from `run-pc-rules`.

Figure 3.25 The family of functions for `compose-rules`.

a.

```
1.  (defun COMPOSE-RULES
2.    (work-names length end-notes channels &optional (remove-objects t))
3.    (if remove-objects (remove-all-objects))
4.    (unless (equal *already-set-works* work-names)
5.      (make-objects work-names))
6.    (setq *available-sets*
7.         (group (get-sets)))
8.    (run-pc-rules (work-lexicons *database*) length end-notes channels)
```

b.

```
1.  (defun RUN-PC-RULES (work-names length end-notes channels)
2.    (setq *work* nil)
3.    (let ((start-set-lexicon
4.         (test-for-end-notes-in-database end-notes work-names)))
5.      (if (null start-set-lexicon)
6.        (message-dialog "Start notes don't have a
7.            correlative in the database!")
8.        (connect-pc-rules length
9.                         (pc-rules-groupings (eval start-set-lexicon))
10.                         end-notes
11.                         channels))))
```

c.

```
1.  (defun CONNECT-PC-RULES (length groupings end-notes channels)
2.    (if (zerop length)
3.      (setq *work*
4.            (set-timings (if *rhythm-overview-rather-than-inherited*
5.                            (break-at-each-entrance *notation-events*)
6.                            (add-rests-to-new-composition
7.                             (break-at-each-entrance *notation-events*)
8.                             (reverse *work*)))))
9.          (let ((new-grouping (get-one groupings channels))
10.                (rule)(new-rule-motion))
11.            (push new-grouping *history*)
12.            (if new-grouping
13.              (setf rule (rule (eval new-grouping))))
14.            (if groupings
15.              (if (not (check-doubling
16.                        rule
17.                        (loop for element in
18.                              (second
19.                               (lookup
20.                                (loop for note in end-notes
21.                                      collect (double-list note))))
22.                              collect (list element))))
23.                (connect-pc-rules
24.                 length
25.                 (my-remove (list new-grouping) groupings)
26.                 end-notes
27.                 channels)
28.                (progn
29.                  (setf new-rule-motion
30.                        (create-a-new-rule-motion
31.                         end-notes
```

Figure 3.25 continued.

```
32                            new-grouping
33.                           channels
34.                           (create-new-rule end-notes rule)))
35.              (if (not (null new-rule-motion))(push new-rule-motion *work*))
36.              . . .
```

d.

```
1. (defun CREATE-A-NEW-RULE-MOTION (end-notes set channels
2.        &optional (rule (rule (eval set)))(save-rule))
3.    (if (member 0 end-notes)
4.      (and (setf channels
5.                 (remove-position (position 0 end-notes) channels))
6.             (setf end-notes (remove-zero end-notes))))
7.    (let ((notes))
8.      (if (and (find-x rule)(not (member 'x end-notes)))
9.        (create-a-new-rule-motion
10.         (extend-end-notes end-notes rule)
11.         set
12.         (remove-duplicates
13.          (append channels (get-x-channel-numbers rule channels))))
14.        (progn
15.          (setf end-notes (remove-zero end-notes))
16.          (let ((associated-rule)
17.                (chan)
18.                (ordered-end-notes
19.                 (place-in-note-order
20.                  end-notes
21.                  (second
22.                   (lookup
23.                    (loop for note in end-notes
24.                          collect (list note
25.                                        (list note)))))))))
26.            (loop for note in ordered-end-notes
27.                  unless (or (null set)(null rule))
28.                  do (setf associated-rule
29.                           (assoc-pc (first note) rule))
30.                  unless (null associated-rule)
31.                  collect
32.                  (list
33.                    (mod (original-location (eval set)) *quantize)
34.                    (setq
35.                     the-note
36.                     (range-it
37.                      (let ((the-rule (second associated-rule)))
38.                        (cond
39.                         ((equal the-rule 'x)
40.                          (find-middle-range
41.                           (third associated-rule)
42.                           (remove-zero notes)
43.                           (remove-y-rule save-rule)))
44.                         ((equal the-rule 'y)
45.                          0)
46.                         (t (get-scale-degree
47.                             (first (second note))
48.                             (second associated-rule)
49.                             *scale-projection*)))) ...
```

The function `create-a-new-rule-motion`, shown in figure 3.25d, must deal with many of the necessary complications of rules to produce the events of new algorithmic composition. Lines 3 to 13 demonstrate one of these complications. Alice uses x's in place of intervals whenever a new voice enters in a composition. This results from the fact that no interval between a previous note and the entering note exists. Alice uses y's to represent notes that disappear from textures in order to announce their about-to-be missing status. Figure 3.26 demonstrates how x and y replace intervals in music of varying textures. The horizontal brackets indicate how y accounts for its associated rest yet pairs up with last- and next-sounding notes to create a voice-leading interval for the ensuing re-entrance. Rules with a y in place of an interval result in 0 for pitches and are removed here in line 5 of `create-a-new-rule-motion`. Notes with an x in place of an interval require Alice to project an entering note if the channel has not sounded previously. In cases in which a former note exists, that note creates an appropriate interval with the newly entered note, as previously discussed. Projecting an entering note requires that Alice have access to the set and to the range of the channel involved, and it then fits the choice of pitch to the `*scale*` being used.

Lines 16 to 25 of `create-a-new-rule-motion` declare variables important for establishing new events. The `ordered-end-notes` variable holds the end notes re-ordered according to their positions in sets rather than according to channel ascendancy. Beginning in line 31, `create-a-new-rule-motion` collects the events by start time, pitch, duration, channel, and respect to the beat, a position that may have been lost by using `*quantize*` initially to create more generalized lexicons.

Observe how notes conform to the contents of the variable `*scale-projection*` in line 49. This ensures that new music will follow the basic scale model of the input music. However, since tonal and some non-tonal music modulates, a more complicated set of functions exists in more elaborate forms of Alice in which interval classes are selected rather than pitches so that the music can modulate appropriately between logical keys. Alice derives scales automatically from its analysis of the database in use. The use of the function `get-scale-degree` (in line 46 of figure 3.25d) highlights this function's role in ensuring that a new chord will abide by the current status of the `*scale*` variable.

Figure 3.27 shows an example created by using the code shown in figure 3.25. The extension here, although brief, contains none of the actual music in the database. This new music is rather simplistic and devoid of context in terms of tempo, dynamics, articulations, and so on, which help make the realization of the voice-leading rules and harmony more musically meaningful. However, the example usefully shows how the previously described processes function contextually, at least in terms of pitch and rhythm, and provides the groundwork for further expansion.

While the music in figure 3.27a consists of three voices overall, the texture varies. Textural unpredictability provides the most difficult environment for Alice's type of algorithmic composition. As mentioned previously, Alice's approach to extending music of such different textures involves representing entering and exiting notes with x and y symbols.

Figure 3.28a shows a more extended musical example: a work called *Transformations* created using a slightly more complex version of Alice than the one just described. Here, the choice of instruments, dynamics, and so on are mine. However, the chords themselves resemble those shown in figure 3.18. The voice leading in this example retains its integrity even with the octave displacements present. Figure 3.28b provides a reduction of the score on a measure-by-measure basis. Note that creating the reduction required some voice interchange since the orchestration has masked an obvious one-to-one relationship.

The program just described derives rules with which it composes entirely from the database rather than from the user. I reiterate this point here for a number of reasons. First, user-provided rules limit

Figure 3.26 An example of how entering and exiting voices get represented by x and y, respectively.

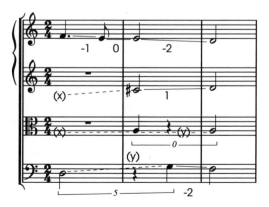

Figure 3.27   (a) User input music; (b) music extended using the code of figure 3.25 and the principles of figure 3.21.

a.

b.

programs to a single style. Second, user-provided rules often derive from a statistical or at least generalized version of a style and rarely reflect the idiosyncrasies that often help define musical style. Third, user-provided rules often require exhaustive amounts of code since rules will occasionally contradict each other and require backtracking or other time-consuming and inelegant processes.

Figure 3.28   An excerpt from *Transformations*: (a) from the score; (b) a reduction map.

Figure 3.28   Continued.

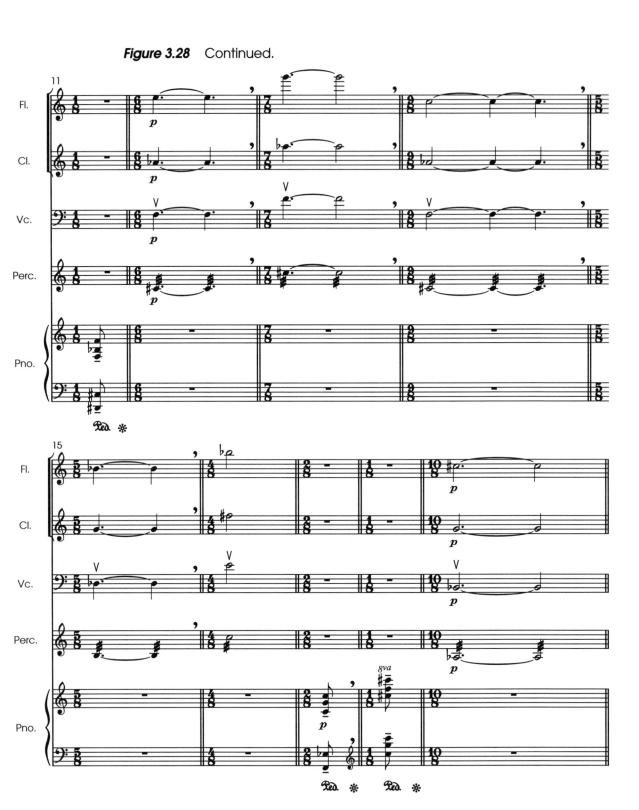

Figure 3.28 Continued.

b.

None of these problems occur in Alice since the rules it uses evolve naturally from the music it analyzes. In effect, Alice expands as new examples are added to the database. In fact, new rules help refine the program's adherence to a style while still creating distinctively new music. Furthermore, added music can create rule duplication. As mentioned previously, Alice weights duplicated rules more heavily and tends to prioritize them over other solutions just as duplicated visual images weigh more heavily in déjà vu. This weighting ensures that the program creates music with the same overall rule tendencies as the original music.

■ MUSICAL EXAMPLES

In *Experiments in Musical Intelligence* (Cope 1996, chap. 7), I discuss the 1992 creation of 5,000 works, including 2,000 piano sonatas and 1,500 symphonies. That discussion includes brief examples from three of the sonatas: numbers 293, 1755, and 3392. The program that created these works, a subset of the Experiments in Musical Intelligence program, began its composing by using a Stravinsky database—the third piece of the *Three Pieces for String Quartet* (1914), a homorhythmic chorale section from the 1947 version of the *Symphony of Wind Instruments,* and the final chorale passage from the *Symphony in C* of 1940—and slowly replaced this database with its own output, a process I call generational composition. Part of the process of creating variations in that program's subsequent output involved the techniques just discussed—the derivation of rules. Figure 3.29 shows an example of this from one of the symphonies—the second movement of number 1383. Coincidentally, this movement juxtaposes extremely loud wind passages against very soft string

Figure 3.29   From the second movement of *Symphony 1383*.

interludes in much the same fashion as Beethoven contrasts the piano and strings in the second movement of his fourth piano concerto.

Once completed, the program that created this music saved movements to the program's database to replace the previously oldest movement present in order to allow observation of how style changes over time. Constantly refreshing the database in this manner allowed variations to apply to variations, so that eventually the original model, the Stravinsky, became generally unrecognizable in the output. Figure 3.30 shows a part of Stravinsky's *Three Pieces for String Quartet* (1914), which was used as database for the creation of the first symphony of this series of 1,500. As can be seen by a comparison between Stravinsky's work and the example from Symphony 1383, the two works still have some stylistic elements in common. This similarity provides a continuity of style, while the differences help create the unique quality of each work.

Symphony 1383 uses other databases and techniques to ensure that all four movements are not simply extensions of the above-named musical sources and thus too similar to provide the contrast necessary for different symphonic movements within the same work. The program used to create this symphony had access to all the Experiments in Musical Intelligence's extant databases at the time of composition with explicit instructions to utilize these databases for contrast whenever necessary. While such access is not directly related to the subject matter of this chapter, it is useful to show fragments of the other three movements of this work to give readers more understanding of the issues at stake when composing large-scale music.

Figure 3.31 shows the beginning of the first movement of *Symphony 1383*. This movement grows additively from the opening cello solo to a climactic tutti. The material used here originates from my own *Arena* (1974) for cello and tape and *Five Pieces for Flute, Violin, and Bassoon* (1965). Because each derived idea has its own distinct and continuous texture, the music of this movement often quotes rather than paraphrases its sources. This results from the fact that, for example, a database consisting entirely of a work for solo instrument combined with a work for a quartet of instruments will allow interchanges only within one work or the other. In effect, once begun, the composing process cannot juxtapose different textures if such juxtapositions do not occur in one of the works in the database. Alice's output can suffer the same consequences when its database contains textures of similar extremes in size without examples of mixtures of these textures.

Figure 3.30   The beginning of Stravinsky's *Three Pieces for String Quartet*, second movement, on which 5,000 works were originally based.

The third movement of *Symphony 1383*, shown in part in figure 3.32, is based on two songs from Mahler's *Des Knaben Wunderhorn* (1898) with orchestration derived from those songs. The quotation nature of both this and the first movement fits well with the *musikalisches würfelspiel* nature of unifications (discussed in chapter 5) and provides style continuity to the work that is as strong as its origins in Stravinsky's voice leading.

The beginning of the final movement of *Symphony 1383* shown in figure 3.33 centers around various trills with an accompaniment of almost random-sounding percussion and piano figurations. The music here seems closely based on the scales that appear at the end of movement 1. The music shown in figure 3.33 eventually splinters

Figure 3.31   Beginning of the first movement of *Symphony 1383*.

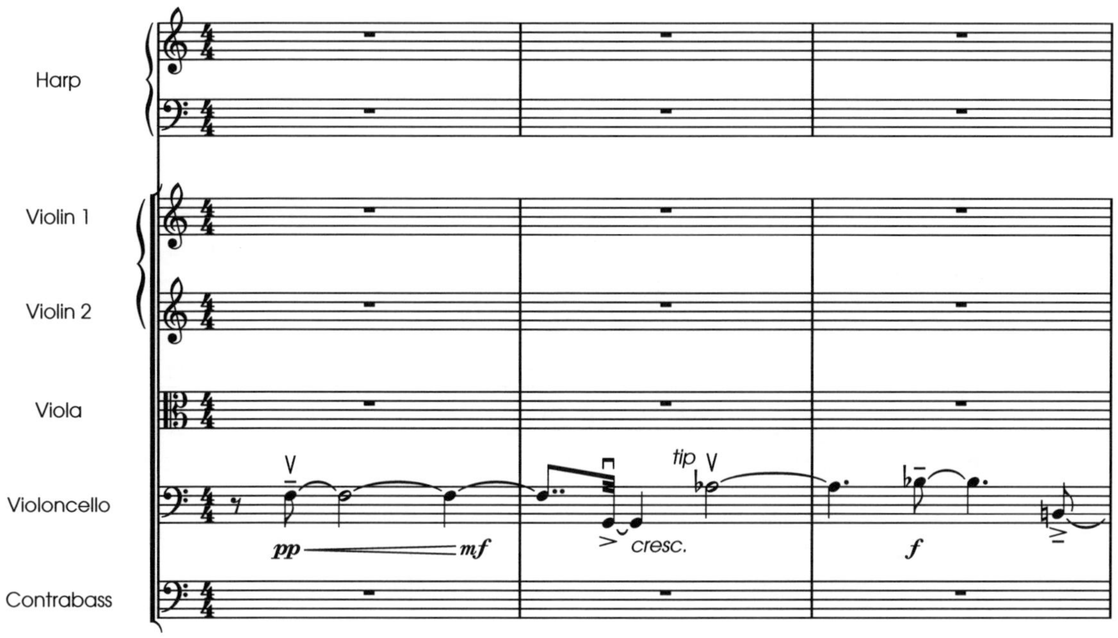

into a distinctly more contrapuntal section. The movement then returns to the first movement's opening material, ending palindromically in much the same way as *Vacuum Genesis* (a 1987 work in Cope style; see Cope 1991b)—a characteristic of many of Experiments in Musical Intelligence's compositions for which no known rationale exists in the code.

Alice, as well as the Experiments in Musical Intelligence program and SARA, expects that musical materials for movements of works will be extremely limited. These programs concentrate on developing a few ideas rather than introducing new ones. This process follows the "most out of the least" principle, which I find rewarding and which I teach my composition students. Luckily, this approach ensures that, while many of the movements of the 1,500 symphonies may be similar, most movements will have their own unique identity within the style constraints provided by the databases. In these ways, the program that composed the 5,000 works differs from the program that composed the more imitative stylistic compositions discussed in Cope (1991, 1996).

Figure 3.32   Beginning of the third movement of *Symphony 1383*.

Figure 3.33   Beginning of the fourth movement of *Symphony 1383*.

Thus far I have not, to any extent, discussed harmonic function, a subject often revered as the centerpiece of musical theory. Instead, I have concentrated on set reduction and voice leading. The omission of harmonic function from this discussion should not suggest that I feel that function is unimportant. To the contrary, extrapolating representations of harmony in tonal music can greatly enhance one's knowledge of that body of music. Also, as described in chapter 5, Alice uses SPEAC as one method of differentiating function. At the same time, I do suggest that notating symbols for chords and their inversions does not represent an end in itself but rather a guidepost on the way to more important goals. Harmonic analysis too often portrays music as static and one-dimensional, as if we listen vertically instead of horizontally over time. Voice leading gives life to the tensions and resolutions of harmonies and thus serves as a wellspring for inference and ultimately creativity, the subject of the next chapter.

FOUR

Creativity

■ CREATIVITY, INTELLIGENCE, AND HEURISTICS

In the first chapter of *Experiments in Musical Intelligence,* I wrote,

> A clear, common link among all these examples is that the *process* of composition, at least in many cases, involves combining elements of previously heard music. This process includes everything from stylistic signatures of a composer's period to actual paraphrases of certain works. These techniques, in combination with possibly more innovative ideas, are then used to create new works. (Cope 1996, p. 23)

In contrast to the Experiments in Musical Intelligence program, Alice (ALgorithmically Integrated Composing Environment) creates these innovative ideas by deriving rules from groupings found in its database and, as we will now see, extrapolating variations of these rules. Since this extrapolation often produces distinctively new music, I consider Alice's output the result of creative-like behavior. While the Experiments in Musical Intelligence program's recombinance does not compete with creativity, Alice's use of rules reinforces creativity by extending the constraints inherent in the original music to new situations.

Creativity, however, is not without constraints (Boden 1991). While innovation certainly represents one possible source, it does not constitute what I believe to be the core of creativity. As with inference, creativity depends on rules, however broadly they may be applied. Such broad interpretation represents, I feel, one of the important cornerstones of both intelligent-like and creative-like behavior and must be understood if we hope to replicate these irrevocably linked but illusory processes.

It seems to me that creative minds are intelligent minds that tend to associate more freely. In terms of the BackTalk program described in chapter 2, creativity ignores, to lesser or greater degrees, the weightings that help guide the program to more meaningful, but possibly less poetic, conversations. BackTalk, then, has elements of intelligent-like behavior but not creativity. Intelligence does not, in my estimation, require creativity. Creativity, on the other hand, requires intelligence.

It would be useful to look at other views of creativity. Douglas Hofstadter describes creativity as having four basic ingredients:

Having a keen sense for what is interesting: that is, having a relatively strong set of *a priori* "prejudices. . . ."

Following it recursively: that is, following one's nose not only in choosing an *initially* interesting-seeming pathway, but also *continuing* to rely on one's "nose" over and over again. . . .

Applying it at the meta-level: that is, being aware of, and carefully watching, one's pathway in "idea space" (as opposed to the space defined by the domain itself). This means being sensitive to unintended patterns in what one is producing. . . .

Modifying it accordingly: that is, not being inflexible in the face of various successes and failures, but modifying one's sense of what is interesting and good according to experience. (Hofstadter 1995, pp. 313–14)

Alice scores highly on the latter three of these ingredients but fairly low on the first. However, I have in fact tried as much as possible to exorcise these *a priori* prejudices that Hofstadter refers to from the program so that it relies solely on the music in its database for its rules of composition. I would be foolish, though, to think that Alice does not possess some of my preferences. At the same time, Alice is ruthless in its unbiased rules derivation and modifies itself—through its use of a BackTalk-type processor—according to adaptive weightings stored in its *character*. If such a learned sense of what is interesting qualifies as Hofstadter's "*a priori* prejudices," then Alice scores high on this ingredient as well.

Hofstadter adds to his definitions of creativity: "Note that this characterization implies that the system must go through its own experiences, just as a person does, and store them away for future use. This kind of storage is called 'episodic memory'" (Hofstadter 1995, p. 314). This description certainly fits Alice. The weights in Alice's lowest-level objects (discussed in the previous chapter) adapt to rejection and acceptance of Alice's output during the interactive composing process. Such experience, while certainly not comparable to the breadth of human experience, nonetheless qualifies, I believe, as episodic memory.

Figure 4.1 shows one of the ways in which humans demonstrate musical creativity and intelligent-like behavior. Here we see a series of four sketches and the final form of a melody by Beethoven for his String Quartet in A Minor, Op. 132. The first sketch (figure 4.1a) shows a phrase of music divided by two subphrases interlocked at the G-sharp in measure 2. The second sketch shows an abbreviation of the first sketch with the original form of the first subphrase appended by a dotted-eighth variation of the beginning of the second subphrase. The third sketch extends the first subphrase cadence (G-sharp) with a transposition of the first measure and a rhythmic augmentation of the original sketch's last two notes. The last sketch in figure 4.1d adds a resolution of the first subphrase's cadential G-sharp (to A) and then provides another ending to the phrase—a sequence of the first three notes in rhythmic augmentation and variation. The final form of Beethoven's music, shown in figure 4.1e, demonstrates extension in a variety of forms, including variations of the original dotted-eighth-sixteenth pattern. Of particular interest here is the return of figure 4.1c's cadence in measure 4 of figure 4.1e and the sequence by third in measures 4 and 5.

The Experiments in Musical Intelligence program, SARA (Simple Analytic Recombinancy Algorithm), and Alice, while not following Beethoven's precise sketching process, demonstrate similar techniques. The manner in which material is extended, varied, and manipulated in Alice resembles, tactically at least, that taken by Beethoven. Interestingly, Beethoven replaces internal measures while sustaining cadence points, which parallels the ATN (augmented transition network) and structural processes that Experiments in Musical Intelligence, SARA, and Alice use to make local choices logically project toward structural nodes (see the structure pointer slot described in relation to figures 3.22 and 3.23). In addition, Alice uses a backfilling subprogram to connect separate musical materials, as will be discussed in chapter 6. In figure 4.1 we see Beethoven heading for the cadential C in measure 4 of all but one of his examples (that example, figure 4.1b, does not extend far enough) while shifting materials and varying his measure 3's, which approach this cadence. This technique is reminiscent of the Experiments in Musical Intelligence program's analysis and Alice's transformational composition discussed in the previous chapter.

To achieve the same type, although certainly not the same quality, of sketching processes used by Beethoven requires not only creativity and intelligence but also the ability to learn. The term *heuristic*

Figure 4.1   Sketches by Beethoven for his *String Quartet in A Minor*, Op. 132.

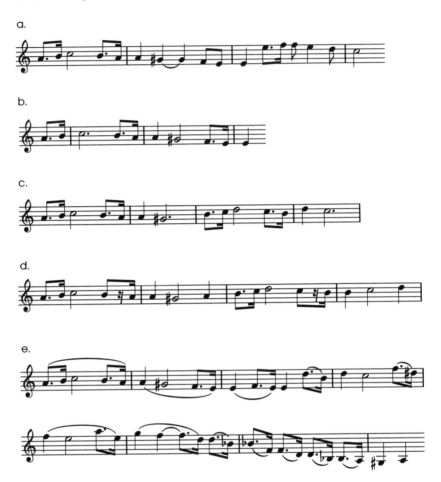

applies here (Michalski 1986). *Webster's New World Dictionary* defines heuristic as "helping to learn, as by a method of self-teaching" (Webster 1984, p. 284). Chapter 7 of *Experiments in Musical Intelligence* (Cope 1996) describes a version of the Experiments in Musical Intelligence program that displays heuristic techniques in its incremental resetting of various controllers for its pattern matcher. This incarnation of the program learns by comparing newly composed music with input music (databases) and statistically cataloging which settings of its controllers prove most effective in producing appropriate signatures.

Alice, unless overridden by composer preference, sets these same controllers to govern processes where more than one possible correct choice exists. Thus, Alice can make independent decisions as well as relying on users for their preferences. However, pattern matching is not the only process in which Alice can make independent decisions. Alice also applies the principles of heuristics to other elements of the composing process expedited by Alice's conversion of voice leading into abstract rules. Thus, the replacement of music by rules provides a unique opportunity to implement creative-like behavior. Abstract rules, represented as they are by numbers, can be manipulated in useful ways that would be cumbersome or impossible with lists of events. However, more important, the moment of conversion from events to rules offers Alice an opportunity to compare similar rules and to create new ones. As we will see, writing new rules can be a powerful mechanism for creating original music.

■ VARIATION AND APPROXIMITY

There are many ways that rules can be varied and still retain their basic integrity. For example, voice motions may move toward as well as away from their chords of origin. Put simply, retrograde voice motion produces effective variations. The only possible consequence of such motions is poor set-to-set ordering. For example, the fact that two successive sets follow correct order protocols does not mean that they will follow correct protocols when reversed. Figure 4.2b shows the retrograde motion of the sets shown in figure 4.2a. If the succession of sets in figure 4.2b violates succession rules, then the process fails. However, more often than not, such progressions confirm or effectively extend such succession rules. This kind of process occurs when Alice analyzes database music for rules at terminal cadence points where a lack of a destination set can produce complications during composition. In other words, the rule object that contains the final set of a database or current work does not have a chord of destination and as such, when used elsewhere in a new composition, can cause the program to abruptly stop. Using the preceding set as a destination allows the program to compose through such dead ends.

A second and more interesting way to vary rules involves reassigning voice motions. This means that chords retain all their motions but that these motions occur in different voices. In a sense, Alice's basic process of composition (described in chapter 3) mixes

Figure 4.2   Retrograde motion (b) of the sets shown in (a).

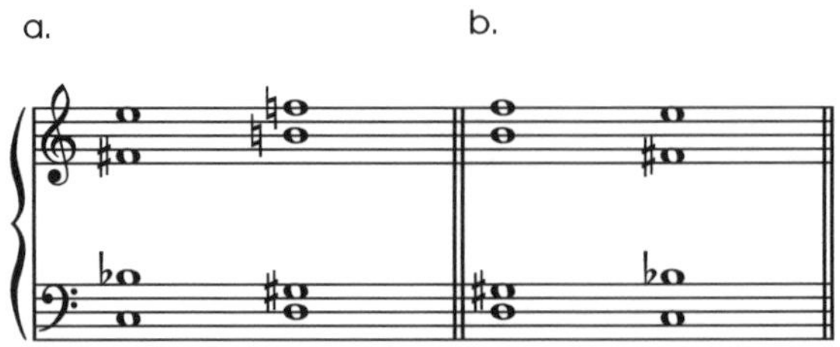

voice motions. However, that process also changes inversions of the destination chords so that voice motions maintain their associations with their original set members. Mixing voices to *vary* rules means that the original groupings do not invert and that voicings do not remain connected to their original set members. Figures 4.3a and b show how this works. In this particular case, the soprano voice motion has transferred to the alto voice, the alto motion has moved to the bass voice, and so on. Note that the chord that results from this process, the second chord of figure 4.3b, must be an allowable set type. In Alice this means that such sets are compared with the variable *available-sets*, whose contents represent all the sets used in the music in the database. Thus, Alice must correlate new chords created by this technique and use only set types that already exist in the materials being used for composition. Nonetheless, even with the possibility that such variations will not work, viable new motions can result from this process and produce interesting variations of set-to-set movements within new compositions.

Another approach to rules variation involves inverting voice motions. Inverting motions means that the intervals between set members move in mirror relation to their original motions. Figure 4.4a and b show an example of this process. Again, the set of resolution in figure 4.4b must exist in the variable *available-sets* for this new progression to work. Unlike mixing voice motions, the set motions resulting from inversion can produce novel motions, quite different from any motions present in the database. Thus, voice inversion extends rules farther than any method described so far.

Figure 4.5 shows a yet more abstract form of rules variation. The principle here follows the notion that we hear or at least comprehend implicit voice motions between prime forms of sets in use even when actually using complex generations of those sets. Regardless of its inherent justification, using such motions as extensions to rules possibilities creates interesting and useful material from which Alice can draw.

Figure 4.3   Voice motions occurring in different voices.

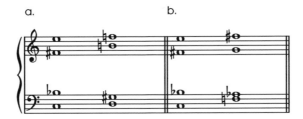

Figure 4.4   Inverted voice motions.

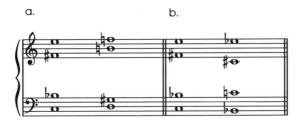

Figure 4.5a shows the same simple four-voice motion between two sets presented in the previous examples with their prime pc set forms given below. Figure 4.5b then shows a list of motions derived from the apparent motions between the two prime forms. This list of motions has been figured by subtracting the respective set numbers from each other. Figure 4.5c shows the originating set and a set derived from using the prime form motions. While no two sets in the database may actually move according to the motions given here, this principle of using prime form motions presumes that such motions occur implicitly in the original movement of sets. Applying prime set motions can produce powerful new ways to view rules and vary them.

These variants may also be used in combination. For example, inversions may be mixed with retrograde motions and so on. Prime form motions may likewise join with other variation techniques. In this way, a rather large number of progressions may be generated from the single voice leading between two sets. Each new motion, while different, adheres to the basic principles of the original.

To this point we have centered on voice motions as a source for variation. It can also be useful to employ pc sets that have approximate as well as exact equivalency. These approximations can produce

Figure 4.5   (a) Simple four-voice motion between two sets with pitch-class prime forms; (b) derived motions; (c) new music based on motion between the prime forms.

a.

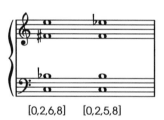

[0,2,6,8]   [0,2,5,8]

b.

[0,0,-1,0]

c.

[0,2,6,8]   [0,2,5,8]

important new possibilities for creative variations of found set orders and voice-leading rules. Concomitantly, it must be cautioned that such approximations may cause style variance and atypical voice motion. For this reason, approximation belongs to Alice's *character,* as presented in chapter 2. To understand how sets can have inexact but closely related structures, it will be necessary to discuss some elemental set theory.

Some sets are similar but not equivalent (Forte 1973; Lewin 1987; Morris 1987; Rahn 1980). One of the ways to have a program such as Alice utilize such similarities involves comparing subsets of sets. For example, two sets can have a number of common or invariant pitch classes. For example, the sets [4,5,9,10] and [3,4,9,10]—the first two chords in figure 4.6—have three invariant pitch classes, the subset [4,9,10]. Replacing set 1 in this example with set 2 will produce a similar but not identical motion with whatever set originally preceded the first set.

Figure 4.6   Two sets with invariant pitch classes.

Exchanging similar sets with different numbers of elements can also produce interesting results when used compositionally, as shown in figure 4.7. In this example, the first set [0,1,2,5,7] has four members of the second set [0,1,5,7]. Implicit resemblance can also be useful for exchanges as the set [0,1,3] occurs in the set [0,1,2,4] as the latter's last three pcs reduced to begin on 0. Obviously, however, the fewer elements two or more sets have in common, the less the sets resemble one another and the more tangential such comparisons become. Such replacements also suggest textural variation where none may logically occur in the current database. While doubling could account for this mismatch, it too may not conform to database style. Thus, these variation techniques must be used carefully and only in situations in which they make musical sense.

Interval vectors and Z relationships (see Forte 1973) can also produce varied sets. Interval vectors represent the complete interval content of a set with the number of minor seconds, major seconds, minor thirds, major thirds, perfect fourths, and tritones indicated in left-to-right order. Thus, the interval vector 121211 indicates that a set has one minor second, two major seconds, one minor third, two major thirds, one perfect fourth, and one tritone. The interval vectors 223111 and 222121 have four interval counts in common: minor seconds, major seconds, major thirds, and tritones. Essentially, one pitch has moved, causing the third and fifth categories to change one degree in each direction. Figure 4.8 demonstrates how two chords with these vectors can be used in succession to enhance their similarities and, possibly, take advantage of their differences, thereby extending and varying a set's appearance in a progression. Alice uses variations in place of originals rather than having them appear side by side. I have presented these examples in this way to allow you to see and hear their relationships and similarities.

Some sets with different prime forms have identical interval vectors. Such sets are said to have a Z relationship, with the letter Z

Figure 4.7   Composition using similar sets with different numbers of elements.

Figure 4.8   Using sets with similar but not equivalent vectors.

having no special meaning beyond vector equivalence. Figure 4.9 provides an example of two sets having a Z relationship. Alice's *character,* as presented in chapter 2, determines whether Alice may substitute a set's Z relation given that the voice leading to and from the Z relation conforms to the constraints of the current style. This conformity results from Alice accessing its *voice-motions* slot, as shown in figure 3.23.

Alice can also substitute SPEAC equivalents (see Cope 1991b, 1996) as a method of variation. These SPEAC equivalents may be contextual, based on the tension relationships found in the database, or non-contextual, based on relationships abstracted in Alice's sets variable located in the *reference* file in the *compose* folder. Figure 4.10a shows two chords that have the same *consequent* prefix. The chords have substantial differences—three different pitch classes. However, their tension component is quite similar, with the minor second in chord 2 as the primary difference. Substituting the first chord here for the second chord in figure 4.10b demonstrates how the process works. While occasionally producing unmusical or atypical progressions, using SPEAC in this way as a variation process can create interesting and often musical results.

Figure 4.11 presents a review of some of the variation techniques discussed thus far. Figure 4.11a shows two sets as they might appear

Figure 4.9   Relationship of two sets having a Z relationship.

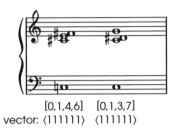

[0,1,4,6]   [0,1,3,7]
vector: ⟨111111⟩   ⟨111111⟩

Figure 4.10   (a) Two chords that have the same *consequent* prefix; (b) possible progression for substituting SPEAC-related sets.

a.   b.

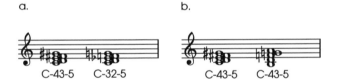

C-43-5   C-32-5   C-43-5   C-43-5

in a simple database. Figure 4.11b then presents three variants. In figure 4.11b(1), the first chord has been altered using invariant subsets and the motions corrected by one half step. Note that this new first chord reduces to the same prime form as the first chord of figure 4.11a. Figure 4.11b(2) shows the same progression as figure 4.11a but with the second chord missing one note (B-flat) resulting in necessary changes to the voice leading. In figure 4.11b(3), both chords have been altered. However, the voice-leading motions have changed only by half steps.

None of these variations preclude pattern matching as a source of comparing or composing variants of pc sets. While it may seem redundant to use such techniques with pitch classes, it can be useful to apply pattern matching to unordered sets to compare their similarities and general contours. However, pattern matching sets to create or to find variations is not routine in Alice. Such processes occur only when more standard procedures have resulted in predictable or unacceptable behavior.

Figure 4.11   (a) Two sets: [0,1,3,5,8,9] and [0,1,3,5,7,9]; (b) three sets of variants.

a.

b.
1.

2.

3.

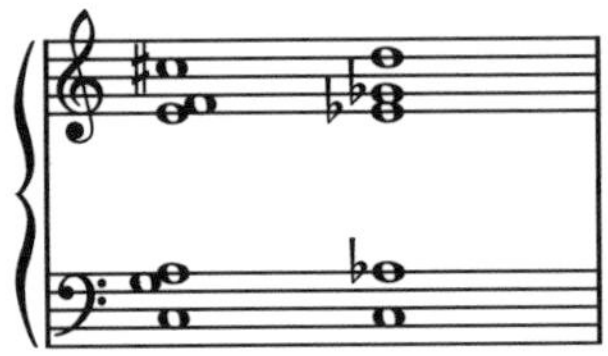

■ NEW RULES

Alice creates new rules on the basis of information it gleans from the music in its database. These new rules are not just simple variations of already discovered rules. Alice creates new rules by storing special information about the rules found in its database and using this information to generate completely new voice motions that have no precedent in the rules or in the music originally used to create these rules. The program uses three separate but related lexicons derived from the database to accomplish this:

1. A lexicon of all pc sets

2. A lexicon of voice motions by channel

3. A lexicon of all combinations of voice directions

With these three lexicons, Alice triangulates new rules. Figure 4.12 shows how this can be accomplished. Figure 4.12a shows examples of the three lexicons described previously. Figure 4.12b shows a new rule formed by accessing the three lexicons. While the second chord in figure 4.12b [0,3,7] already exists in the database, the combination of voice motions and set orders do not. Thus, the motions create a new rule that, because of the consultation with the various lexicons, meets the generalized requirements of the database. Since the values in the lexicons change depending on the music in the database, the process creates new rules according to the style found there.

Extrapolating new rules from a rules base can powerfully extend Alice's compositional processes in logical ways. I believe that these new rules represent the kind of deductive and adaptive (by

Figure 4.12 (a) Three lexicons required for creating new rules; (b) a new rule formed by triangulating the three lexicons.

a.

```
*available-sets*
((7  0  3  7) (0  7  3  7) (3  0  7  7) (5  8  0  1) (7  0  2  7) (7  3  0  7)
 (7  3  0  3) (8  0  5  2)(3  0  3  7) (4  0  4  0) (1  5  0  5) (2  0  7  7)
 (0  3  0  7) (4  4  0  4))

*channel-motions*
(((1) (0  1)) ((2) (3  0  1)) ((3) (0  4  1)) ((4) (1  3  0  4)))

*voice-directions*
((up same down down) (up same up down) (same same down same)
(down same down up)
 (same down same same) (down down down up) (same same up up)
(down down up up)
 (same up same same) (same same up same) (down same up down)
(same down down same)
 (down up up down) (out out out out))
```

b.

```
(((0  3)-1  1)((0  7)  3  2)((4  0)  4  3)((4  7)-1  4))
```

including new rules in the rules base) processes indicative of creative and intelligent minds. To view the techniques described here from within Alice, readers should open the file called *new rules* in the folder of the same name on this book's CD-ROM after composing with a database in Alice and run the function `create-new-rule`.

Generalizing voice motions to direction only and then applying these motions without respect to original interval amounts can produce more extensive variations. This approach requires only that subsequent chords meet the criteria of chord types in the database. Figure 4.13 demonstrates how this process works. Figure 4.13a shows unordered motions derived and generalized from a database along with a set of allowable intervals. These intervals are then freely applied in the allowable directions to produce the new sets of motions shown in figure 4.13b. Figure 4.13c presents a progression that does not otherwise occur in the database. However, the second chord here meets the pitch-class requirements for set types. Figure 4.13d then shows the new rule created by the process presented in figure 4.13c. In brief, Alice abstracts the composite directions of voice motions, catalogs the allowable horizontal interval motions, mixes these, and uses the mixture to produce acceptable new motions.

This generalizing rule-creating process requires a number of steps. First, Alice collects groupings of voice-movement directions from its database. Then Alice takes a set of voice motions and reduces them to their absolute equivalents (i.e., disposes of their direction). Alice freely applies these motions to one of the previously collected groupings of voice directions. The program then calculates the new motion from a given set to a new set and checks to see whether this new set occurs in the lexicon of already extant pc sets. If this set exists in this lexicon, Alice calculates a new rule. If this set does not exist in the lexicon, Alice may either attempt to match the set using the previously discussed variation techniques or reiterate the process until a new rule produces an acceptable set.

■ RULES ABOUT RULES

To this point, I have discussed ways in which Alice creates and varies rules. While many of these techniques produce interesting and even occasionally engaging results, they still fall short of intelligent-like behavior. Few if any of these techniques produce any unexpected or insightful results. The technique just discussed, that of

Figure 4.13   An example of generalized rules.

a. (+ + 0 +)(0 1 2 4)

b. (4 0 1 1)

c.

d. (((7 7) 5 1) ((7 0) 0 2) ((3 7) 1 3) ((0 3) 2 4)))

separating rules into component parts and carefully constructing new but logical versions, comes closest to the kinds of creativity that I, at least, explore while composing. Further generalization is required for a program such as Alice to uncover some of the insights that composers achieve when they intuitively compose.

As an example, it would be hard to believe that composers, when adding notes to their compositions, explicitly consider the kinds of rules discussed to this point. Such consideration would be prohibitively time consuming. For example, it is hard to imagine the following process occurring in a composer's mind:

> Moving up one half step in voice 1 means moving one half step down in voice 2, up a major second in voice 3, and down a minor second in voice 4 to ensure arriving at a logical set type.

More likely, one would imagine a composer thinking the following:

> Use stepwise contrary motion.

This latter approach, a less specific version of the former, provides a simple set of pointers to more detailed instructions of which there may be many slightly different iterations.

Figure 4.14 shows how Alice attempts to acquire and utilize such generalized rules. Figure 4.14a provides three progressions in event format. Events represent the notes of music in Alice. In left-to-right order, the numbers in an event indicate its beginning time in thousandths of a second, MIDI pitch number, duration in thousandths of a second, channel number, and dynamic ranging from 0 (silence) to

Figure 4.14   Forming more general rules: (a) three progressions in event format; (b) these three progressions reduced to rules; (c) generalized information about these three progressions for producing new but style consistent music.

a.

```
((0 47 1000 4 67) (0 55 1000 3 67) (0 65 1000 2 67) (0 72 1000 1 67)
 (1000 50 1000 4 67) (1000 55 1000 3 67) (1000 65 1000 2 67) (1000 71 1000 1 67))

((0 47 1000 4 67) (0 56 1000 3 67) (0 65 1000 2 67) (0 72 1000 1 67)
 (1000 50 1000 4 67) (1000 55 1000 3 67) (1000 65 1000 2 67) (1000 71 1000 1 67))

((0 47 1000 4 67) (0 56 1000 3 67) (0 65 1000 2 67) (0 71 1000 1 67)
 (1000 50 1000 4 67) (1000 55 1000 3 67) (1000 65 1000 2 67) (1000 71 1000 1 67))
```

b.
```
(((7 0) −1 1) ((0 6) 0 2) ((2 8) 0 3) ((6 3) 3 4))
(((7 0) −1 1) ((0 6) 0 2) ((3 8) −1 3) ((6 3) 3 4))
(((6 0) 0 1 ) ((0 6) 0 2) ((3 8) −1 3) ((6 3) 3 4))
```

c.
```
if (((7 0) −1 1) ((0 6) 0 2) ((6 3) 3 4)) then either ((2 8) 0 3) or (( 3 8) -1 3)
or
if ((0 6) 0 2) ((3 8) −1 3) ((6 4)3 4)) then either ((7 0) −1 1)or ((6 0) 0 1)
```

127 (loudest possible sound). For example, the event (5000 60 1000 1 100) refers to a relatively loud C³, beginning on the fifth second of a work, with a duration of one second, on channel 1 (see also Cope 1996, chap. 2).

Figure 4.14b shows how the three progressions of figure 4.14a reduce to rules in Alice. The pc sets in these rules remain in contextual form rather than reduced to prime order. Figure 4.14c demonstrates how Alice approximates information about these three progressions in ways that can produce new but style consistent music. The rules shown here take the form of conditionals. The *then* portion of the rule provides the consequences of the *if* condition. Since, especially with larger rules bases, this *then* portion of the conditional may have many different options, the best possibility can be chosen to fit a particular circumstance. Generalized rules provide the kind of flexibility that allows programs such as Alice to, for example, harmonize given melodies, a process often required during Alice's backfilling processes. Each note of the melody provides the *if* portion of the conditional with the consequences gauged in terms of the local choices and their longer-term implications.

With larger databases, Alice can dispense with using explicit rules altogether and concentrate entirely on using the derived generalized rules. While the program provided on this book's CD-ROM does not have the capacity to run generalized rules, it does, using the approach described under the previous subheading, separate elements of rules and recombine them to create new rules. I have opted to restrict this public version of Alice from using rules about rules since the processes needed to develop these rules and then to use them effectively in composition requires, at least initially, significant amounts of time and memory. Alternatively, I include here a leaner version of the program that composes, although less interestingly, on a much more reasonable time scale.

The use of *if...then* clauses in figure 4.14c suggests that Alice creates new code for their execution since those clauses differ substantially from rules. For decades programmers have romanticized about programs that write their own code in this way since this process suggests the epitome of adaptation, an especially important aspect of intelligent-like behavior, as we have seen. Early on in the process of creating the Experiments in Musical Intelligence program I too wrote code that created code. One of my programs, called *Darwin,* actually took over a mainframe computer for three days before it could be stopped. It re-wrote files, grew in size tenfold, and utilized 100 percent of the time-sharing computer's central processing unit. However, as exciting as this process may be to some, and as easy as it is in LISP to implement programs that themselves write programs, having Alice decipher *if...then* conditionals does not require such an approach. It is much easier and more transparent to simply organize data properly. For example, by placing all *if* data at the heads of lists that contain as their tail the *then* data, Alice simply associates—using the LISP primitive *assoc*—its situational data with its generalized rules database to accomplish its goal.

In their most abstract form, rules about rules interlace non-specific parameters in ways that produce rules. For example, each of the variables shown in figure 4.12a can be further generalized, as shown in figure 4.15. Figure 4.15a shows how the available sets in a database can be reduced to a list of possibilities for each set element. The set numbers here are listed in prime set order. Thus, this listing represents sets [0,1,5,8], [0,2,5,8], [0,3,5,8], and so on. Figure 4.15b lists absolute motions in channel order. The list here states that channels 3 and 4 move a major third or less in either direction, channel 1 moves by only a minor second in either direction, and channel 2

Figure 4.15   The formation of generalized rules based on figure 4.12: (a) sets listed in prime set order; (b) motions listed in channel order; (c) directions listed in (up same down) order.

a.
```
((0)(1 2 3 4)(5 7)(8))
```

b.
```
(1 3 4 4)
```

c.
```
((1 1 2)(2 1 1)(0 3 1)(1 0 3)(2 2 0)(2 0 2)(1 3 0)(0 2 2))
```

moves a minor third or less in either direction. Figure 4.15c shows possible directions listed in up, same, and down order. The file *generalize functions* in the folder of the same name on this book's CD-ROM provides functions that create generalized rules of this type. Note that this file uses the data of figure 4.12 as input to show the steps taken to create rules about rules from more specific rules.

Since numbers are the primary currency of machine programs, these rules about rules retain the general appearance of rules. However, in reality these rules about rules more typically resemble the previously described notion of "stepwise contrary motion," although in this case the contrary motion has greater flexibility.

Having Alice reduce databases to sets of voice-leading rules and saving abstractions of those rules requires significantly less storage space, easier access, and more potential for creative yet stylistically representative composition. This kind of rules form generalizes database music in ways that more easily invite manipulation and, for the programmer (if not the program itself) at least, a clearer avenue for amplifying the possible variations, which still follow the basic rules present in the original.

■ NON-PITCH CREATIVITY

To this point, discussion of Alice's creative-like abilities have been relegated almost entirely to pitch. Alice can also extrapolate rules and definitions concerning rhythm and, to a lesser degree, dynamics and articulations. To understand how non-pitch parameters are organized and processed in Alice, it will be necessary to re-visit Alice's object system.

The database object, the top-level object in the Alice composing program (see figure 3.22), provides detailed information about the works it contains. This object has access to voice leading rules and sets organized both by timing in relation to beats and by set type. This information is invaluable when Alice attempts to create new voicings and new rules, as already seen. Each work in the database also contains general attributes, such as meter, tempo, and maps of dynamics and texture (see figure 3.23). This information, mostly in the form of collections of data, serves as a prime focus for non-pitch creativity. The work database object also contains timing lexicons. As previously stated, timing lexicons are named according to their relation to beats. A -300 suffix to the name of a timing lexicon indicates, for example, that it contains a list of set lexicons which begin at 300/1000 of a beat after their respective beats. As will be seen, these timing lexicons serve as one source for rhythmic creativity.

Alice determines rhythm in one of three ways. In its simplest incarnation, Alice imposes a rhythmic template derived from one or more of the works in the database or the work in progress. This approach serves best when using very small databases in which inheriting durations individually can cause unstylistic results by creating uncharacteristic juxtapositions. The state of the variable `*rhythm-overview-rather-than-inherited*` determines whether Alice uses rhythmic imposition. The rhythm template is stored in the variable `*rhythm*`.

Figures 4.16 to 4.18 provide an example of this process. Figure 4.16 shows a small excerpt of an early work of mine called *Concert for Piano and Orchestra* (1980). I grouped this passage roughly and Alice analyzed it, as shown in figure 4.17. Alice then composed the music shown in figure 4.18. Note how all the rules of set progression and voice leading have been followed carefully by the program even though the actual music is different from that shown in figure 4.16. The rhythm in figure 4.18 follows the composite rhythm of measure 1 of figure 4.16 with some subtle refigurings.

A second and more typical approach to rhythmic invention involves inheriting begin times and durations directly from rules objects as a natural consequence of the manner in which these objects are stored. Since Alice composes music by selecting objects residing in timing lexicons (see figure 3.23), the program operates best by determining its current temporal location in a new work and choosing from the appropriate beat-relative lexicon. This timing-sensitive approach reflects relationships between harmonic materials and on-beats that composers may have incorporated into their style.

Figure 4.16   An excerpt from *Concert for Piano and Orchestra.*

Both of these methods are available in the version of Alice that appears on this book's CD-ROM. A more elaborate form of Alice also employs techniques for authoring original but still database-related rhythmic schemes. In general, Alice creates these new rhythms by deriving succession rules from the music in the database and the work in progress and creating rhythms on the basis of these rules. Figures 4.19a–e demonstrate how Alice accomplishes this. Figure 4.19a presents a simple rhythm from which the succession rules shown in figure 4.19b were derived. The durations to the right of the followed-by sign ≈ indicate which individual duration can acceptably follow the duration to the left of the sign. These simple first-order Markov succession rules can produce some rather awkward rhythms, as shown in figure 4.19c. Avoiding such problems requires deeper-order Markovian rules, such as those shown in figure 4.19d. Here, the third succession rule of figure 4.19b, the problem rule, has been modified such that an eighth note is followed by a half note only if the half note occurs on a subsequent beat. Figure 4.19e shows a new rhythm that follows the rules of figures 4.19b and d but that is different than figure 4.19a. For the most part, such rhythmic variation does not produce new rhythms but, rather, subtle variations of rhythms already present in the music in the database.

Figure 4.17   Analysis of passage from figure 4.16.

```
((c-18-4 (0 1 3 7)) (c-24-4 (0 2 5 7)) (c-10-4 (0 1 3 5)) (c-16-4 (0 2 4 6))
 (c-23-4 (0 2 4 7)) (s-13-4 (0 3 4 7)) (c-18-4 (0 1 3 7)) (c-26-4 (0 1 5 8))
 (c-15-4 (0 2 3 6)) (c-22-4 (0 2 3 7)) (c-22-4 (0 2 3 7)) (c-8-4 (0 1 2 4))
 (c-20-4 (0 1 5 7)) (c-31-4 (0 3 6 9)) (c-28-4 (0 2 5 8)) (c-19-4 (0 1 4 7))
 (c-11-4 (0 1 4 5)) (c-25-4 (0 1 4 8)) (c-15-4 (0 2 3 6)) (c-29-4 (0 2 6 8))
 (c-23-4 (0 2 4 7)) (c-20-4 (0 1 5 7)) (c-13-4 (0 1 3 6)) (e-3-4 (0 1 2 6))
 (c-27-4 (0 2 4 8)) (c-10-4 (0 1 3 5)) (c-16-4 (0 2 4 6)))
```

   Alice can further vary rhythms by adding or subtracting durations from one another. Figure 4.20a shows a simple rhythm as presented in a database. Figures 4.20b–d then demonstrate how this
rhythm can be used as a springboard for three different variations.
In the first variation shown in figure 4.20b, the rhythmic values have
been eroded by subtracting succeeding values from one another
whenever this results in a positive number above zero. The second
variation of figure 4.20c results from the reverse process: the addition of subsequent durations. The third variation in figure 4.20d
shows a combination of these techniques. As with rule abstraction
for pitch, this form of Alice creativity may produce unstylistic
music. At the same time, such variations can create much needed
contrast in situations that have become monotonous or predictable.
   Dynamics pose particular problems for programs using abstract
rules as a compositional paradigm. Groups that connect well in
terms of destination notes seldom connect well in terms of dynamic
continuity. Individually stored dynamics left to the exigencies of the
rule process would typically terrace from one level to another and

Figure 4.18   New music based on figures 4.16 and 4.17.

likely represent little of the style of dynamics in the original music in the database. For dynamics to have any real value to newly composed music in terms of style inheritance, they must be treated separately from pitch. This means extracting dynamics from the original music, deriving overall patterns, and reuniting the dynamics with newly composed music in logical ways. The object system of Alice, as it appears in figure 3.22, shows how lexicons store various attributes for entire compositions, such as dynamic and texture maps.

Figure 3.22 also reveals that the work lexicons in Alice store complete dynamic maps of works in the database. In their simplest configuration, these dynamic maps serve as templates that are superimposed on newly created music and that then follow the exact dynamic contours of one or more of the works in the database. Logical segments of music in the database suffice for shorter segments of newly composed music.

However, dynamics often occur in relation to formal considerations rather than just in terms of individual notes or pairs of notes. Concomitantly, the dynamics of individual phrases often have unique stylistic meanings. Thus, Alice creates a list of phrase lists of contiguous dynamics and reapplies these lists of dynamics to newly composed phrases. Since these newly composed phrases may be of

Figure 4.19   (a) A simple rhythm; (b) derived rules; (c) a new rhythm following the rules of (b); (d) an extra rule to prevent offbeat half notes; (e) a logical new rhythm following the rules of (b) and (d).

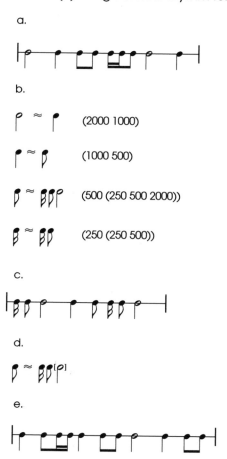

different lengths than those in the original music from which the dynamics were extracted, Alice applies these dynamics proportionally rather than literally. This proportionality requires omitting some repeating dynamics if the new phrase is smaller than the original or extending some dynamics by proportional repetition if the new phrase is larger than the original.

Figure 4.21a shows a user-composed phrase of music with the dynamics clearly shown. Figure 4.21b presents a list of these dynamics expressed roughly in terms of Alice-related event dynamic numbers (in which 0 to 127 represent the complete gamut of possibilities). Figure 4.21c shows a machine-composed passage

Figure 4.20 Three variants of a given rhythm (a); (b) subtractive; (c) additive; (d) combinative.

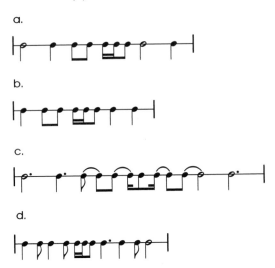

Figure 4.21 Dynamics used by relative overall shape in the creation of a new phrase: (a) piece 3 from *Three Pieces for Clarinet*; (b) a list of dynamics; (c) new phrase with same general shape as in (a).

b.

(50 50 75 65 65 65 65 65 60 65 72 72 30 50 50 75 75 75 75 75 100 100 30 30 30 30 30
38 42 48 55 64 79 75 79 80 75 72 50 50 75 100 100 100 100 25)

Figure 4.21 Continued.

c.

in the style of the original but of a different length. Note how the dynamics retain the general shape of the original music but do not explicitly repeat on a note-by-note basis.

Dynamic changes occurring on long-held single notes cannot be adequately represented in MIDI. However, as discussed in chapter 7 of Cope (1996), Experiments in Musical Intelligence events—and thus Alice events—can be extended to include any desired information. Thus, Alice can store the dynamic shape of a single pitch. Note, however, that Alice does not compose using this information. New works inherit it verbatim on an event-by-event basis for eventual translation to standard notation.

The better method for incorporating dynamic shapings of individual notes may well be to compose without them and then, after the music has been transferred to traditional notation, to figure the appropriate hairpin dynamics. This process avoids having to decipher the sometimes haphazard arrangements of dynamic changes occurring on individual notes that can occur during algorithmic composition. This inclusion-by-hand alternative seems especially appealing when using Alice, where, unlike the Experiments in Musical Intelligence program and SARA, there is no need to preserve the integrity of the computer-composed music; in other words, users may freely adapt Alice's output in any way they choose.

Articulations and other effects require similar special notations if they are to accompany their pitches through the machine-composing process. In general, the use of mutes, microtones, glissando, pizzicato, and so on can be so notated. However, as with hairpin dynamics, Alice does not compose using articulations or other effects, nor will MIDI perform them during playback—they will simply be ignored. In some cases, the program may translate these effects into traditional notation.

■ TEXTURE

Alice, the Experiments in Musical Intelligence program, and SARA do not orchestrate music. None of these programs has awareness of the human factors that govern the performability of the music they compose. Such knowledge would require an amount of code rivaling and perhaps superseding that of these composing programs themselves. Programming such constraints would also be a never-ending task in which rules would likely conflict with other rules, just as they do in real life. One would have to constantly shoehorn in new gradations of rules on the basis of ever better interpretations of just what exactly constitutes the idiomatic use of standard and non-standard orchestral instruments.

However, one of the benefits of recombinancy in Experiments in Musical Intelligence and SARA includes the fact that their algorithmic output inherits orchestration as well as pitch and rhythm. This means that these programs do not require lists of instrument ranges, fingering charts, or appropriate instrument combinations. All these attributes transfer, at least in principle, from the database and often occur in newly composed music as idiomatically as the original composer composed them. However, Alice requires special care in this regard. First, structural or rule constraints can force out-of-range notes. Second, as described earlier in this chapter, Alice's *character,* as presented in chapter 2, can cause the program to create music beyond the range of one or more instruments in the ensemble of the work being composed. Alice must transpose music to registers within the ranges of instruments in the ensemble of this in-progress work.

To avoid creating unplayable music, Alice keeps a record of each channel's range extremes as dictated by the database. Whenever the program transposes music because of any of the previously named situations, the program consults this range record and transposes notes that fall outside that range in the direction necessary to bring them back into proper range. This may occasionally cause uncharacteristic inversions with other instruments as well as collisions or problematic doublings. However unthinkable some of these may be, I have spent far less time making appropriate changes in the resulting music than I would have by entering the ranges of each instrument and the constraints governing the transposition of out-of-range notes myself.

Figure 4.22a provides an example of this process from a database in which a simple texture occurs within the framework of a very specific circumstance: wide-register, rhythmically diverse music. In a subsequent compositional passage by Alice (shown in figure 4.22b), the program has not consulted the ranges in the database, thus the out-of-range low F-sharp in the violin. However, in figure 4.22c, the ranges found in the database have been referenced, and thus the music falls more reasonably in range.

Alice's algorithmic composing program also recomposes music by channel. This transformational process exchanges channels between like-functioned segments in much the same way that the use of rules exchanges groupings. This transformational process adds complexity and variety to algorithmically composed passages and resembles MATN (micro ATN) in both the Experiments in Musical Intelligence program and SARA.

Transformational processes cannot work directly on inferential composition since exchanging the various voices would simply undo what the program just accomplished. However, after-the-fact transformational changes with larger segment sizes can produce further variations in output. This can be especially useful if Alice's output continues to sound derivative rather than new. However, such transformations cannot produce miracles, and new output may still reflect the input music's influence and thus reflect the style and content of either the current work or one of the works in the database.

With transformations added to the already extensive collection of possible variants derived from inferential rules composition, the palette of possible right choices becomes large. Random selection from all these possibilities seems haphazard and irresponsible since such care has been invested in their creation. Thus, Alice makes such choices on the basis of its *character,* as discussed in chapter 2.

One of the less routine ways in which Alice varies output involves adding or subtracting voices. Such addition and subtraction is not done arbitrarily. In general, musical voices are omitted when the resulting newly created textures imitate textures found elsewhere in a database. For the most part, such texture alterations do not substantively change music but rather reduce, double, or embellish.

Figure 4.23 shows two passages from Beethoven and two from Alice. In figure 4.23a and 4.23b, Beethoven has arranged two different

Figure 4.22   (a) An example from a database of a three-voice texture; (b) composition by Alice; (c) better results based on register consultation.

a.

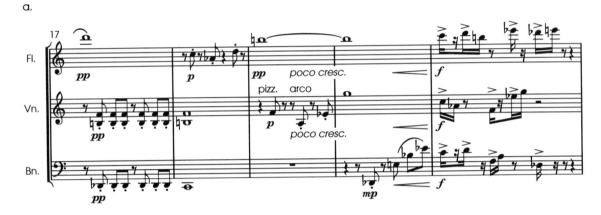

b.

c.

measures of his *Tempest* sonata in similar but texturally different ways. Figures 4.23c and 4.23d show how an initial Alice composition appears and then later varies in a similar manner to the music presented in figures 4.23a and 4.23b. Note that in each case added

Figure 4.23   Two passages from Beethoven (Op, 31, No. 2, mm. 31 and 99) (a, b) and two from Alice in *Transformations* (c and d).

a.

b.

c.

Figure 4.23   Continued.

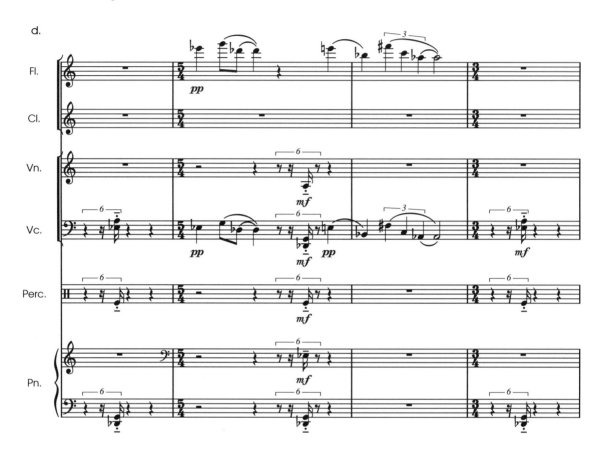

materials are not substantive—they do not harmonically or melodi-
cally alter the inherent musical meaning of the original passages.
However, the texture changes produce a different take on the material and thus provide another way for Alice to vary its output.

This process of adding and subtracting voices can be especially
useful when combining materials of different textures. Where recombinancy requires two joining segments to have the same texture,
Alice's ability to alter texture makes it possible to successfully join
segments regardless of their textural differences. Thus, Experiments
in Musical Intelligence would not likely join figures 4.23a and b even
though most of the material in these measures match and seem possible candidates for recombination with certain register adjustments.
Subtracting a voice from figure 4.23b along with transposition, as
shown in figure 4.24, allows the measures to smoothly connect. In

Figure 4.24   The two measures of Beethoven from figure 4.23 connected logically using voice subtraction.

this case, the program found similarly textured music elsewhere in one of the two compositions or in Beethoven's style, as exemplified in the database used for composition, permitting the measures to be recomposed. Alice uses rules for this process rather than recombinancy, but the principle remains the same.

In more dramatic circumstances, Alice may create completely new textures from material in its databases. For example, two-part counterpoint could result from four-voice music with the subtraction of two voices. Alternatively, four-voice textured music could result from various alternating doublings of a two-voice counterpoint. In some cases, even vertical recombination of two two-part textures can occur, resulting in four-voice counterpoint. However, the possibilities of such counterpoints following the inherited rules from a database seem highly unlikely.

Alice consults databases and in-progress works extensively to decide whether texture changes are appropriate both in terms of style compatibility and the context of the passage being extended. This approach distinguishes Alice from its predecessors—Experiments in Musical Intelligence and SARA—both of which change textures according to foreground (beat-to-beat) recombinancy.

As previously mentioned, Alice employs texture variations by way of its *character,* as presented in chapter 2. The variables associated with Alice's *character* can be ratcheted to 100 different levels, each providing incremental degrees of variation. At zero or quite low settings, such variables allow very little use of the techniques described here. At very high settings, most if not all of the variation types are used to their fullest. In general, low settings produce the most stylistically faithful output, while higher settings create the most imaginative.

Composing using high levels of *character,* especially over a long period of time, can be tricky. It can also be exciting. In effect, any voice motion can occur, given the existence of a proper harmonic vocabulary. With just a few examples, Alice can use rule abstraction to create immense amounts of diverse music. Much of this new music will not conform to the voicing and doubling present in the database and, as such, may not be usable or effective. At the same time, such music may provide precisely the variation necessary. Obviously, only users of Alice can determine which of these outcomes occur. High levels of *character* were used effectively during the creation of the 5,000 works discussed in chapter 7 of *Experiments in Musical Intelligence* (Cope 1996) and many of the examples presented in this book. Such levels often provide the variety needed to allow style to develop over time and not remain stagnant.

Figure 4.25 provides an example of how Alice's approach to creativity can produce distinctively new music. On the surface, the relationship between figures 4.25a and b appears tenuous. The two phrases bear little resemblance, and the fact that figure 4.25b was derived from figure 4.25a seems obscure at best. However, following each of the connecting lines proves that the sets evolve logically following the principles outlined in this and the preceding chapter. The rhythm, dynamics, and orchestration originate from other works in the database. The resultant new phrase has a unique musical flavor owing as much to the process that created it as to the music that preceded it.

Figure 4.25   An example of how Alice's approach to creativity can produce distinctively new music (b) from music in a database (a).

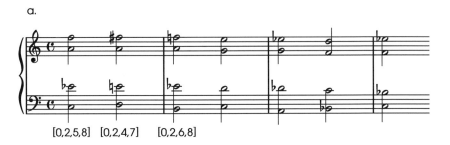

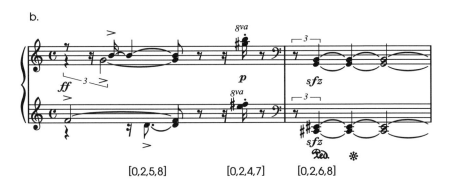

FIVE

Structure and Coherence

■ OVERVIEW

The following chapter contains an extensive list of subprograms used by Alice, in some cases the version of Alice which I use rather than the one that appears on this book's CD-ROM. In many instances (as with structural analysis), the variously-described subprograms act as successive alternatives to find solutions to complex problems. In such cases, readers should not imagine these subprograms functioning simultaneously or even often. In other cases (especially those involving various forms of pattern matching), subprograms act in concert but at widely-spaced times during the composing process. Thus, while these subprograms may occasionally seem competitive, most of them actually occur in sequence rather than in parallel and in ways which eventually prove simple rather than complex.

Most of these subsections also deserve significantly more explanation than I afford them here. However, I have left their descriptions intact since in-depth explanations would not only require immense amounts of space but many of these subprograms would also require previous musical and programming experience that I cannot expect most readers to have. I include figure 5.37 to help provide readers with a summation of how these various subprograms integrate in hopes that, in some small way, it will help forgive the otherwise whirlwind tour of the supportive code that surrounds the already-described basic foundation of the Alice program.

■ SIGNATURES AND PATTERN MATCHING

Deriving and varying chord-to-chord rules from music in a database ignores the possibility that some aspects of musical style occur at larger levels. The approach that Alice (ALgorithmically Integrated Composing Environment) takes to texture presents one situation in which global issues often overrule local constraints. There are aspects of pitch that also require special care. For example, Alice protects musical signatures—patterns derived from matching processes described in Cope (1991b, 1996)—from being broken into smaller groupings for rules composition. Such protection ensures that stylistic signatures survive the composition process.

Signatures are contiguous note patterns that recur in two or more works of a given composer, therefore indicating aspects of musical style (Cope 1991b, 1996). Signatures often change over time and provide a microcosm of stylistic development. Figure 5.1 shows an example of this kind of development with a signature found in Mozart as it appears in different guises over a fifteen-year span. Figure 5.1a shows the signature in a rudimentary form with a simple harmonic statement. This is followed by a more elaborate version from a sonata composed four years later (figure 5.1b). In figure 5.1c, the melody has returned to a more simple form with a rhythmically elaborated version of the accompaniment. Both this and the following version (figure 5.1d, which presents a more elegant and developed melody) were composed around the same time, six years after the version shown in figure 5.1b. In figure 5.1e, the melodic line matches that of the version shown in figure 5.1b but an octave lower and with a slightly more developed accompaniment. The last version of this signature shown here (figure 5.1f) has a fully developed melody and accompaniment and is by far the most elaborate of those shown. Most of these versions of this signature appear in cadences in fast movements of Mozart's sonatas and concerti.

Observing a signature develop over time can provide valuable insights into how a given style matures and how one can aurally differentiate the various periods in the musical life of a composer. While such style analysis cannot supplant other forms of harmonic, melodic, or structural analysis, it can augment them in important ways. Interestingly, most forms of standard analysis tend to articulate the ideas and materials composers have in common. On the other hand, studies of signatures tend to define what makes composers different.

Placement of signatures can be an extremely important strategy in creating structural logic. Figure 5.1g shows five examples of a Viennese signature used by Mozart (second movement of his piano

Figure 5.1   Versions of a Mozart signature from his (a) *Piano Sonata* K. 280 (1774), mvt. 1, mm. 107–108; (b) *Piano Sonata* K. 330 (1778), mvt. 3, m. 110; (c) *Piano Concerto* K. 453 (1784), mvt. 1, mm. 162–163; (d) *Piano Concerto* K. 459 (1784), mvt. 2, mm. 114–116; (e) *Piano Sonata* K. 547a (1788), mvt. 1, mm. 63–64; (f) *Piano Sonata* K. 570 (1789), mvt. 2, m. 4; (g) *Piano Sonata* K. 284, mvt. 2: m. 16; m. 30; m. 46; m. 69; m.92.

sonata K. 284) that I describe generally in my book *Computers and Musical Style* (Cope 1991b, pp. 157–69) and verified by occurrence in other of Mozart's works. This signature can be analyzed as a premature tonic bass note under a dominant chord or a late-sounding dominant chord over a tonic pedal tone. Each iteration of the signature shown here appears at the end of a two-phrase period whose first phrase does not cadence with the signature. Note how the spacing and number of dissonant notes provide differing tensions to the signature, with the final version having the most prominent dissonance of the five shown. These variations of tension help delineate the rondo form in this movement, with the signatures in the key of the movement weighted more strongly toward dissonance than those appearing in the dominant key. Thus, signatures not only may be location dependent at the local phrase level but can also provide structural glue. Experienced listeners can hear these subtle relationships and become confused when composers or machine-composing programs misplace or leave out such important signatures in certain styles.

To discover musical signatures requires pattern matching. Musical pattern matchers work best using intervals rather than pitches in order to avoid mistaking similar patterns in different keys for different patterns. For pattern matchers to recognize other types of variations, they must also have variables that allow certain numbers and amounts of mismatches to occur. These variables, which I call controllers, must be set wide enough to allow some patterns to surface as signatures but not so wide as to permit non-signatures to match. Musical pattern matchers should also consider rhythm and harmony as well as melody (see Cope 1991b, 1996).

Patterns from at least two different works that match are not necessarily signatures. Figure 5.2 shows how this can be true. Using a single controller that allows for one-half-step interval differences permits figure 5.2b and figure 5.2c to match figure 5.2a. However, figure 5.2b and figure 5.2c themselves do not match using the same criteria. Thus, only figure 5.2a counts as a matched pattern.

Once discovered, signatures cannot simply be inserted randomly into any context, for doing so would result in inconsistencies so stylistically uncharacteristic as to counteract any stylistic integrity their use was meant to preserve. Thus, Alice, as well as the Experiments in Musical Intelligence program and, to an extent, SARA (Simple Analytic Recombinant Algorithm), recomposes signatures to match the context of the surrounding music into which they are placed. This process closely resembles that of backfilling (discussed in chapter 6), in which the program composes part but not all of a

Figure 5.2   Three patterns in which (a) matches (b) and (c) while (b) and
(c) do not match (using a level of 1 in the `*amount-off*`
controller).

given passage. In this re-composition, the melody of signatures usually survives relatively unchanged while the harmony and accompaniment change to match the context provided by the entering and exiting material of the surrounding music.

Figure 5.3a shows how a signature can sound when forced into place without regard for its surrounding context. Here the sixteenth notes in measure 3 protrude from the otherwise eighth-note motion of the music. However, in figure 5.3b the signature conforms to the rhythm and texture of its neighboring music. Interestingly, the music here resembles the music of Mozart's Sonata K. 282, mvt. 3, measures 24–5 which falls in relatively close proximity to the location of the actual signature which appears in figure 5.3a, measure 3 (m. 36 of the Mozart sonata).

One of the attractions of using rules rather than events for composing is that the process does not include event data. However, signatures present special cases. For example, while generalized rules can be used in many places, signatures are context dependent. In addition, many elements of rhythm, dynamics, and so on become abstracted and separated from their sources during rules composition, which can render signatures less recognizable. Thus, while signatures often must be recomposed to fit their new contexts, submitting them to the same constraints as rules composition provides few advantages. Consequently, signatures in Alice are saved and re-used as events rather than as rules. This ensures that many of their characteristics—rhythm, dynamics, and channels—will remain intact.

Some patterns in music have importance separate from pitch. While possibly not contributing significantly to style definition, these non-pitch patterns often represent musical character worth preserving. For example, figure 5.4a shows a short passage by Brahms, a composer noted for his use of hemiola. Contemporary composers, especially those dedicated to obscuring the bar line in their composition, often use similar rhythmic techniques. Figure 5.4b

Figure 5.3   Examples showing a poorly situated signature (a) and the same signature recomposed according to context (b).

shows how a newly composed second measure to the first measure of figure 5.4a renders the hemiola nearly impossible to recognize. To rectify this problem, Alice ensures not only that ties in significant voices of such found patterns remain intact across grouping boundaries but also that new groups mirror the rhythmic patterns found in original destination groups without the rhythmic variations presented in previous chapters. Figure 5.4c shows how the original Brahms hemiola retains its overall structure in a more logical recomposition of the original music shown in figure 5.4a. In this way, Alice does not interrupt the flow of ideas in styles where rules composition might otherwise confuse important non-pitch patterns.

Alice must also recognize pattern repetitions in newly composed or database music. Such repetitions not only help define an aspect of the character of a current thematic idea but also can mark certain styles (i.e., certain types of minimalism). Thus, Alice's algorithmic analysis program keeps track of the frequency of such pattern repeats and produces like numbers of repeats when necessary in its algorithmic extensions. However, Alice counts and composes such repeats only if they occur contiguously. The program also imposes harsh limits on rhythmic variations in such repetitions, insisting that the rhythms of such patterns retain their integrity.

Alice employs a number of useful variations to pattern matching. One of the most important of these variations uses an incremental

Figure 5.4 Hemiola in Brahms' *Variations on a Theme by Joseph Haydn,*
Op. 56a: (a) mm. 14–15 from Variation VIII; (b) a poor recombination of mm. 14 and 10 of Variation VIII; (c) a successful
recombination of mm. 14 and 7 of Variation VIII, which retains
the hemiola present in (a).

pattern-recognition process. This process assumes that there are patterns too small to produce signatures—less than four-note pattern
sizes—or too large to produce successful matches—beyond ten to
twelve notes (melodic signatures most likely occur when their number exceeds three but not ten). This incremental pattern-recognition
program also assumes that increasing pattern sizes within these
boundaries will produce a decreasing number of matches since larger
patterns require more matching constituents. To test for patterns, the
incremental pattern matcher sweeps through the entire database successively, with incrementally increasing pattern sizes stopping when
the match numbers agree with variable levels established by the

program's user or the program itself. This approach avoids the often haphazard method of testing for signatures that users often employ when pattern matching, and resembles the approach taken in the stand-alone version of the Experiments in Musical Intelligence program (described in Cope 1996, chap. 7), with the exception that the earlier matcher also automates the other controllers, which affect the number of variances, size of variances, and so on. Alice, on the other hand, continues to make these controllers available to users.

Because incremental pattern matching returns sets of patterns of varying sizes, it is necessary to further screen these sets for potential signatures. Even a second sweep may produce a number of successfully matched patterns. This result varies significantly from those produced by the pattern matchers discussed in previous volumes of this series (Cope 1991b, 1996). Determining which patterns qualify as signatures then falls to either the user's ear or the automatic processes described in chapter 7 of Cope (1996).

One method of making incremental pattern matching more efficient involves a combination of incremental processes and the sublisting of events into groups the size of the largest pattern sought. This process assumes that if a large pattern matches, then any subset of that pattern will also match. This combination of processes also reduces the number of pattern searches required. Figure 5.5a shows a pattern of five intervals grouped successively. Figure 5.5b shows three interval patterns of five, four, and three intervals, respectively, sought in a matching sequence. The largest of the three patterns (five) matches the first interval collection. Thus, the successive search for smaller matches of the remaining two groups need not take place since the larger pattern contains both of these groups. This *decremental* pattern-matching process then removes subgroups of the successful patterns from the lists of patterns to be further tested. This process reduces the number of pattern comparisons and thus makes the entire process more efficient.

There are numerous other ways to make pattern matching more efficient. The simplest of these approaches involves saving found signatures and re-loading them to avoid repeating the pattern-matching processes each time one requires these signatures. However, while signatures as well as signature settings can be saved in this way, I have found that separate pattern-matching sessions with even the same database can provide increasingly more sophisticated results. Such sessions also help ensure that the program's output will continue to be different since it will not depend on the same signatures. Pattern matching certainly requires time and patience. However, such time is usually well spent. My logs of various pattern-matching sessions and lists of different signatures also indicate that

Figure 5.5 A more efficient method of pattern matching: (a) pattern; (b) since the first pattern matches (a), the remaining subsets must automatically match.

a.

b.

the best results often come near the end of a series of attempts rather than near the beginning (see figure 6.6).

Storing music in ways more conducive to pattern matching can also reduce processing time significantly. Figure 5.6 shows how. Figure 5.6a lists a small fragment of music in event form that will serve as a simple example. Figures 5.6b–f provide a more elegant technique for pattern matching than previously described. In figure 5.6b, pitches have been removed from their event lists and stored contiguously in a separate list. Figure 5.6c shows these pitches converted to intervals. In figure 5.6d, the intervals are sorted into sublists that consist of their location in the initial list and the number of intervals allowed by the equivalent of a *pattern-size* controller. In figure 5.6e, these sub-lists have been reorganized according to their initial interval classes. For example, the first group begins with perfect fifths (7). Finally, in figure 5.6f we see how a simple pattern can be retrieved from this new list and quickly returned to its former event status.

The process in figure 5.6f deserves more careful explanation. For example, instead of matching a pattern against all possible combinations of patterns, this matcher needs to find only the groupings that its head matches within the parameters of the controller setting. Here this means that only two patterns need be consulted, given the respective controller settings. This process saves up to 70 percent of the processing time required by more brute-force approaches. Instead of having to shuffle through numerous nonmatches, the program eliminates poor candidates on the basis of testing only a few intervals. Such optimization not only uses time more efficiently but also represents a more elegant and thoughtful way of coding.

One drawback to this process involves increased storage space since the notes and intervals do not replace the original events but must be stored separately. The resulting signatures here also need

Figure 5.6   A more efficient pattern-matching method: (a) events; (b) extracted pitches; (c) pitches converted to intervals; (d) intervals sublisted by location and initial pattern size; (e) intervals grouped by interval class (high to low); (f) matching a pattern against appropriate interval class only.

a.
```
((250 60 250 1 127) (500 62 250 1 127) (750 64 250 1 127)
(1000 65 250 1 127) (1250 62 250 1 127) (1500 64 250 1 127)
(1750 60 250 1 127) (2000 67 500 1 127)  (2500 72 500 1 127)
(3000 71 500 1 127) (3500 72 500 1 127) (4000 74 250 1 127)
(4250 67 250 1 127) (4500 69 250 1 127) (4750 71 250 1 127)
(5000 72 250 1 127) (5250 69 250 1 127) (5500 71 250 1 127)
(5750 67 250 1 127) (6000 74 500 1 127) (6500 79 500 1 127)
(7000 77 83 1 127) (7500 79 500 1 127)  (8000 76 250 1 127)
(8250 81 250 1 127) (8500 79 250 1 127) (8750 77 250 1 127)
(9000 76 250 1 127) (9250 79 250 1 127) (9500 77 250 1 127)
(9750 81 250 1 127))
```

b.
```
(60 62 64 65 62 64 60 67 72 71 72 74 67 69 71 72 69 71 67 74 79 77 79 76
81 79 77 76 79 77 81)
```

c.
```
(2 2 1 -3 2 -4 7 5 -1 1 2 -7 2 2 1 -3 2 -4 7 5 -2 2 -3 5 -2 -2 -1 3 -2 4)
```

d.
```
((1 (2 2 1 -3)) (2 (2 1 -3 2)) (3 (1 -3 2 -4)) (4 (-3 2 -4 7))
(5 (2 -4 7 5)) (6 (-4 7 5 -1)) (7 (7 5 -1 1)) (8 (5 -1 1 2))
(9 (-1 1 2 -7)) (10 (1 2 -7 2)) (11 (2 -7 2 2)) (12 (-7 2 2 1))
(13 (2 2 1 -3)) (14 (2 1 -3 2)) (15 (1 -3 2 -4)) (16 (-3 2 -4 7))
(17 (2 -4 7 5)) (18 (-4 7 5 -2)) (19 (7 5 -2 2))
(20 (5 -2 2 -3)) (21 (-2 2 -3 5)) (22 (2 -3 5 -2)) (23 (-3 5 -2 -2))
(24 (5 -2 -2 -1)) (25 (-2 -2 -1 3)) (26 (-2 -1 3 -2))))
```

e.
```
(((7 (7 5 -1 1)) (19 (7 5 -2 2)))
((8 (5 -1 1 2)) (20 (5 -2 2 -3)) (24 (5 -2 -2 -1)))
((1 (2 2 1 -3)) (2 (2 1 -3 2)) (5 (2 -4 7 5)) (11 (2 -7 2 2))
 (13 (2 2 1 -3)) (14 (2 1 -3 2)) (17 (2 -4 7 5)) (22 (2 -3 5 -2)))
((3 (1 -3 2 -4)) (10 (1 2 -7 2)) (15 (1 -3 2 -4))). . .
```

f.
```
pattern sought: (7 5 -2 2)
matched against: (((7 (7 5 -1 1)) (19 (7 5 -2 2)))
return: ((5750 67 250 1 127) (6000 74 500 1 127) (6500 79 500 1 127)
(7000 77 83 1 127)(7500 79 500 1 127))
```

to be rebuilt into events. However, these trade-offs do not seriously counteract the efficiency created by the reductive technique. In general, any method that saves processing time helps users see and hear the results more quickly.

In previous discussions of pattern matching, I describe the process of listening to the results of a pattern-matching session for signatures as if this were a hereditary skill that most users normally possess. Obviously, this is not the case. Signature recognition comes only after achieving intimate familiarity with a composer's style and music. Even then, such recognition can be difficult. The decision as to what constitutes a signature and what does not may ultimately be personal rather than empirical. After all, signature recognition has not yet been universally recognized as a predictable measure of musical style.

However, familiarity should not be a problem when pattern matching one's own music, as most likely occurs with Alice. Universal acceptance of signatures as a critical element in style recognition is also not an issue since users can bypass pattern matching if their doubts about the process override their curiosity. Indeed, pattern matching for signatures can become a laborious pursuit challenging even the most patient user. In addition, some music may not have useful signatures. While automated matching can alleviate this problem, relegating pattern matching solely to Alice guarantees approximation, not accuracy. Also, the search for signatures, however unproductive it may seem, usually produces rewarding discoveries of other patterns besides signatures and reveals further elements of personal style.

The fact that some music contains no clearly recognizable signatures does not indicate a lack of style but merely a lack of readily accessible patterns to provide clear recognition of that style. In addition, many composers consider signatures as clichés and pattern match in hopes of not finding them. Those who want to find signatures but are unsuccessful in doing so should note that signatures often appear in musical parameters besides pitch and duration. Orchestration, for example, may reveal a composer's identity. Signatures occurring in orchestration are extremely difficult to find with Alice's pattern matcher since timbre, and thus orchestration, only appears in the channel portion of event notation. Channel patterns cannot be easily revealed since events are not typically organized in a way that facilitates channel matching. Even if channel choices were organized in ways suitable for pattern recognition, matching these channel lists would, at best, produce typical harmonic combinations rather than useful signatures. Melodic channel patterning—the pattern of channels switching on and off, the most parallel process to pitch matching—does not usually produce significant results either. Thus, users should not be disappointed if their many hours in searches for personal signatures prove unsuccessful.

■ HIERARCHICAL PATTERN RECOGNITION

Since the music resulting from rule inheritance generally wanders with little sense of balance or development, Alice-composed music requires a larger formal logic. As previously mentioned, Alice inherits structure from the music in its database to achieve this logic. This inheritance requires a relatively deep hierarchical analysis and a specialized search for structural patterns.

Since the overall shape of phrases, or phrase equivalents, may be integral to either the style of the current composition and/or the style of the music in the database, Alice must derive information from the database beyond the scope of an ATN (augmented transition network) program (see Cope 1996, chap. 5). One of the ways in which Alice discovers phrase shapes involves meta-patterns, patterns whose members occur non-contiguously. Meta-patterns are discovered by hierarchical pattern-matching processes. Alice then makes signatures and rules conform to the general, if not specific, shapes of these meta-patterns.

Alice utilizes a different kind of pattern matcher for matching hierarchical patterns. This pattern matcher reduces the actual number of matchings necessary by first evaluating foreground material in terms of importance and then using only those notes and intervals that surpass certain thresholds. This hierarchical pattern matcher is substantially more productive than previously described models because it reveals patterns that note-to-note processes miss.

Figure 5.7 provides an example of this process. Figure 5.7a shows an original phrase of music composed by a user of Alice. Figure 5.7b then presents the meta-pattern discovered by the hierarchical pattern matcher. This pattern surfaces from the matching process where others do not by virtue of its agogic weightings, placement in the metrical structure, and its relevance to the key or scale in use. The legend below figure 5.7b gives the sources of the shown notes by measure and beat number. Figure 5.7c presents a newly composed phrase based on the meta-pattern. Figure 5.7d then shows how the meta-pattern of figure 5.7a surfaces in an hierarchical analysis of figure 5.7c. The new melodic notes of figure 5.7c then represent new melodic extrapolations or prolongations based on the identical superstructure as the music of 5.7a. This obviously simplistic example nonetheless demonstrates the basic principles of deriving meta-patterns and reusing them for new compositions.

Figure 5.8 shows a less transparent example of the use of meta-patterns. Here, the various patterns in the music at the top in the figure have lines drawn to connect them to their correlates in newly

Figure 5.7   (a) A phrase of music; (b) a meta-pattern discovered by the hierarchical pattern matcher; (c) a newly composed phrase based on the combination of local patterns and the meta-pattern; (d) the meta-pattern of (c).

Figure 5.8   An example of the use of meta-patterns (Mozart *Piano Sonata* K. 331, first mvt., mm. 1–4).

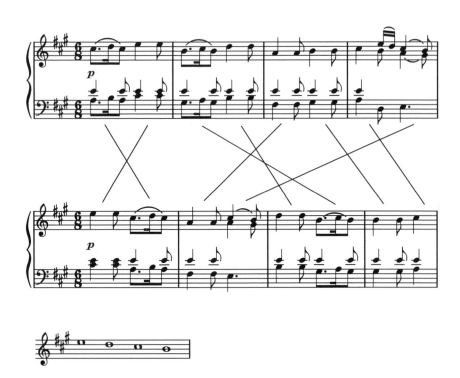

composed music. The lower music demonstrates how, through the composition process, the fragments reorganize while concomitantly retaining much of their original coherence. However, this new music varies from the original. Note how the meta-pattern shown at the bottom of the figure serves as a general guide for the composing program. While only half the notes fall in the same place in their respective measures, this variation of the original works effectively because the meta-pattern occurs so prominently in each example.

The hierarchical analysis that produces meta-patterns resembles the process that Experiments in Musical Intelligence uses to find patterns with interpolated notes. Figure 3.7 of *Experiments in Musical Intelligence* (Cope 1996, p. 89) shows how Chopin can bury repetitions of his themes in extremely ornamented variations. In such cases, two extremely varied patterns can match because of the high setting of the controller designated to allow interpolated notes. While effective for matching patterns in music by composers who, like Chopin, use such ornamental techniques for variation, the high setting of the interpolation variable also allows all manner of noise to enter into the pattern matching of music of composers who do not use such techniques. Hierarchical analysis, on the other hand, does not depend on what approach composers may take for variation in their music. The process rather takes a single pattern and weights its contributing notes and intervals such that the important elements become more clear.

However, both brute-force and hierarchical pattern-matching techniques have their own unique analytical contributions to make to algorithmic composition. Hierarchical analysis would not, for example, effectively reveal the basic identity of the previously mentioned Chopin example since many of the important notes in the embellished version have little metric weight. On the other hand, hierarchical analysis can produce quite revealing results when applied to individual patterns, such as that shown in figure 5.7a, where the basic imprint of the passage occurs on weighted notes that likewise would probably not surface in a more standard pattern match for signatures.

Meta-patterns can serve another very useful function: varying signatures to match their new contexts. This process requires two steps. The first step involves creating a meta-pattern from the signature. The second step uses recombinancy to fit various forms of the signature together to create a new version while maintaining the integrity of the signature by following the meta-pattern. Figure 5.9 shows these processes at work. Figure 5.9a presents the various forms of a found signature in Chopin's mazurkas. Figure 5.9b reveals a meta-pattern derived from these signatures. Figure 5.9c shows how various parts of the patterns of figure 5.9a (labeled by opus and measure number) roughly fit together to create a new version of the signature while following the basic interval dictates of the meta-pattern. In this way, signatures of varying types can be developed contextually in a new musical environment while concomitantly retaining their fundamental character and recognition.

Hierarchical pattern matching in Alice involves generating weightings. These weightings result from a combination of analyses of approach interval, duration, dynamic, metric placement, and scale degree (if appropriate). Each of these factors is measured by levels determined by the user of the program. Weightings in Alice fall between 0.0 and 1.0 (floating point numbers), with 0.0 representing no weight and 1.0 indicating the most important note in the pattern.

Figure 5.10 shows a simple melodic line for demonstration. Figure 5.11a presents a chart for establishing the weights of each note in figure 5.10. While these weightings are somewhat arbitrary, they do reflect my personal estimate. Alice allows users the option of overriding

Figure 5.9   (a) Various forms of a found signature in Chopin's mazurkas: Op. 6, No. 1, m. 1; Op. 50, No. 1, m. 18; Op. 7, No. 2, m. 3; Op. 17, No. 4, mm. 13, 15, 29; Op. 6, No. 4, mm. 9–10; (b) a meta-pattern from the last of these signatures; (c) how the patterns of (a) fit together.

default settings of such parameters. In figure 5.11a, off-beat refers to notes one sixteenth note before or after beats. Sub-beats refer to "ands" of beats. Weak-beats are on-beats not occurring at the beginning of measures. These weightings' categories could include other relevant musical parameters, such as harmony, consonance, dissonance, and so on, but are limited to four here simply for demonstration. Figure 5.11b shows the results of applying the weightings of figure 5.11a to the music of figure 5.10.

Figure 5.10   A simple tune (*My Bonnie Lies over the Ocean*) for demonstrating hierarchical pattern matching.

Figure 5.11   (a) Chart showing the values attributed to the various parameters; (b) weightings for the notes of the melody of figure 5.10.

a.

Approach Interval:

second	third	fourth	fifth	sixth	seventh	octave
.05	.07	.09	.1	.15	.2	.25

Duration:

sixteenth	eighth	quarter	half	whole
.05	.075	.1	.15	.25

Metric Placement:

off-beat	sub-beat	weak-beat	down-beat
.05	.1	.15	.25

Scale Degree:

1	2	3	4	5	6	7
.25	.1	.18	.15	.2	.13	.11

b.
.45, .7, .325, .55, .5, .55, .45, .5, and .65

Figure 5.12 presents a plot of the weightings of figure 5.11b to better show their relationships. Alice then filters these weightings at various levels to produce a variety of hierarchically weighted patterns. For example, setting a threshold of .6 allows just the second and ninth notes to survive the screening process. On the other hand, setting a threshold of .4 produces a list of all notes but the third. A setting of .5 allows all but the first, third, and seventh notes to survive. These patterns are shown in figure 5.13.

Typically, Alice analyzes at least three different weighting levels to find a meta-pattern. In the previously mentioned tests, only two notes survive all three filterings: high and low E. However, three other notes—C of full measure 1 and D and C of full measure 2—survive two of the tests and as such may be usefully included in the resultant meta-pattern. Alice then matches these meta-patterns to discover ideas that have underlying similarities.

Figure 5.14 shows two different simple folk melodies that will be used to more fully demonstrate how hierarchical matching works— *Go Tell Aunt Rhodie* in figure 5.14a and *Three Blind Mice* in figure 5.14b. Using the settings provided in figure 5.11a produces the weightings for these two melodies, shown in figure 5.15.

Interestingly, these two melodies are in separate keys and look somewhat different. However, establishing a high threshold reveals their similarity—both have a I-to-V motion at the background level using .55 and .6 thresholds, respectively, as shown in figure 5.16. In fact, when transposed the notes of figure 5.16a match almost exactly the notes of figure 5.16b.

Such similarities do not suggest compositional influence except as all simple folk songs bear some resemblance to one another. However, it does suggest that using hierarchical pattern-matching processes can reveal interesting structural resemblances where few might appear at the surface level. In a more typical case—that of two patterns that do have surface similarities—hierarchical weighting can verify or discount such similarities. In short, pattern-weighting processes provide insights into music that other, more note-by-note methods do not.

This hierarchical weighting process is not unlike that used in Schenkerian or layer analysis (Schenker 1933). Typically, however, Schenkerian analysis follows a middleground pattern of descending scale degrees. Alice makes no such assumptions about the music it analyzes. The program simply assigns its various weightings to notes and then attempts to apply useful thresholds. Such thresholds typically produce results that, on the one hand, have more notes than those usually provided by Schenker-type middlegrounds

Figure 5.12   A chart showing the weightings of figure 5.11b.

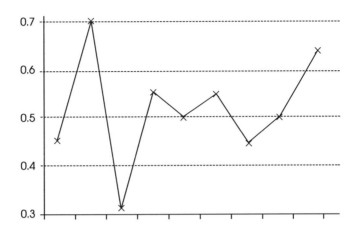

Figure 5.13   The melody of figure 5.10 with threshold set at (a) .6, (b) .4, and (c) .5.

and, on the other hand, fewer notes than the foreground or surface of the pattern being analyzed.

The weighting process just described demonstrates how the hierarchical approach reveals patterns with little foreground similarities but with strong resemblance when viewed structurally. Hierarchical pattern matching can also reveal whether patterns that sound similar in their foregrounds are actually similar when viewed structurally. Figure 5.17 presents two examples, the first from Brahms's *Intermezzo No. 3,* Op. 117, and the second from Rachmaninoff's

Figure 5.14   Two folk melodies, (a) *Go Tell Aunt Rhodie* and (b) *Three Blind Mice* used to demonstrate hierarchical pattern matching.

a.

b.

Figure 5.15   Weightings for figure 5.14a and figure 5.14b, respectively.

a. Go Tell: .53/.405/.325/.65/.5/.5/.325/.395/.555/.325/.55/.65/.425/.375/.55

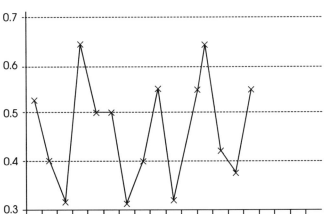

Figure 5.15   Continued.

b. Three Blind: .53/.4/.7/.6/.4/.7/.65/.425/.325/.63

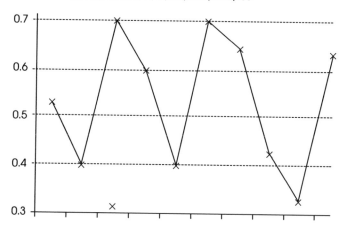

Figure 5.16   Results of figure 5.15 applied to figure 5.14 with thresholds set at (a) .55 and (b) .6.

a.

b.

Piano Concerto 3, Op. 30. While in different keys and meters, these themes sound very similar, at least to my ears.

Singing through these two melodies will verify their general similarity. The two themes have many similar patterns, such as the first six notes of figure 5.17a being almost the same (types of seconds vary) as the six notes of figure 5.17b, beginning in its second measure. Note as well the small range of each melody and the extensive use of seconds. These two themes sound so similar to me that I often sing one from memory while intending to sing the other. A standard structural analysis would probably (depending on the analyst) emphasize a prolongation of the tonic (C-sharp in figure 5.17a and D in figure 5.17b) moving to the leading tone or dominant function.

Figure 5.17   The beginnings of the (a) Brahms *Intermezzo*, No. 3, Op. 117; (b) Rachmaninoff *Piano Concerto 3*, Op. 30.

Figure 5.18 shows the two melodies of figures 5.17a and b in graph form based on the previously discussed weightings shown in figure 5.11a. Using a threshold of .5 produces the versions shown in figure 5.19. Note how the first background shows a rising stepwise pattern falling a minor third to the subdominant note of the key. However, the Rachmaninoff weightings display none of this motion but rather prolong the tonic note—a note not even present in the Brahms reduction. Thus, these melodies appear quite different when reduced to their most important notes, revealing that their similarities to the ear may be superficial. Alice takes such differences into consideration when pattern matching hierarchically and includes only those patterns that have similarity in both their foreground and background forms, thereby making pattern recognition more effective and convincing.

Figure 5.20 shows how hierarchical (structural) pattern matching can be applied to signatures, with the result of not only extraordinary savings of processing time but also the return of fundamental rather than superficial matches. Figure 5.20a shows the significance of figure 5.20b (also figure 5.1a) reduced to a hierarchical pattern using the method just described. The matches found by comparing two hierarchical skeletons take only a fraction of the time required of standard pattern-matching processes. In addition, the matches produced represent more logical similarities than do the standard note-by-note or interval-by-interval brute-force processes.

Figure 5.18   Graphs for (a) Brahms *Intermezzo* Op. 117, No. 3; (b) Rachmaninoff *Piano Concerto 3*, Op. 30.

a. Brahms: .4, .25, .555, .3, .33, .375, .45, .25, .52, .33, .3, .33, .375, .38, .3, .575, .35, .35, .505, .4, .28, .385, .42, .28, .545, .4, .35, .387, .4, .485.

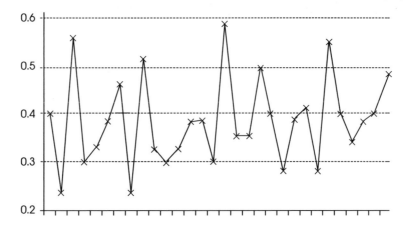

b. Rachmaninoff: .425, .45, .25, .475, .46, .4, .325, .537, .25, .6, .25, .405, .405, .355, .45, .4, .36, .48, .26, .475, .475, .4, .25, .625, .31, .4, .375, .5, .465, .405, .475, .475, .41, .4, .31, .28, .36, .4, .37.

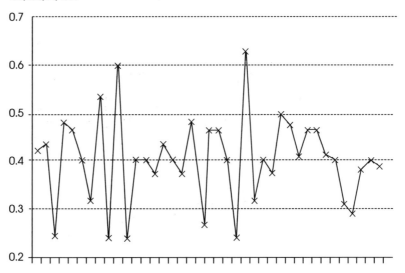

The file *Hierarchical Pattern Match,* located in the *Hierarchical Pattern Match* folder on this book's CD-ROM, contains the functions

Figure 5.19   Results from using a .5 threshold on (a) Brahms *Intermezzo,* Op. 117, No. 3; (b) Rachmaninoff *Piano Concerto 3,* Op. 30.

a.

b.

Figure 5.20   How hierarchical (structural) pattern matching can assist in standard matching techniques.

a.

b.

required to discover meta-patterns following the principles provided here. Running the function `threshold-the-weighted-events` with the argument types shown in the documentation in the folder produces the output shown in the examples presented in this section.

Alice's pitch-class pattern matcher works similarly to the hierarchical pattern matcher but differs in two fundamental ways. First, the pitch-class pattern matcher uses collections of musical groupings for matching. In effect, these groupings are themselves collections of events. These groupings may be identical to the groupings used for composition (i.e., vertical collections of events), or they may be horizontal collections or combinations of horizontal and vertical groupings. For horizontal or combinational grouping, users should devise some standard on which to base their grouping process. Second, Alice's pitch-class pattern matcher can match either pitch-class sets or their interval vectors. The variables `*number-wrong-in-set*` and `*amount-wrong-pc*` require quite different settings, depending on whether sets or vectors are chosen as the match criteria.

The basic function for matching pitch-class sets, `get-set-match` in the file *match pc,* uses three arguments, as shown in figure 5.21a. The first argument defines the type of matching sought: set or vector. The second argument should be a list of groups of events that serve as the patterns to be matched. The third argument is a list of groups of events representing an entire database that serves as the target of the search. When finished, `get-set-match` returns a list of analyses that have successfully passed the matching test on the basis of the current settings of `*number-wrong-in-set*` and `*amount-wrong-pc*` (see lines 11 and 12 of figure 5.21a). Note that the sets used in this hierarchical pattern-matching tutorial use standard terminology rather than Alice's SPEAC-based approach. I have avoided the latter so as not to unnecessarily confuse the pattern matching process here.

The file *match pc* also contains the function `match-set-against-the-database` (see figure 5.21b), which requires users to supply only the type (set or vector) and a set name (e.g., 3-2). This function returns a list of complete sets from the database of sets that match the argument following the current settings of `*number-wrong-in-set*` and `*amount-wrong-pc*`. These returned sets can be useful when analyzing music for set pairings that match within certain tolerances.

■ UNIFICATIONS

Alice searches for other kinds of patterns in its databases besides signatures and meta-patterns. For the most part, signatures and meta-patterns are seen as global commonalties in that they must appear in at least two, and preferably more than two, of the works stored in the database. Such patterns contribute to the recognition of the *style* of the composer whose music the program is attempting

Figure 5.21   The functions `get-set-match` and `match-set-against-the-database`.

a.
```
1. (defun get-set-match (type set-group-1 set-group-2)
2.    (setf type (converter type))
3.    (group
4.     (loop until (null (nthcdr (1- (length set-group-1)) set-group-2))
5.           do (setq save-set set-group-1)
6.           collect
7.           (let ((test (find-matching-sets
8.                        type
9.                        set-group-1
10.                       set-group-2
11.                       *number-wrong-in-set*
12.                       *amount-wrong-pc*)))
13.              (if (all-truep test)
14.                 (list (firstn (length set-group-1) set-group-2)))))
15.          do (setf set-group-2 (rest set-group-2)))))))
```

b.
```
1. (defun match-set-against-the-database (type set-name)
2.    (setf type (converter type))
3.    (let* ((set-list (second (assoc (first (explode set-name)) sets)))
4.           (full-set-name (assoc set-name set-list)))
5.      (match-sets type full-set-name set-list)))
```

to emulate. However, some patterns that are critical to the Alice composing processes have greater local importance and relate to harmonic, thematic, and rhythmic elements only of one work: the work in progress. Discovering such patterns can be quite important. Otherwise, the new material that Alice composes, no matter how relevant it might be to the rules and general style of users, would be irrelevant to the local motivic content of the current work.

I have named such motives *unifications*. Unifications are patterns found most frequently in a single work in a database. They represent motives that unify that work and that make it different from other works in the database. Unifications are discovered by number as well as by type. Alice then takes a naturally recurring motive or unification in a work in progress and attempts to coerce the program toward like numbers of unifications and their variations in the new music the program creates. Such use helps maintain unity in new works at the foreground level.

Alice uses three basic techniques to find unifications in the music it extends. First and most obviously, actual patterns are collected only from the music of the current work being composed. In effect, for this process at least, Alice ignores the music in the database. Second, Alice matches patterns only in defined regions. These regions have been separated by structural identity (discussed further in chapter 6). Finally, Alice looks for patterns that conform to controller-prescribed limits *within* individual phrases rather than *between* phrases. In effect, Alice seeks to find patterns integral to the basic continuity of the music of the work being composed to extend that music in logical and musical ways.

Alice ascertains the numbers, location, and variance types of unifications in the music in the database. For example, knowing that a certain pattern has repeated during a passage is of little use if one does not also know that this pattern repeats few or many times, repeats only in certain circumstances, repeats only after predictable delays, and repeats only with certain variations, such as sequence.

Interlacing unifications with rules voice leading can cause significant problems. To avoid many of these problems, I have the program coerce voice leading choices (particularly the choice of rule variants and new rules as discussed in chapter 4) toward unifications rather than forcing unifications into already-composed music. In this way, the two processes proceed hand in hand rather than from opposing perspectives. Unifications may be quite numerous, and rather than spreading their use over entire sections of compositions, Alice uses unifications in close quarters, even in combination by using them contiguously and in sequence. In each case, however, the program assumes that their positioning is rule sensitive.

Unifications help Alice extend in-progress music in natural rather than artificial or mechanistic ways. Thus, a mid-stream phrase will, it is hoped, sound fulfilled and not interrupted when completed by the program. To help ensure this, Alice utilizes a hierarchical analysis of the incomplete phrase as a template along with the previously mentioned local patterns in unification-prescribed numbers and orders. This typically creates better continuity with user-composed music. In this way, Alice integrates unifications and meta-patterns while composing.

Unifications can also be effective in helping Alice devise contrasting music for new sections of a work in progress. Again, the program accomplishes this by carefully cataloging already-composed music into unifications and then representing these unifications in numbers and types of variations as represented in the music found in the database. Presuming that the order of contrast necessary may require a different unifying factor, Alice may use a contrasting set of unification numbers for contrasting machine-based composition.

Unifications do not presuppose that all music consists of small local patterns. However, it does assume that music itself constitutes patterns and that all music can be analyzed as patterns, even if these patterns are quite large and occur rarely. In fact, the larger the pattern Alice discovers, the easier it becomes for the program to use as a model in a newly composed passage. In this way, music that does not utilize obvious pattern replications as a prototype of musical style does not suffer from Alice's mode of composition.

◼ STRUCTURAL ANALYSIS

Alice utilizes a multifaceted approach to structural analysis. Initially, the program seeks out major thematic areas, a technique that often succeeds with classical music. If that process fails, the program looks for contrast, changes in density, and/or shifts in composite rhythm. Alice also attempts to map cadences, finally using an approximation process if all else fails. Each of these processes deserves further explanation.

In many musical styles, the main formal sections follow the melodic ideas that initiate them. Often in these styles, the basic texture and harmonic rhythms remain constant across the boundaries of sections. Alice uses a variation of its conventional pattern matcher to detect such melodic contrasts when other techniques do not suffice. Since this pattern matcher seeks differences between patterns rather than similarities, new sections are detected when the program encounters no matches between ongoing and newly found patterns.

If this thematic analysis fails to determine sectional boundaries, the program looks for principal areas of rhythmic and dynamic contrast to differentiate found elements. While the voice-leading rules of such materials can contribute to the overall rules base of the composition in progress, the rhythms—figured as on-times and durations—and dynamics (in particular) help create contrasting music. Channel assignment, phrase length, and form also assist Alice in differentiating new material from previous ideas.

If this process also fails, Alice uses density as a principal factor in determining when sections end and new sections begin. Alice finds the density of a passage by breaking it into contiguous groupings the size of the passage's shortest durational element. Thus, a phrase with a sixteenth note as its shortest member will be broken into continuous sixteenth-note-length groups.

The formula used for determining the density of a passage appears in figure 5.22, where T represents the texture of each segment in

Figure 5.22   Formula for determining the density of music.

$$\overline{A} = \frac{\sum\limits_{K=T_1}^{K=T_N} K}{N}$$

$$N = \frac{D}{S}$$

number of voices, N represents the number of segments, D represents the duration of the passage, and S represents the duration of the shortest duration in the passage. The file called *density* found in the folder named *density* in the *tutorial* folder provides an example of functions that incorporate this formula. Loading any phrase from the standard databases provided with Alice and running the top-level function in the *density* folder/file demonstrates this process.

Composite rhythm can also play an important role in distinguishing sections from one another. Alice collects all the sectional entrance times for the work under analysis, as determined by the previously discussed density principles, and then parses these entrances into spatial and numerical categories. Figure 5.23 demonstrates graphically how this produces the characteristics necessary to differentiate musical materials of one section from another. In figure 5.23a, entrance times appear as linear dots proportionally distributed in a defined time frame. Figure 5.23b then shows how figure 5.23a can be segregated into various logical groupings. Here, three possible candidates help substantiate aspects of this formal process.

While thematic separation, density, and composite rhythm provide excellent resources for discovering contrast in music, they are not typically sufficient to distinguish all the various elements of form. This insufficiency can be especially noticeable when analyzing works with transitions between sections rather than abruptly contrasting ideas. For such works, as well as for other works in which structure evolves transitionally rather than incrementally, texture and other formal analyses must be combined with cadence mapping to produce a formal plan. Such mapping indicates more precisely where the ideas of one section end and another section begins.

Figure 5.24 shows the same eight-beat phrase of Bach and ATN representation as in figure 5.15 from *Experiments in Musical Intelligence*

Figure 5.23   (a) Sectional entrance times as linear dots proportionally distributed in a defined time frame; (b) how these entrance times can be segregated into various logical groupings.

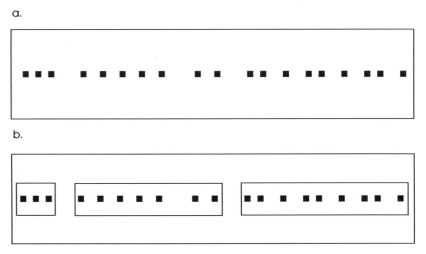

(Cope 1996). This figure demonstrates a simple form of inheritance in the creation of a new Bach-like phrase (figure 5.24b) from the beginning of an actual Bach phrase (figure 5.24a; for more details about this process, see the discussion about the original figure in Cope 1996). Cadences represent the hierarchical linchpins of most musical styles and thus form the backbone of their structure. Arrows have been added to this newer version of figure 5.15 from Cope (1996) to explicitly show how cadences at the phrase level in the Experiments in Musical Intelligence program result from decisions made early on in phrase composition. The creation of movements and works in Alice follows roughly the same techniques as that of the Experiments in Musical Intelligence program and thus corroborates those principles.

However, in SARA and especially in the Experiments in Musical Intelligence program, the approach to cadences is governed by an elaborate ATN (see Cope 1996, chap. 5) process, which requires extensive computation time and thus detracts from the composing process. While Alice does not compose in real time, the program still attempts to produce algorithmic composition as quickly as possible to effectively assist in the collaborative composing process. Thus, while ATNs must still be used to guarantee a logical beginning to each phrase, the transition to cadence, a much more complicated process, requires a somewhat different approach.

Figure 5.24   (a) Bach's *Chorale No. 140* beginning; (b) an ATN re-creation.

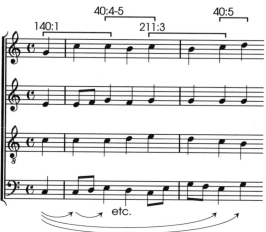

Figure 5.25a shows a larger structural view of Bach's Chorale No. 6. This phrase is followed by the cadences of the succeeding phrases in the work. Note how the logic of the original phrase dictates future cadence choices in the replication in figure 5.25b, with the first cadence affecting both the next cadence and the final cadence of the work. Viewed tonally, this process pairs incomplete authentic cadences with complete authentic cadences, half cadences with full cadences, and so on (for further information on this standard technique of classical tonal music, see Cope 1991b, chap. 2). While the notes

Figure 5.25   (a) Bach's *Chorale No. 6* overview; (b) a re-creation showing the inheritance of larger-scale form.

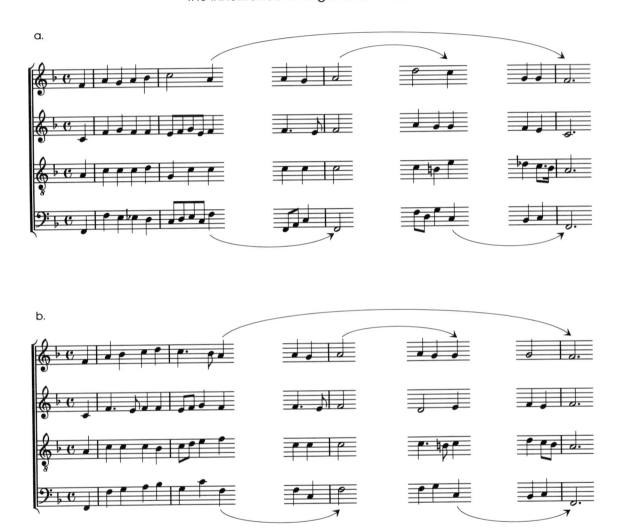

differ between figures 5.25a and b, the relationships between the various cadences do not. Thus, large structures proceed by forward chaining the cadence types in logical succession.

However, discovering the precise locations of cadences can pose many problems. Figure 5.26 demonstrates why. In figure 5.26a, Mozart arrives at simple harmonic and rhythmic cadences in measure 4, beat 2, and measure 8, downbeat, which clearly define the end points of his phrases. Such points are relatively easily analyzed by algorithmic composing programs. However, figure 5.26b shows a passage by Bach in which the harmony suggests the presence of a cadence in measure 4, for example, but the rhythm does not. In fact, Bach has cadenced one phrase while simultaneously beginning another. Since the chord progression here can also be found at noncadence points in Bach, analyzing such music for cadences can be challenging if not impossible for human experts no less than for computer programs. Texture analysis does not help here because the passage moves smoothly through this material without textural variation.

As previously discussed, Alice accounts for the difficulties created by texture discontinuities across cadence points by using proportions in its analysis. Believing that composers, no matter what their approaches to cadences may be, create phrases according to certain basic principles of balance as well as antecedence and

Figure 5.26   (a) Mozart *Piano Sonata* K. 333, mvt. 2, beginning; (b) beginning of Bach's *Prelude XX* in A minor from the *Well-Tempered Clavier*, Book II.

a.

Figure 5.26   Continued.

b.

Figure 5.26 Continued.

consequence, I have programmed Alice to utilize the proportions of the music from which it derives its analysis to help determine where cadences occur. Then, using one or more of the previous techniques that seem to hold true—texture, harmonic analysis, and so on—Alice attempts to analyze more difficult passages. Figure 5.27 provides an example of how this approach deciphers the previous Bach work shown in figure 5.26b. Figure 5.27a shows a model for analyzing cadences. In this case, the model follows the repeats of the descending chromatic scale in the bass voice of figure 5.26b. Figure 5.27b then shows how this model matches the harmonic cadences present.

Obviously, some musical styles do not yield their structure sufficiently even when these processes are used in combination with other evaluative information, such as cadence locations. In other words, such music resists these more or less standard analytical procedures. In these cases, Alice resorts to creating a best approximation using the form of one of the smaller elements found in the database music. In other words, rather than make an arbitrary choice, Alice relies on proportions found in other aspects of the work being analyzed. For example, the contours of a notable signature might serve as the basis for choosing a found textural pattern, as shown in figure 5.28. Here, the signature contour suggests a strong level of contrast (leap up) followed by a return or resolving motion (step down). This contour is best mirrored in the first of the three possible graphic representations shown in figure 5.28b, and thus it becomes the one chosen. Alice may select such verifying patterns from

Figure 5.27   Principles of proportions, balance, and antecedence/ consequence used to decipher cadences in the Bach example of figure 5.26b.

a.
model: short   long   medium

b.

cadence:	location:	phrase length:
E minor (full)	4 downbeat	(3+)
G major (plagal?)	9 downbeat	(5+)
A minor (full)	13 downbeat	(4+)

Figure 5.28   Proportions used to create textural contours: (a) signature contour; (b) three textural interpretations of (a).

a.

b.

signatures, unifications, or any other found pattern. However, in each case the principle remains the same—the modeling of materials of one level based on selected attributes of another level. The hope is that, while the ear may not directly recognize such hierarchical imitation, the resulting music will subtly reveal its structure, and thus will sound logical rather than haphazard. Ultimately, while many forms will fail to inherit form properly because of Alice's imperfect analysis, the program will still create integrated structures on the basis of the databases that it accesses.

Alice must occasionally reconcile the differences between an in-progress form and the possibly different forms encountered in its database in order for the program's composing algorithm to usefully create new material. When Alice cannot account for such differences on the basis of proportions (i.e., the same form but different durations of material), the program assumes that the current work, the one in progress, should retain a semblance of the formal concepts present in the works in its database. Thus, Alice generalizes the database forms and applies these generalizations to the currently in-progress music. Figure 5.29 shows an example of this. Two abstracted forms are shown in figures 5.29a and b, the first from a work in progress and the second from a single work in the database at the time of composition. As can be seen, the in-progress work has already presented three consecutively different ideas, while the work in the database has a clear-cut two-theme tripartite form. No amount of proportional relativity can equate the two forms, even though one of the forms is incomplete. However, generalizing that the complete work represents an example of a recapitulative form allows Alice to complete the form of figure 5.29a, as shown in figure 5.29c, where the C material of the current work becomes an extension of the B section with the first two themes restated as a recapitulation. While this may not be what the user would compose, this kind of form extrapolation provides one legitimate possibility for the completion of the work in progress.

■ EARMARKS

While studies of timbre, harmony, and form can produce quite useful results, they often neglect phenomena that may indicate other possibly important meanings in music (Agawu 1991; Gjerdingen 1988). As an example, one type of pattern matcher I use has revealed gestures in certain styles that seem to foreshadow important structural events. For example, the two principal cadential trills—end of the second exposition and pre-cadenza—in the first movements of the last twenty-two of Mozart's piano concerti belong to this category. These location-specific gestures can provide deeper understanding of musical structure and ultimately reveal why some works possess a sense of inevitability. I call these patterns *earmarks*.

Earmarks provide structural guides beyond repetition and contrast, key relations, and so on. Earmarks indicate, at least to the experienced listener, important attributes about one's temporal

Figure 5.29   Two abstracted forms (a, b); (c) how Alice might complete (a).

a.

b.

c.

position in a work and foreshadow especially important structural events. Earmarks can even contribute to expectations of when a movement or work should reach a point of arrival or return to earlier materials. Earmarks are icons holding little interest in themselves but great interest for what they tell us about structure and what they can foretell about ensuing events.

My pattern-matching programs have located earmarks in the first movements of Mozart's piano concerti (Mozart 1978) numbers 6 through 27: the tonic $^6_4$s, which precede the trills at the end of expositions and recapitulations just prior to cadenzas. Figure 5.30 shows six examples of this pattern. Note how the first measures in each example vary yet adhere to simple scalular or arpeggiated designs. While these examples are simple, possibly obvious, it is clear that with even a limited listening experience one can become accustomed to the harmonic and melodic substance of such material and begin to anticipate the eventual culmination of the exposition in the first occurrence and the cadenza in the second occurrence.

Such earmarks produce structural anticipations requiring fulfillment without which the antecedent-consequent implication will fail to convince listeners of a movement's formal integrity. Alice thus analyzes for earmarks and ensures that, once found, these structural patterns remain intact and are not shuffled to other, inappropriate locations in the music the program composes.

Earmarks appear in such general forms that standard pattern matching typically does not reveal them. In other words, the controllers normally used in pattern matching need to be set so wide that the resulting extensive numbers of successful matches will obscure the structurally significant patterns. To find earmarks, Alice utilizes a special program capable of recognizing pattern similarities at a variety of levels. This pattern-matching algorithm operates independently and quite differently from Alice's signature pattern-matching program. Earmarks surface by pattern matching a single work—unlike the two or more necessary for finding signatures—and eliminating all the more numerous pattern matches relevant to thematic development. Typically, earmarks occur only once or twice in a movement or work and appear as lone survivors after all other matched patterns have been discarded.

Earmarks often go undetected because they can get lost amid similar melodic motions. The distinguishing characteristic of earmarks is their location—that they appear at particular points in compositions just after an important event and just before another important event. In the case of signatures, position sensitivity is typically local to a phrase (e.g., cadence). Earmarks have global position sensitivity,

Figure 5.30   A recurring pattern from the first movements of Mozart's piano concerti: (a) K. 238, mm. 86–87; (b) K. 449, mm. 318– 319; (c) K. 450, mm. 277–278; (d) K. 482, mm. 196–197; (e) K. 595, mm. 326–327; (f) K. 459, mm. 371–372.

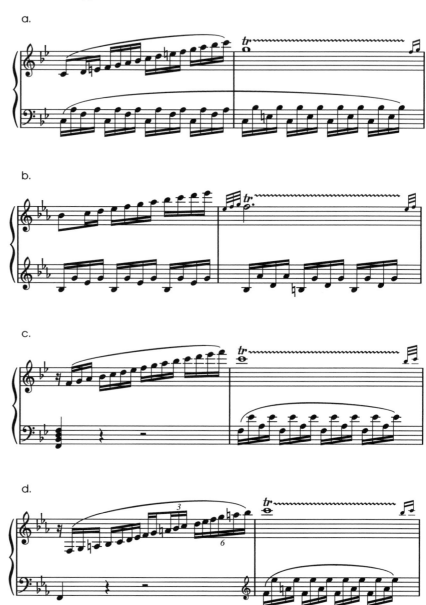

Figure 5.30 Continued.

usually to the ending and/or beginning of a major section of a movement or work.

The examples shown in figure 5.30 are typical of the type of variations earmarks demonstrate. In general, these variations point out the *gestural* nature of earmarks. Here, this can be described as a scale or arpeggio followed by a trill as opposed to an upward second followed by a downward third and so on, more typical of descriptions of signatures. As such, one can say that the relationships between signature variations are explicit, while the relationships between earmark variations are implicit.

Figure 5.31 shows how Experiments in Musical Intelligence integrated the earmark shown in Figure 5.30 into its own piano concerto in the style of Mozart. The second measure of this earmark closely resembles those in figure 5.30. The first measure here varies from the first measures in figure 5.30, but no more than the first measures of figure 5.30 do from one another.

Earmarks play a critical role in Alice's ability to generate logical musical structures. Using earmarks appropriately in algorithmic composition tends to enhance stylistic integrity, formal and structural balance, cohesion, and, ultimately I feel, aesthetic value. As mentioned previously, earmarks are also location sensitive. To be effective, they must reappear in logical temporal locations in new compositions. Like signatures and unifications, earmarks are saved

Figure 5.31   A portion of an Experiments in Musical Intelligence piano concerto in the style of Mozart demonstrating the use of an earmark, mm. 312–313.

as events rather than as rules and recomposed contextually to match their new surroundings.

Misplaced earmarks can cause disruption in an educated listener's perception of musical structure. For example, earmarks that do not precede anticipated events—that occur out of sequence or that otherwise are ill-timed—can cause a rift between the antecedent-consequent motion so important for maintaining musical coherence. For example, there is an oboe concerto attributed to Haydn that has numerous earmarks scattered about the first movement, earmarks that typically foreshadow or precede the cadenza. None of the uses of this earmark subsequently moves to the cadenza, with the result that the movement, at best, sounds disconnected and, at worst, appears to constantly stumble about unsure of its destination. Given that Haydn was undoubtedly aware of the proper use of this earmark, at least if one can go by the numerous examples of concerti of his that use this earmark logically, it would seem unlikely that this work's attribution is correct (for more on attribution, see chapter 7).

Interestingly, Alice attempts to *create* earmarks when they seem lacking in the music found in a database since Alice assumes that style replication depends on the existence of such patterns. When Alice creates aspects of work not inherent to a given style, the program graduates to a level beyond that of a mere imitator. I am often struck by the importance of such artificial pattern injection—in so doing the program becomes a truly equal partner.

During the rehearsals of the piano concerto in the style of Mozart, part of which appears in figure 5.31, a single measure continually bothered both the conductor and the members of the orchestra. This measure seemed out of context, causing much confusion. During one session, the conductor stopped and took a poll, which resulted in a decision to have me re-write the measure, an earmark, prior to performance and final recording. I subsequently spent more than five hours attempting to graft a new measure in place. When I finally completed an acceptable but fairly innocuous new version, which I then documented carefully, I discovered that I had a new-found respect for composing in styles—Mozart's *and* my program's. The displacement of one note can cause severe consequences to both style and musical compatibility. I have since fixed this measure into place and noted its alteration.

Figures 5.32a and b show, respectively, the beginnings of the second and fourth movements of the Experiments in Musical Intelligence program's Mozart symphony composed in the spring of 1995. This work, like the concerto composed in the same year, uses earmarks as well as signatures for creating structure- and style-sensitive music. However, both earmarks and signatures are

Figure 5.32   The beginnings of the Experiments in Musical Intelligence program's Mozart's *Symphony* movements 2 and 4.

so melded into the fabric of this work that I rarely find them without a computer analysis. Interestingly, analysis of the symphony produces substantially different earmarks than those found in the concerto.

Figure 5.33 shows a fourth-movement earmark found in type, if not character, in many of Mozart's symphonies and later found in the symphony just described. The earmark begins here on the fourth beat of measure 82 and concludes on the final half note of the example. Three fourth movements of Mozart's symphonies were used in the pattern matching that found this earmark. Each of these movements possessed a version of this earmark at roughly the same structural point. Again, as with the earmark found in the concerti, the music here is not especially distinguished. Interestingly, after hearing the passage, the earmark stands out from the surrounding material with enough integrity to make its structural importance clear to the ear. The orchestration, inherited from the original scores on which its composition was based, helps blend the earmark with the surrounding material so that the pattern occurs naturally rather than artificially. This earmark forms the basis on which Mozart announces, in this case, the recapitulation of the first theme in the movement's original key.

To compose longer segments of music, Alice must adhere to structures beyond that of simply using earmarks appropriately. As previously noted, Alice refers to forms in the databases that most closely approximate the form of the work being extended. Alice compares proportions and makes best possible choices among those available. Proportions involve structural elements from the phrase level up to and including full movements. To make this process more efficient, Alice incorporates SPEAC.

■ SPEAC

There are many methods for analyzing non-tonal music. These range from quasi-tonal functional representations to pitch-class set theory and beyond. While each of these approaches can be revealing, few relate to other parameters besides pitch or define significant hierarchical connections. Further, most contemporary analytical techniques provide little useful information about actual musical function. In short, no single method seems appropriate as the ideal choice for analysis.

In contrast, SPEAC (discussed at length in Cope 1991b, 1996) analysis uses the context provided by elements such as beat placement,

Figure 5.33   An earmark from the fourth movement of the Experiments in Musical Intelligence program's *Symphony* (mm. 82–85). The earmark begins on the fourth beat of measure 82 and ends on the half note of measure 85.

duration, location, and vertical tension to differentiate between groupings that visually appear the same but that sound different. For example, a chord used as a pickup to the first measure of a work can play a significantly different role than the identically spelled chord appearing as the penultimate chord in the final cadence of the same work. The tonic $^6_4$ chord in tonal music provides another good example of this difference in approach. The cadential tonic $^6_4$ chord has a dominant function, is location specific, and poses severe voice-leading requirements. The passing tonic $^6_4$ chord, however, usually has a tonic function with different but nonetheless strict voice-leading requirements. The pedal tonic $^6_4$ chord can be considered tonic, dominant, or without function with yet different voice-leading restrictions. In traditional functional analyses, all three of these chords are usually labeled identically. SPEAC analysis, on the other hand, provides the means for differentiating these three separate musical ideas.

The SPEAC approach abstracts musical notes and harmonies on the basis of ideas derived from the work of Heinrich Schenker (1935). SPEAC is an acronym for *statement* (S), *preparation* (P), *extension* (E), *antecedent* (A), and *consequent* (C). SPEAC analysis allows notes and chords to vary in meaning, depending on context. Thus, the analysis of C–E–G in C major can change, depending on its use. For example, at the beginning of a phrase in C major, C–E–G may be a statement, S, whereas in a cadence it may be a consequent, C. Thus, while traditional functions provide analysis of surface detail, the SPEAC system provides insight into the deeper meaning of music.

I do not argue here that SPEAC analysis should replace other types of analysis. Rather, I suggest that SPEAC can enhance these other types of analysis since SPEAC differentiates between otherwise identical analyses. SPEAC can also be used in parallel with any other analytical approach.

As a simple example, figure 5.34 shows the first two phrases of Bach's Chorale No. 1 (Bach 1941). The standard roman-numeral analysis given below each chord shows seven different tonic (I) chords. With the exception of the first-inversion tonic chord on the downbeat of measure 6, the analysis of these chords does not indicate that they have different musical meanings. Even the two chords that repeat in precisely the same voicings (e.g., tonic chords 4 and 5 and tonic chords 1 and 7) have different implications if not meanings. Each tonic chord here has different preceding and following chords, different beat placement, different durations, and/or different location in regard to their phrase and section context. The SPEAC identifiers shown below each chord function in figure 5.34 demonstrate how SPEAC differentiates meanings of chords that otherwise have similar or equivalent functional analyses.

SPEAC identifiers function in the following ways:

Figure 5.34   First two phrases of Bach's Chorale No. 1 with tonic chords marked in function and SPEAC analysis showing how SPEAC differentiates between chords of like function.

S = *statement;* stable—a declaration of material or ideas. Statements can precede or follow any SPEAC function.

P = *preparation;* active—an introductory gesture. Preparations precede any SPEAC function but more typically occur prior to statements and antecedents.

E = *extension;* stable—a continuance of material or ideas. Extensions usually follow statements but can follow any SPEAC function.

A = *antecedent;* very active—requires a consequent function. Antecedents thus directly or indirectly precede consequents.

C = *consequent;* conclusive—results in consequent gestures. Consequents must be preceded directly or indirectly (with intervening extensions) by antecedents.

Thus, progressions of identifiers such as P–S–E–A–C and S–E–A seem logical, while progressions of identifiers such as A–E–P–S and S–A–P–C, while still possible, are less plausible. SPEAC identifier assignments follow an A–P–E–S–C progression of stability, with the most unstable function to the left and the most stable function to the right. Thus, A and P require resolution, while E, S, and C do not. SPEAC is multidimensional as well. For example, no two groupings labeled A have precisely the same amount of A-ness. Typically, this multi-dimensionality appears when producing structural levels of SPEAC analyses (see the section "Analysis" in chapter 6). Labeling pitch groupings with SPEAC functions is also *personal* rather than universal. Some assignments of these identifiers may seem more obvious than others.

SPEAC identifiers also stand for relationships between groupings of any musical parameter or parameters. As with pitch-class set analysis, grouping requires great care for SPEAC analysis to work effectively. In Alice, SPEAC identifiers represent dissonance or tension relationships. To accomplish this, Alice calculates a tension weighting for each grouping of event pitches. This weighting requires variables defined by users that take into consideration variations due to octave displacement. Each grouping receives an identifier based on its tension within its local and global context. Basically, this identifier assignment depends on the values and identifiers of the preceding and following groups. Thus, identical groupings may have any SPEAC identifier attached to them, depending on their context. Hierarchical groupings of identifiers show tension at larger and larger levels using the same procedures. These hierarchical analyses are not based on succession orders but purely on SPEAC analysis.

I have programmed Alice this way because tension is one of the ways in which I listen to music, and few existing methods of analysis view tension as a significant factor. I am also partial to analytical approaches that incorporate personal interpretation. Different variable settings for intervals in Alice will lead to distinctly different SPEAC analyses.

Figure 5.35 shows an example of SPEAC used both as a phrase and as a formal analysis tool. Alice uses a bar graph to show SPEAC phrase analysis with tension levels listed above and SPEAC identifiers presented below these graphs, as shown in figure 5.35a. Figure 5.35b demonstrates how Alice represents hierarchical SPEAC using a separate tree-structure diagram that resembles those shown in figures 2.4, 2.7, and 2.9 of *Computers and Musical Style* (Cope 1991b). The initial letters of each node indicate the SPEAC analysis, with the immediately following number representing the level in the hierarchy. The hyphenated suffixes differentiate between two otherwise like-analyzed points, as in the third tier from the top, where two C3's occur. The curved connectors at the bottom of figure 5.35b relate phrases containing similar material. Thus, a single chart can capsulize a variety of important structural relationships.

Figure 5.35   (a) SPEAC column chart; (b) an example of SPEAC structural analysis.

a.

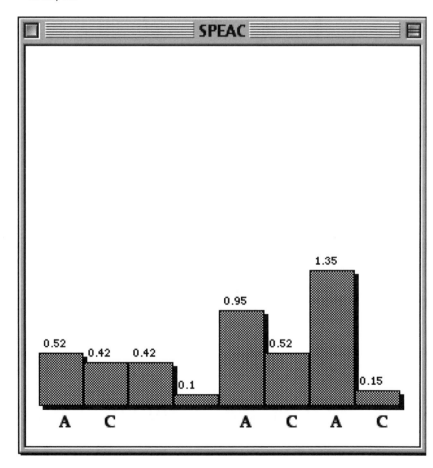

Figure 5.35 Continued.

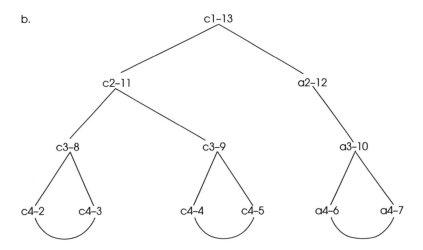

b.

As previously mentioned, the Alice SPEAC program is not intended to supersede any other analytical approach but rather to augment such approaches. I have found that comparing my own intuitive interpretation of a score to the program's analysis produces very useful results. Viewing diagrams of different phrases and works shows how some music has logical and elegant organization of tension while other music appears haphazard.

Alice uses SPEAC analysis in many different ways when composing. For example, in-progress phrases inherit the SPEAC tension contours of music in the database. While rules and meta-patterns contribute to correct motions of voices throughout a phrase, new phrases can still sound random or ineffective in terms of their ordering of tensions. Figure 5.36 provides just such an example. Here, an original phrase of Scriabin appears in both music and in terms of SPEAC identifier analysis (figure 5.36a). Figure 5.36b shows a newly composed phrase intended to be in the style of Scriabin. Voice leading follows that found in Scriabin's style. However, as can be seen, a SPEAC analysis indicates that the two phrases move in quite different directions. The original Scriabin increases in tension as it drives toward a point of arrival and then eases toward a cadence with incrementally decreasing levels of tension. On the other hand, the newly composed phrase in figure 5.36b has no real point of arrival, and the orders of tension seem arbitrary. Figure 5.36c shows a newly composed phrase that takes into account the original SPEAC analysis of figure 5.36a. This new music has no less attention paid to rules and

Figure 5.36 (a) Scriabin, *Prelude No. 1*, Op. 16, and SPEAC analysis; (b) new phrase with different SPEAC analysis; (c) new phrase with complementary (to (a)) SPEAC analysis.

a.

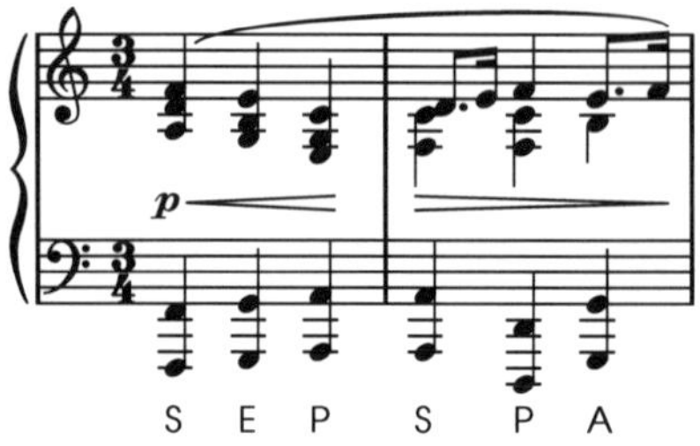

b.

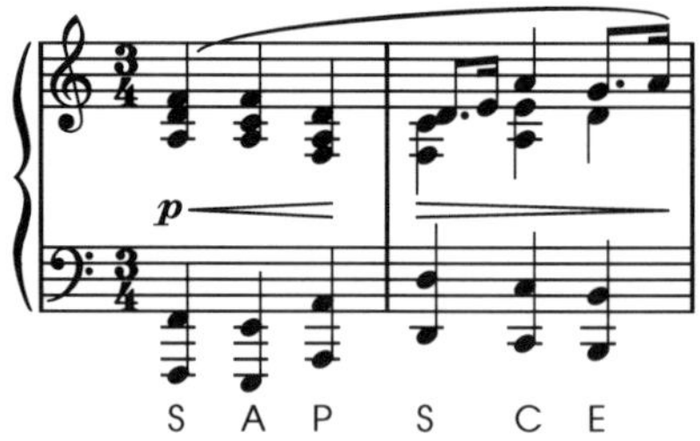

c.

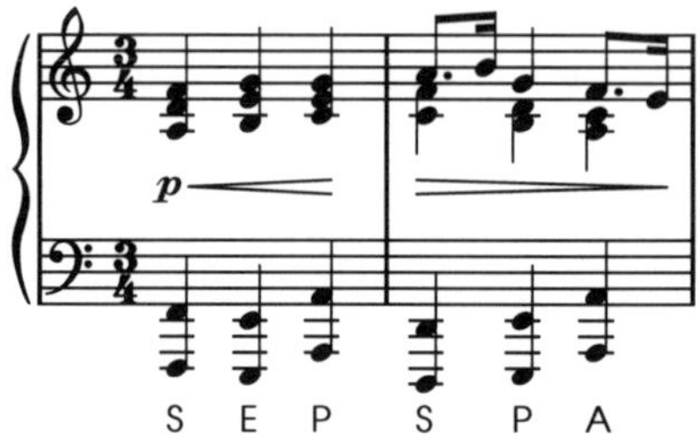

meta-patterns, with the voice leading as correct as that in the preceding example. However, as the SPEAC analysis shows here, this new phrase follows the same directions in terms of tension as does the original music by Scriabin.

The machine-created music in figure 5.36c results from SPEAC-coerced choices in which many correct possibilities exist at decision-making points during composition. Thus, SPEAC is most effective when using a rich and deep database. With smaller databases, often only one possible choice exists, and even using SPEAC the program cannot compose new music very effectively.

While mapping SPEAC on a phrase-by-phrase basis helps create a certain logic at upper hierarchical levels, it does not guarantee it. Some works and/or styles have distinct approaches to tension on a larger scale than phrases. For example, two contiguous phrases in a database may have the same general tension contour as a newly composed pair of phrases, but the point of arrival of the two sets may occur in quite different locations. For example, the second point of arrival of a database pair of phrases may serve as a consequent to the previous phrase's antecedent. However, a machine-composed pair of phrases could still maintain the tension contours of the two phrases but actually negate the roles of the two points of arrival by reversing their tension relationship. Alice avoids such reversals by measuring the smallest and largest tensions and ensuring that the newly composed music follows the same order. Such hierarchical comparisons take place at successively larger and larger levels. This ensures that, for example, the point of arrival for an entire work will occur at an appropriate point rather than out of sequence. One could imagine, for example, a Ravel *Bolero* or a Barber *Adagio for Strings* in which all the basic tension relationships were carefully followed but the point of arrival for each work came near the beginning instead of near the end. Such misplacements would have serious musical consequences.

As previously mentioned, SPEAC may be used in conjunction with virtually any type of analysis. For example, using SPEAC with functional harmony can help differentiate various uses of given functions, uses that otherwise may remain hidden (for more information regarding this use of SPEAC, see Cope 1991b, chap. 2). SPEAC can also be applied to every level of structural analysis—from measures to sectional relationships—in ways other than tension. In all these cases, useful analysis occurs only with proper assignment of SPEAC identifiers. While such assignments can sometimes seem vague, especially when compared to, say, assignment of traditional harmonic functions, SPEAC can, for each analyst, produce significant insights.

At this point, some readers may be overwhelmed with the various methods Alice uses to analyze music as well as the processes it uses for composing extensions to works in progress. Figure 5.37 hopefully provides some clarity on how these various techniques work in concert. Here we see signatures, earmarks, unifications, meta-patterns, SPEAC, and so on, interlocking to create new music.

Figure 5.37 An overview of how the various analysis and pattern-matching programs work together in Alice.

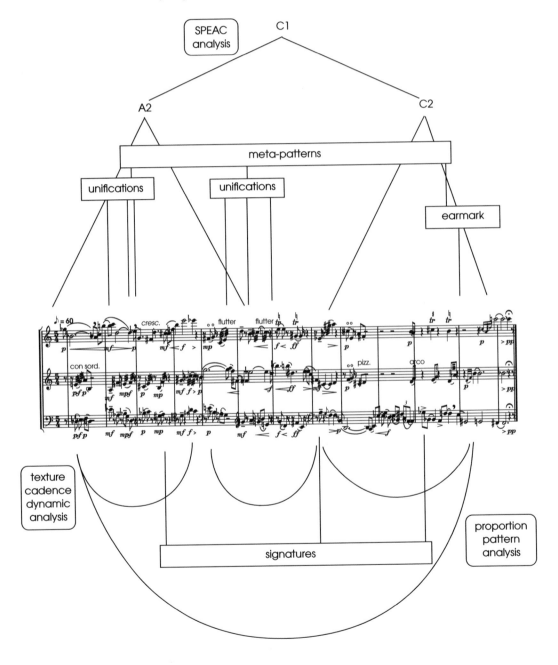

Signatures help produce stylistic continuity. Unifications ensure that compositions in progress will continue developing similar materials. Earmarks provide clues for major structural events. Texture, cadence, and dynamic analyses help formulate structure. Meta-patterns and SPEAC contribute to the overall formal logic. Proportion and pattern analyses ensure that the overall variations and contrasts of existing sections make sense.

Figure 5.38 shows the entirety of the third movement of my *Five Pieces for Flute, Violin, and Bassoon* (1965), the musical example used for figure 5.37. Although brief, this movement has a clear-cut three-part form with the middle section (mm. 5–8) being a relatively simple variation of the opening material. The initial minor sixth downward motion in the flute with the tremolo minor third in the violin describe the initial thematic material. This opening material is mirrored beginning with the anacrusis to measure 5. The recapitulation begins with the bassoon pickup to measure 9. A small coda appears in the final two measures.

Figure 5.39 shows the beginning of the third movement of my *Songs from the Navajo* composed in collaboration with my version of Alice and using my *Five Pieces for Flute, Violin, and Bassoon* as a part of the database. This example shows rule inheritance—note the initial minor sixth downward motion in the clarinet and the opening tremolo minor third in the cello—and structural influence. This latter may be better described as structural *resemblance* since this movement from *Songs from the Navajo* embellishes the structure of the movement from *Five Pieces for Flute, Violin, and Bassoon* shown in figure 5.38 by introducing more contrast. However, during the composition of *Songs from the Navajo*, Alice constantly reminded me of the original music's form whenever I called on it for composition. These reminders served as foils against which I constantly struggled. Without them, the movement would have turned out much differently and, I feel, less effectively.

Songs from the Navajo contains signatures, earmarks, unifications, meta-patterns, and SPEAC contours as discussed in this chapter. Approximately 10 percent of the completed song in figure 5.39 was composed by Alice, although it would be difficult to identify exactly which music the program actually created. The fact that the instrumental music of this movement from *Songs from the Navajo* breaks into two groups of three instruments each (clarinet, viola, and cello in one group and harp, percussion, and piano in the other) directly results from Alice's creation of three-voiced composition. Again, the machine-composed music produced a resistance against which my coercing and prodding exemplifies the ideal collaboration for me. It

Figure 5.38 Piece 3 from *Five Pieces for Flute, Violin, and Bassoon.*

Figure 5.39   The opening of the third movement from *Songs from the Navajo* showing various types of inheritance from the music in figure 5.38.

is hard not to react rather fiercely when such machine-composing partners create music so fluently, without the self-examination and doubts so innate to human composing.

SIX

The Alice Program

■ GENERAL ALGORITHM

Figure 6.1 shows an overview of the Alice (ALgorithmically Integrated Composing Environment) program. Initially, composers must establish a database of previously composed works and set the various program variables. Music of a new work is then input using Alice's standard notation program and output by performing, printing, or saving in a variety of formats. This process follows the primary vertical line in the center of the overview in figure 6.1. The analysis program (discussed more fully later in this chapter) presents composers with statistical models of their music and informs them of the signatures of their style, the SPEAC contours of their music, the hierarchical structure of their work in progress, and various other analyses of their music. The algorithmic component of Alice, at the user's discretion, uses previously composed music, the currently in-progress composition, and values of the various program variables to compose new music. Composers may initiate the algorithmic composing program at any time and use it for extending their music or, in my version of Alice, backfilling incomplete areas of their scores.

Alice utilizes many of the same basic compositional algorithms as does the Experiments in Musical Intelligence program, although it does not possess some of that program's more intricate ATN (augmented transition network) algorithms and incorporates rules rather than recombinancy. These differences result in part from the fact that ATN and recombinancy deal directly with event semantics that require immense amounts of processing time, thereby diminishing interactive potential, and operate best in the context of creating

Figure 6.1   An overview of the Alice program.

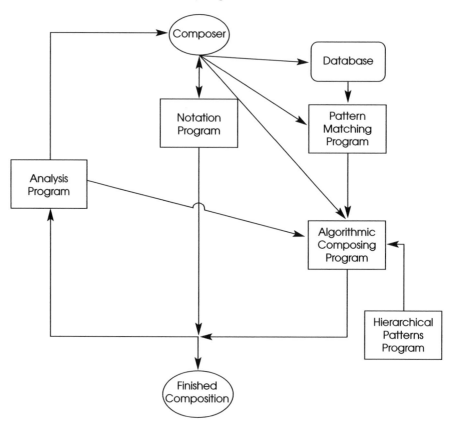

whole compositions rather than passages of otherwise incomplete works. Concomitantly, however, Alice can track a work in progress and continue it at any given point with few transitional errors. As has been pointed out, Alice's approach to abstracting input music to rules offers significantly more creative potential than does recombinancy.

Alice requires the same interaction as does the Experiments in Musical Intelligence program: appropriate databases, setting pattern-matching controllers, selecting best output, and so on. Beyond these, however, Alice depends on the user to provide the work in progress, the precise amount of required machine-composed music desired, and feedback on the successes and/or failures of Alice's algorithmic music.

The Alice program that appears on this book's CD-ROM represents a simplified version of the one I use myself, just as SARA (Simple Analytic Recombinant Algorithm) is a simplified version of the

Experiments in Musical Intelligence program. However, most of Alice's basic capabilities exist in this simpler version, and users should be able to vary and extend the code in ways that will ultimately make the application more personal and more personally valuable to them. This simpler version results from three basic constraints that necessarily affect any public software. First, the version of Alice provided here must be compatible with various Macintosh models. Thus, the program requires design simplicity and as few in-progress experiments as possible. My own version represents the opposite—I am constantly varying the program in ways peculiar to my personal needs. Second, this simpler version of Alice must be bug free. As a programmer and the creator of Alice, I can easily live with problems if they occur as a result of risks taken for substantial gains. However, users of the version of Alice that accompanies this book cannot live with such problems. Whereas the Alice that I use is constantly being improved and varied, the published Alice must stand as a kind of final document. Finally, this simpler version of Alice must be interface friendly and ultimately usable without significant investment of time by first-time users. The greater the number of variables, the greater the probability of failure. Thus, options have been kept to a minimum for the sake of universality; on the one hand, these limited options make the software more immediately accessible while, on the other hand, at least for some, they make the program less immediately useful.

However, the simplified nature of the Alice software provided here should not deter the truly interested user. Since I have included source code, users can personalize their versions of the program by altering or adding code on the basis of the suggestions provided by this book and the two volumes that precede it. Some of these alterations include varying and/or personalizing the structural analysis code, extending the pattern-matching code to include dynamics and/or channels, adding other subprograms such as graphical inputs, and so on. Chapters 3 and 4 of *Computers and Musical Style* (1991) and chapter 4 of *Experiments in Musical Intelligence* (1996) also inform readers of ways to use LISP to alter or add code. Likewise, Steele (1990) and the Macintosh CommonLISP user's manual, as well as the numerous LISP tutorial books (see this book's bibliography), should provide users with sufficient tools to produce truly personal versions of Alice.

Thus, I sincerely hope that those acquainted with LISP will revise and augment the source code presented on this book's CD-ROM and devise more elaborate versions of the program. Beyond my explanations in this book, I have liberally documented the code and provided examples and tutorials whenever possible and useful. This should ensure that programmers will not have to reverse engineer the program (an often hostile and fruitless endeavor) but, rather, will enjoy an immediately rewarding opportunity to customize and make Alice their own.

A perfectly prepared (i.e., right databases, best settings on pattern-matching controllers, and so on) Alice-like program should produce the sensation that one is collaborating with oneself. The program-composed music should extend the work in progress with compatible, appropriate, and relevant ideas both to that work and to the style of the works in the database. The program itself should be as invisible as possible, and users should never be aware of the process of composition, only the result. The current Alice—the one provided with this book—cannot boast of such seamless operation. However, the Alice-like program of the future, the type of program that I predict will accompany many contemporary composers through the twenty-first century, will approach these goals. Composers using such software will find their interfaces as easy to use as the notation software of the present day. Listeners of works composed in part by such software programs will be unable to distinguish any machine aspect of the style or content of these works.

Some users of Alice, as well as the Experiments in Musical Intelligence program and SARA, will be dismayed to discover that producing good music using this software nonetheless remains a difficult and trying task. Entering and melding viable databases, discovering the best settings for controllers during pattern matching, and deciding the quality of the many different choices of output are but a few of the critical and time-consuming tasks that users face. Most if not all of these tasks require as much musical experience as would be required for composing without a computer program. Ultimately, getting programs such as Alice to create stylistically credible music requires immense effort. Getting such programs to create *good* music can often seem unachievable. Those who imagine that computer programs such as Alice provide opportunities for the musically illiterate to compose great masterpieces will be disappointed. Indeed, it may take longer to create a masterpiece using this software than to *become* musically literate and then create your own masterpiece.

■ INPUT

Alice offers two possibilities for inputting music: a notation program written in Common LISP or using a commercial notation package. Alice's LISP notation program has been kept simple since a complex program would slow Alice significantly, add to the program's already large footprint, and unnecessarily re-invent the wheel, for comprehensive notation programs already exist that, through extensive testing, have proven themselves more than worthy. However, the Alice notation program is sufficient for relatively straightforward composition.

Using a commercially available notation application and loading the resultant standard MIDI files into Alice offers users the opportunity to create, edit, and ultimately incorporate algorithmic composition in a notational environment of their own choosing. However, using this approach requires saving documents from one program and then loading them into Alice, a two-stage task that requires time and that occasionally can be disconcerting.

As previously stated, users must furnish Alice with previously composed works for use as a database. Any work or group of works stored as standard MIDI files may be loaded directly into Alice for such purpose. Chapter 2 of *Experiments in Musical Intelligence* (Cope 1996) describes in detail how database works must resemble one another in terms of meter, dimension, tempo, and so on. Carefully selecting works for databases and entering them appropriately can greatly enhance resultant algorithmic composition (again see Cope 1996, chap. 2). As an alternative to standard MIDI file format, users can also input database music with Alice's soon-to-be-discussed music notation program.

Alice databases need not consist of entire works. It can even be useful to seed databases with smaller style-similar sections from various works rather than only using whole compositions. However, at least one complete composition should be included in the database to be used as a model for structural analysis. This work should be identified appropriately (see the Alice manual for instructions) when loading databases in Alice. Sections of works act as material for continuity so that algorithmic composition does not continually reproduce previously composed material and create a kind of quotation rather than new music. I often use fragments from various compositions, some involving different numbers and types of instruments, to create a database that will, once honed, produce extensive amounts of successful composition. As pointed out in *Experiments in Musical Intelligence* (Cope 1996), a well-chosen database can produce a significant variety of successful output, while a poorly created database will continually produce poor music. Since even a single mistake in a database becomes magnified in output, users should check and recheck their database music many times for accuracy.

In the version of Alice that I use and the one described in Cope (1997a), the Alice notational input window allows notes to be placed anywhere in a given measure without regard to associated rests, which then appear automatically in the more readable score window. Choice of note value, accidentals, channels, dots, ties, and dynamics is made by way of an independent palette. Any note can be further edited by clicking on it directly and entering a new on-time, pitch, duration, channel, and/or dynamic. However, since this approach requires significant processing time, I have opted for a more standard input interface for use with the version of Alice that accompanies this book, as shown in figure 6.2a. The score window (figure 6.2b) then produces a printable version of the notated music.

Figure 6.2 The Alice notation windows: (a) the Alice Input window; (b) the Alice Score window.

a.

Figure 6.2 Continued.

b.

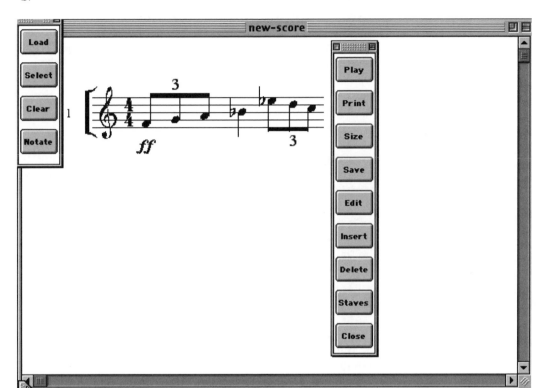

Music created with separate programs can conflict with Alice's somewhat limited notation program. For example, the version of Alice on this book's CD-ROM cannot produce extremely complicated notations. As a result, some transferred music may invoke an error or produce output that suffers occasionally severe quantization. To minimize incompatibilities, users should avoid improvising or using other input techniques that involve extremely complex on-times and off-times. While to some this requirement may seem overly limiting, I remind readers that traditional notation is itself limiting and that any program that uses this type of input and/or output must necessarily have inherent restrictions.

Another, less immediately obvious form of program input involves user access to, and altering of, Alice's code. Both *Computers and Musical Style* (1991b) and *Experiments in Musical Intelligence* (1996) provide tutorials for various aspects of LISP programming that make understanding such code less formidable than it might otherwise seem. Unlike SARA, Alice utilizes a particular process called *loop,* which requires some explanation to be understood.

Recursive functions in LISP (see Cope 1991b, chap. 3) can occasionally suffer from poor readability. Figures 6.3a and b demonstrate this by showing two definitions for the same function: one recursive and the other iterative. Figure 6.3a's recursive function requires that users wanting to understand the function detect the recursion in the final line—the function calling itself. However, the same function written with the LISP `loop` macro, shown in figure 6.3b, has a more transparent meaning.

The `loop` macro, like recursive code, begins with a terminating or qualifying statement. The `loop` macro does not require the same number of parentheses as does traditional LISP, although most standard LISP primitives must still be called parenthetically. Non-listed `loop` function calls and interpolated words can help make the `loop` code appear more readable. Figure 6.3c presents just such a case. Here, the statement `for number in` calls the function `for`, names the variable `number`, and includes the word `in` for readability. The second line uses the function `collect` and the argument (`1+ number`). In effect, the function `collect` collects each iteration of the variable `number` as it increments through the variable `number-list`. With the exception of the lack of parentheses, an added word for readability, and the substitution of `collect` for `cons`, the code for the `loop` macro is not that different from the equivalent recursive LISP code (here shown below the `loop` code in figure 6.3c). This latter code defines a new function (`add-one`) since the function must recursively call itself. However, as can be seen, the `loop` version does not require the same number of instructions as does the recursive version and is more immediately understandable.

While it is important to remember that the `loop` macro often produces more readable code, it occasionally can create less elegant code. Figure 6.3d uses double recursion to evaluate all the symbols in arbitrarily nested lists. These five lines of code read much more clearly than the seven lines of code necessary for the `loop` version of this function, shown in figure 6.3e. On balance, one should choose recursion or iteration, depending on which approach provides the most readable functions. Readers can test the functions shown in figure 6.3 themselves by loading the *loop versus recursion* file in the *loop* folder on this book's CD-ROM.

Those individuals new to LISP will find the `loop` macro easier to read than the code for recursive functions. Those experienced in other programming languages will also find the `loop` macro appealing in that it also resembles iterative processes in those languages. Experienced users of recursion in LISP typically find the reverse to

Figure 6.3 Various readability trade-offs with recursion and `loop`: (a) a
traditional LISP recursive function; (b) the same function written
with the `loop` macro; (c) a `loop` macro and its recursive
equivalent; (d) a double recursive function in LISP; (e) a double
recursive function written with `loop`.

a.
```
(defun create-transpose-down-list (note)
   (if (<= note 47) nil
       (cons (- note12)
             (create-transpose-down-list (- note 12))))))
```

b.
```
(defun create-transpose-down-list (note)
  (loop until (<= note 47)
        collect (- note 12)
        do (setf note (- note 12)))))
```

c.
```
(defvar number-list '(1 2 3 4))

(loop for number in number-list
      collect (1+ number))

(defun add-one (numbers)
   (if (null numbers) ()
       (cons (1+ (first numbers))
             (add-one (rest numbers))))))
```

d.
```
(defun eval-everything (instance-lists)
  (cond ((null instance-lists) nil)
        ((atom instance-lists) (eval instance-lists))
        (t (cons (eval-everything (first instance-lists))
                 (eval-everything (rest instance-lists))))))
```

e.
```
(defun eval-everything (instance-lists)
  (cond ((atom instance-lists) (eval instance-lists))
        ((null (listp instance-lists)) (eval instance-lists))
        (t (loop for instance in instance-lists
                 if (atom instance)
                 collect (eval instance)
                 else collect (eval-everything instance)))))
```

be true. Conservative LISPers generally frown on iteration, believing
that recursion still represents an important distinguishing feature of
LISP and a powerful and more elegant coding procedure. However,
most programmers using LISP have skills in both forms of coding.
Many of the programs on this book's CD-ROM provide example functions using the `loop` macro. Readers should acquaint themselves
with the variety of statements that can be used with `loop` and the

ways in which variables can be altered using the LISP function `setf` before they attempt to rewrite or add to Alice's code.

■ ANALYSIS

Alice's analysis interface includes statistical graphs; pattern matching variables and results; mappings of SPEAC, texture, and rules; and lattice-type tree structure representations of user-chosen works. The choices of analytical techniques, from an obviously wide palette of possibilities, is entirely personal and reflects those that I have found most useful.

Figure 6.4 shows the graphs of the basic statistical analyses that Alice provides. Pitch distributions, weighted by duration, are shown visually as a pie chart (figure 6.4a). Such information can be useful in determining scalular content, pitch use percentages, missing or seldom-used pitches, and potential functional relationships. Scales are shown with a bar graph (figure 6.4b), with Alice providing best guesses as to the scale in use from a large collection of available scale choices. A line graph demonstrates the rates at which different pitches unfold (see figure 6.4c). This can be helpful for following the pace at which new pitch material appears and can reveal, for example, heard but otherwise not easily defined stagnant passages. Texture (figure 6.4d) is plotted in terms of the number of simultaneous voices per unit of harmonic rhythm. A scatter chart (figure 6.4e) cross-references duration (bottom to top) and pitch (left to right), which can be especially useful for interpreting how rhythm and pitch interrelate. A MIDI channel chart (figure 6.4f) provides a view of how and to what extent various channel (timbral) choices occur. Users may configure the scope of the analysis to any amount of the work in progress or any work in the database.

Some users will find that they access Alice's statistical analyses more often than they utilize algorithmic composition. The feedback that such objective information provides can often produce valuable insights into certain habits, misperceptions, and forgotten details. Being able to designate exactly which and how much music requires analysis has proven to be especially valuable. For example, note-use percentages can vary substantially between an analysis of an entire work and a similar analysis of a much shorter section of a work. Likewise, observing the unfolding of texture as it drapes across a longer passage provides composers with a different yet complementary perspective of their composition than the same

Figure 6.4 Analysis charts provided by Alice: (a) pitch distribution; (b) scale weightings; (c) pitch chronology; (d) texture map; (e) cross-referencing chart; (f) channel chart.

a.

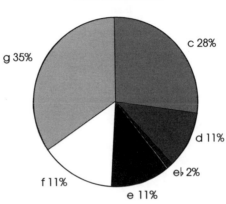

Pitch Occurrence

c 28%

g 35%

d 11%

e♭ 2%

f 11%

e 11%

b.

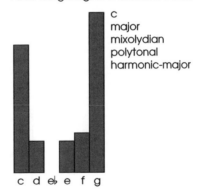

Pitch Weightings to Determine Scale

c
major
mixolydian
polytonal
harmonic-major

c d e♭ e f g

c.

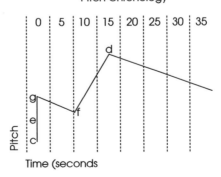

Pitch Chronology

0   5   10   15   20   25   30   35

d

g

f

e

c

Pitch

Time (seconds

Figure 6.4   Continued

d.

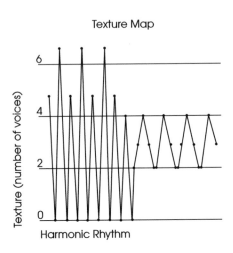

e.

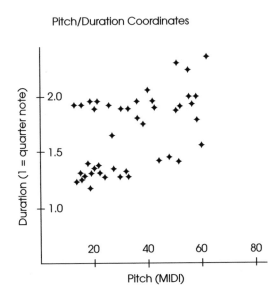

Figure 6.4 Continued.

f.

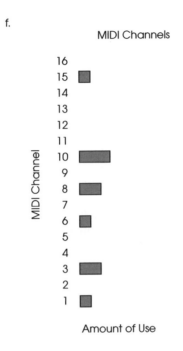

MIDI Channels

MIDI Channel

Amount of Use

analysis of a shorter passage. While any of these analyses are possible by hand, using Alice requires a fraction of the time and produces results with an accuracy beyond that of most human analysts. In fact, many composers would never dream of applying such analyses to their music simply because it would be too exhaustive and time consuming. However, analyses of this type typically helps even advanced composers recognize difficult-to-perceive problems.

The Alice program also produces mappings of texture using piano roll notation. While this mapping duplicates to some extent the texture display in the statistical analysis program, this more extensive map includes pitch names and shows their precise on/off times. Alice also provides a display for all the rules the program has discovered in the database and in the work in progress. This listing can produce occasionally unexpected revelations if one is adept at reading rules notation (see chapter 3).

Aside from the routine but nonetheless often insightful statistical analyses, Alice offers pattern matching and tension mapping. Both of these analysis techniques include a complement of user-controllable variables to account for the variation in styles that the program may encounter. While pattern matching was discussed at length in chapter 5, tension mapping is new in Alice and requires more explanation. To create a tension map involves calculating vertical tension—dissonance—at a rate consistent with a passage's harmonic rhythm. Alice presents this data in a column chart format (see figure 5.35a). Each column receives a SPEAC identifier (see also chapter 5 and Cope 1991b, 1996) indicative of its function with the identifier determined by context. This context derives from the local and global progressions of harmonic tensions, each of which results from calculating interval dissonances on the basis of user-established values. The resulting chart allows composers to view a kind of tension map of their work (again see figure 5.35a) and enables Alice to extend the current work more appropriately when called on for algorithmic composition. Relating these context-sensitive SPEAC assignments to the context-insensitive assignments given to prime forms of sets (as discussed in chapter 3) can provide users with insights into how Alice's SPEAC identifiers dynamically change to fit their environment.

Alice automatically utilizes a hierarchical pattern-matching program capable of recognizing the previously discussed meta-patterns. This hierarchical pattern-matching program resembles a signature-identifying pattern matcher but operates independently of and somewhat differently than the signature pattern matcher. This hierarchical program also recognizes *earmarks* by seeking unique patterns that do not match other patterns in a given work. Since not all works have such unique patterns, the Alice hierarchical pattern matcher can fail to detect earmarks. This matcher occasionally discovers false earmarks when a unique pattern exists only because, for example, its size fails to match any other similarly sized pattern. Pattern matching for earmarks using default controller settings usually produces the best results, and continuing to adjust the earmark controllers after failing to detect earmarks typically produces only frustration on the part of any but the most experienced users. The earmark pattern matcher, like other pattern matchers, is especially sensitive to channel selection. Selecting a channel with little activity or one that does not contain important information for matching will yield few if any useful matchings. The earmark pattern-matching program must use most, if not all, of a complete work. Pattern matching phrases or similar-sized numbers of events will consistently fail to detect earmarks. The Alice pattern matchers also find unifications, which assist the composing program in producing logical continuations of works in progress.

The structure component of the Alice program on this book's CD-ROM represents a simplified variation of the version I use. The differences between these two implementations depend primarily on hierarchical analysis and processing time. Instead of analyzing data-base music for phrases, a time-consuming and often risky process, the version of Alice provided here uses music stored by phrase and named according to user-defined formal designations. Thus, `phrase-a-1` indicates that the stored events represent an initial phrase of formal designation "a," while `phrase-b-6` indicates that phrase 6 consists of formal designation "b" material. Music of works in progress are saved in much the same manner. When called on for composition, Alice looks in the current folder for information about the form of the work in progress and compares it with all the possi-ble forms in the database, selecting the one in the database that best fits the work in progress. Alice then analyzes the chosen data-base work for its SPEAC components and builds a simple hierarchy on the basis of that analysis. Figure 5.35b shows an example of this hierarchy as it appears on screen in the program. As mentioned pre-viously, the lattice structure in this figure represents the SPEAC hier-archy, and the curved arch-like lines below that structure represent the form relations between phrase repetitions or near repetitions. These repetitions need not appear contiguously or even in the same section of music. Alice discovers such repetitions in the foreground and connects them for easy recognition. Middleground analysis appears as SPEAC identifiers and results from groupings of tension-related material intermixed with groupings of contrasting material. The top single SPEAC identifier represents a complex interpolation of contrast, repetition, and variation.

Alice's analytical techniques automatically influence the produc-tion of algorithmically composed music. While a detailed examina-tion of how each technique integrates into the composing process falls beyond the scope of this book, it should be noted that analysis of texture, pitch use, and so on contribute significantly to the algo-rithmic composing program's ability to extend music entered by the user as seamlessly as possible.

The analysis program can also act like a provocateur during the composing process. For example, knowing that a work in progress uses only eleven pitch classes or that more than 40 percent of the notes equate to a single pitch class can have immense effect on one's in-progress composing. I have found that an Alice analysis of my music to a certain point in a composition can reveal many dis-crepancies between what I have imagined occurs and what actually exists. I often find that were I not to have consulted the analysis pro-gram, I would have composed quite differently and probably less effectively.

While using Alice's analysis program, I find that a kind of consult-ing pattern emerges over time. The tempo of this pattern accelerates when I am less confident and slows at times when I have more conviction about my work. Consulting the analysis program usually confirms my suspicions or reinforces my point of view toward certain aspects of my music. On the other hand, I am occasionally surprised by one or more aspects of the analysis. This surprise can inspire me to re-think an area of my composition that I may have otherwise felt secure about.

■ COMPOSING

Alice composes music following the processes described in chapters 3 to 5. These processes ensure that new music will be unique but stylistically related to the works provided in the database and the work in progress.

Figure 6.5 shows a simple flowchart of one possible composing session using Alice. Note that the results of many of Alice's operations may be saved to files and reloaded later to avoid duplicating time-consuming processes. In addition, some of the processes can be controlled by either the user or the program. Pattern matching, for example, will run automatically (including the setting of controllers as described in Cope 1996, chap. 7) unless explicitly controlled by users. With other processes, users have options that may save them time and help preserve their concentration on composing. For example, loading presaved signatures avoids long pattern-matching sessions that can otherwise occupy the majority of an initial composing session. Storing rules instead of events in the database, as is possible in my personal version of Alice, significantly increases loading speed and reduces memory. Thus, one or more of the processes in this flowchart may be eliminated, with the result that users can spend more of their time composing.

Note, however, that when certain processes such as pattern matching or structural analysis become fixed, as is the case when they are saved to a file and then reloaded at a later time, Alice-composed output can occasionally become monotonous. In short, the more variables that have established settings, the less opportunity Alice has to compose freely. In general, then, a healthy mix of previous and new analyses generally produces the most interesting results.

A typical composing session with Alice, at least for me, resembles composing with my favored commercial notation package. This means booting the program by double-clicking on the relevant file, adding or subtracting notes to the music found there, occasionally

Figure 6.5   Flowchart demonstrating one possible composing session with Alice.

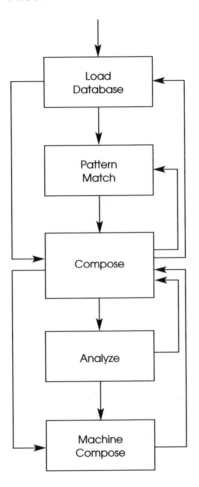

listening to the results, and saving my progress to disk. However, the differences between using Alice and a notation program become noticeable when I consult one or more of the analysis tools available in Alice. This difference becomes yet more exaggerated when pattern matching and playing signatures, earmarks, or other found patterns—opportunities far removed from simply notating music on appropriate staves in a notation program. When curiosity or a temporary pause in inspiration causes a break in the continuity of my composing, I then seek out algorithmic composition, a feature yet further removed from the realm of possibilities of most other music programs. In the case of Alice, because of its attempts at stylistic semblance and continuity, my appetite is usually not whetted easily. In its original recombinant form, Alice often created recognizable music obviously derived from the music in the database. In its current rules form, Alice often surprises me with its attempts to please my intuitive tastes and, when failing, surprises me further by slowly adapting to whatever direction my work happens to be currently following.

I save newly composed music in phrase size or smaller amounts. Each saved phrase has suffix letters and numbers indicating its structural status and ordering, as in *work-a-1*. Saving and loading by phrase further avoids my having to sort through many screen pages of notated music at one time. A simple phrase number index that I keep in a separate file provides me with enough information to identify any unopened phrase whenever required. Since my version of Alice, when called on for algorithmic extensions and backfills, automatically accesses the database and the rest of the work in progress directly from the folders marked *databases* and *work*, I do not need to explicitly load any files. However, Alice requires me to explicitly load files for use with the notation program. Loading phrase-size files of a work in progress increases the speed of Alice's subprograms that analyze loaded music. In turn, this analysis may require quantization and other more cosmetic detailing necessary for producing readable music notation.

The manual for Alice can be found on this book's CD-ROM. However, a number of fundamental issues require discussion here. First, as mentioned previously, the databases that Alice uses for composition must have what the user perceives to be a distinguishable and consistent style. Such style consistency may include mixing music of similar tempos, meters, registers, textures, and so on. The axiom "garbage in means garbage out" (GIGO) should be strictly observed when using Alice. A hastily compiled database produces music of little interest. One mistake in a database will be severely magnified in the output. Users expecting immediate results from Alice will be quite disappointed to find that, as with all forms of composition, satisfying results require significant amounts of time and thoughtfulness. This is especially true when choosing, entering, and proofing music for databases.

Composing music is hard work for both humans and machines. While I have streamlined every aspect of Alice's operation to make it run faster, Alice still requires time to compose. Such delays can be frustrating for some users and may occasionally create poor rapport between human and machine. When combined with the time required to listen to new material in context with previously composed music, Alice's processing can create unfortunate breaks in the composing process not present when one composes without the program. Improvements in hardware and system software will no doubt eliminate most of these problems in the future. At present, however, one can only hope that the quality of Alice's composing will occasionally compensate for the alienation caused by the sometimes snail's-pace interaction.

Interestingly, however, I have found that some of these delays actually cause me to rethink my score in positive ways. In fact, being a slow composer to begin with, I find that most of the delays that Alice causes have beneficial consequences.

Since Alice is also designed to be a provocateur, much of what it produces will get rejected. This is as it should be. In the best of all worlds, even a real-time Alice would typically serve as a foil and rarely as an actual contributing partner. However, plagiarizing Alice is not only legal but can be reasonable and logical as well.

Keeping fairly accurate logs when using Alice can be helpful since users will often find it desirable to reuse more successful settings of variables. The log entries shown in figure 6.6 provide a sampling of what, in this case for me personally, was a seminal moment in the creation of the Experiments in Musical Intelligence's first Mozart sonata emulation (see Cope 1991b). This partial log provides information on pattern matching, output quality, indirect reference to machine used (useful since I replace equipment regularly with newer models but keep and maintain old equipment as well), and number of attempts made before and after successful composition. I have left the misspellings and abbreviations in place for purposes of authenticity. The latter reference to Unix indicates how in 1988, for larger forms at least, I had to abandon my personal computers to take advantage of the higher processing power of mainframe computers.

Alice does not require such elaborate record keeping. One can even use Alice without documenting its settings or output. However, I have found that keeping such logs has value not only for immediate benefit—reusing successful settings—but also for future consultation to reproduce conditions that created successful composition. The short log presented in figure 6.7 is indicative of such documentation. This log resembles that shown in figure 6.6 but comments on different aspects of the compositional processes. Here, more attention is paid to the contents of the database being used and to the presence of earmarks. Should I ever need to reconstruct the conditions under which this particular algorithmic composition took place, I can do so with some expectation that the level of quality in the program's output will not diminish significantly.

Figure 6.6   A computer composing log. The more important abbreviations include pm = pattern matching, sigs = signatures, and mvt = movement.

July 18, 1988 at 2:45p,
mozart second movement
1 (pm 8 1 2 1 2) hmm sigs too easy? poor database
reload (pull the K. 281 2nd mvt - too unique for database!
2 (pm 8 1 2 1 2) better but still something off about dbs
reload (first half only)
3 (pm 8 1 2 1 2) good results but db not big enuf
start coding new music at 4pm

July 19, 1988 at 8:30 am (no run today)
trying Mozart now that new music coded
1 (restarting n.s) (pm 8 1 2 1 2) good results - actually may be it!!!!!
2 (pm 8 1 2 1 2) no new to work on sigs
3 (pm 9 1 2 1 2) fewer sigs and better but output not there
4 (pm 9 1 2 1 3) no way
5 (pm 9 1 2 1 2) ok for now - good piece may be as good as 1 not sure
6 (pm 9 1 2 1 2) no way
relistening to days work with new performance settings - better than I thought

July 20, 1988 at 9:30am or so
1 (pm 9 1 2 1 2) okay, signs okay something else wrong - form? vars??
2 (pm 9 1 2 1 2) adjust texture map and atn better will try to play myself
3 (") excellent - just me?? quit while Im ahead at 12

July 20, 1988 10pm
will work on unix at univ at 12.
1) downld and play at about 2am - great stuff must work here all of the time!
at least for pm.

Figure 6.7   An example of a summary documentation for a computer composition.

Dec 14, 1995 3:45
ext. of mnemonics from m12 1 (pm 9 1 1 1 1) - fair using Five Pieces, Triplum and Arena.
2 same as above but adding Requiem - better but had mistake and no apparent earmark
3 better for sigs (pm 9 1 2 1 1) sv for possible use
4 good rslts rm Arena fm db (pm")
5 okay going on - good take but I can compose this (sv 3 tho)

Dec 15, 1995 11:10 am
1 m 14 good results from same as 5 yesterday

In general, I make sure that each log entry contains the name of the work and date of composition, including time of day completed. I also typically include where it was composed and what machine(s) were used for composition. I further mention editing (if any), works used in the database for composition, signatures and signature settings found during pattern matching, original source of the structure for the piece, and where the master file is located. I occasionally list the version of system software and version of the program used for composition. At junctures where I change locations, I often include the name of the sampler used for playback, including settings and the location of saved files. These data have proven very useful when I have long since forgotten the information.

Alice allows users to set the location and amount of algorithmic composition desired. The program then produces music of any amount and can graft this music into any location. In a more elaborate version than appears on this book's CD-ROM, this grafting includes backfilling between already composed sections, completing partially finished music by channel or in groups of channels, extending irregular combinations of vertical and horizontal materials, and other complicated non-linear projections.

Alice also composes phrases in non-linear order when more than one phrase has been requested by the user. This process helps ensure that destinations required by the use of earmarks, structural signatures, and other formal necessities, sound smooth and logical. This approach occasionally resembles backward chaining, by which materials are generated from destination cadences back toward their origins, and follows a similar process to that of fugue creation as described in *Experiments in Musical Intelligence* (see Cope 1996, chap. 5).

In backfilling especially, Alice uses a combination of forward and backward chaining processes to plot a series of possible correct paths between two known points. To accomplish this, the version of Alice which I use projects a tree of fragmenting branches. Each branch represents a possible succession of groupings derived from the groupings from which they themselves branch. The program keeps track of each branch so that when the various branches have traversed the required distance between origin and destination, Alice can trace each correctly ending branch to its origins and use the resulting progression as a template for composition. This process is even more complicated than it may sound. Fortunately, LISP provides an elegant method for resolving this complication. Figure 6.8a shows a doubly recursive function that traverses the arbitrarily nested lists in its argument and returns all possible paths that connect these lists. The double recursion is seen here as the function `get-lexicon-tree` calls itself in both lines 5 and 6, ensuring that the function applies `get-lexicons` only when its argument equates to a LISP `atom`. Figure 6.8b shows a graphic example of how this branching process works.

It is important to distinguish between the branching process used here and backtracking. Backtracking occurs when a program reaches a point where no correct choices exist. Such dead ends require backtracking to a fork that provides alternate routes. Alice does not backtrack. The function shown in figure 6.8a reveals all possible routes, thus allowing the program to choose one of the successful links between two end-pin groupings. Where it may appear to backtrack—choosing a correct route after already making connections—in fact contradicts backtracking where a program actually encounters an irresolvable problem from which it must recover. Alice's approach avoids such traps in the first place. This branching process works effectively when backfilling—in other words when both a beginning

Figure 6.8   (a) The function `get-lexicon-tree`; (b) graph showing right-projecting tree with correct path from A to D.

a.
```
(defun get-lexicon-tree (lexicon-lists)
  (cond ((null lexicon-lists) nil)
        ((atom lexicon-lists)
         (get-lexicons lexicon-lists))
        (t (append (get-lexicon-tree (first lexicon-lists))
                   (get-lexicon-tree (rest lexicon-lists)))))))
```

b.

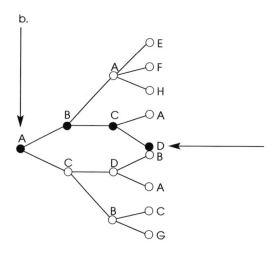

and an ending group act to severely constrain the intervening possibilities.

As previously discussed, backfilling in this way is not trivial. Whereas extending music requires Alice to correlate general style, unifications, and structure, composing material to fit amorphous incomplete passages requires all these same processes as well as a precise sense of which horizontal and vertical elements remain unfinished and what music would justly complete them. Imagine, for example, that you had finished all but the harmony for two successive measures and all but the melody for the next two measures and that you have called on Alice to complete both. The program must not only construe the overall nature of your music, as it does to extend a passage, but it must also discern the details of the harmonization of one set of measures and the melodic continuity of another set of measures and then produce the appropriate music to fit these measures.

Alice's backfill process serves other purposes as well as providing the user with specialized composition for completing unfinished music. For example, location-dependent signatures and earmarks must be approached and left with viable voice leading and logical functional succession orders to avoid sounding sudden or out of place. Alice uses its backfill functions to create transitions between a current context and the context that begins and/or ends signatures and earmarks. Even unifications require this type of special handling to ensure that they occur naturally and not abruptly, voiding the rationale for their use in the first place.

Alice can compose using very little musical data. The program, for example, takes best guesses at scales in use and can create logical notes not already present in the data. Alice can also develop new motives and produce cadences at logical junctures even when the music present has not yet reached a cadence. However, users desiring more original algorithmic composition from Alice should provide the largest database possible to ensure that the program has an optimal number of choices available during machine composition. A large database also reduces the number of possible quotations or paraphrases in the output. Orchestra-sized ensemble music requires exponentially larger databases because the possibility of logical connections between non-contiguous measures in large works can be astronomically small. Other techniques, such as employing Alice's *character* as presented in chapter 2 and including only stylistically homogeneous music in the database, can also help produce original output.

Some composers appreciate the self-referencing that quotation can bring to their compositions. Quotation is a traditional staple of many musical styles of the past. In the case of Alice, quotation results from the nature of the music stored in the database. For example, unique textures in the database tend to foster close imitation in the output. On the other hand, consistency of textures throughout a database promotes variation and originality. Thus, to a degree at least, quotation in Alice's output can be dictated by the program's human collaborator.

However, users of Alice must be aware that they will listen to Alice's output with very different ears and minds than they might listen to any other music. After all, Alice must satisfy many different criteria simultaneously. For example, besides the appearance of quality, Alice's music must complement the composer's style, and, as previously noted, the program (unlike the Experiments in Musical Intelligence program) must pass the severest test of all: evaluation by the world's experts—the composers themselves—on what constitutes that style. Alice must also be original enough not to imitate the music in the database too closely but not deviate so much as to detract from the continuity of the work at hand and, again, the overall style of the composer using the program. This can be a delicate balance.

In most cases, however, quotation, paraphrasing, or self-referencing of music in the database will probably disassemble during machine composition. This can be useful since such quotes might trigger direct recognition of the work in the database. Unfortunately, quotation can also consist of extended whole-cloth reiterations of the original music. However, eliminating such quotes risks losing some aspects of the fundamental style of the music being replicated (Nattiez 1990; Sebeok 1977). Thus, certain styles that depend on quote recognition for all or part of their style identification represent one of the more difficult types of music for Alice to emulate. As will be seen in chapter 7, large multi-composer databases may represent one solution to such problems.

Alice deftly balances the use of rules and the incorporation of earmarks and signatures while simultaneously keeping track of a work that is constantly changing because of newly entered events. Alice updates the current composition and figures the most efficient and reasonable route for re-analyzing and pattern matching without bringing the program to an impasse.

However, it should be noted that Alice is not well suited to initiate or continue fugues, canons, or other strict contrapuntal forms. While I could have included a separate module to make such composition possible, as I have done with both the Experiments in Musical Intelligence program and SARA, doing so would seem anachronistic, given that Alice is intended for contemporary composers more interested in non-historical forms and styles and given that I have otherwise tried to avoid coding predetermined rules into the program.

Alice also has problems maintaining extensively repeated patterns unless such patterns qualify as unifications. Alberti basses, to cite a very simple example, succumb to Alice's creative revoicing and variation techniques and quickly lose their integrity. Thus, styles that depend on exactly repeating patterns, such as minimalism, will not replicate well in Alice. These styles will be better served with programs such as Experiments in Musical Intelligence or SARA, which use recombinance, since these programs are far less likely to deconstruct repeating patterns.

On the other hand, Alice's structural analysis may create approximate or exact repetitions of whole phrases in a work in progress. Such repetitions can prove disappointing to some users who expect strikingly new music to appear when requesting algorithmic extensions from Alice. However, one must remember that this program models its output on an analysis of one of the complete works in the database and inherits the logical necessity for materials to recapitulate as well as to vary or contrast. Thus, even complete reiterations of already composed material do not represent an Alice failure but rather an important response to what the program interprets as structural necessity based on the analysis of a user's previous works.

Alice's output, like output from the Experiments in Musical Intelligence program and SARA, varies in quality as well as in originality. This is especially true when using small databases where the number of available choices is limited. For example, the Experiments in Musical Intelligence program's emulation of a Mozart piano concerto (1995) presents a good case of extremes in originality. Some of the material in this work is strikingly original. Other passages nearly quote from Mozart's concerti and can sound dislocating for those familiar with the original works. In almost all cases, such apparent quotes, on closer examination, paraphrase rather than copy note by note. However, the contextual referencing is nonetheless strong and disconcerting.

Certain types of rests cause special problems in Alice. For example, the program ignores full ensemble rests in terms of voice leading. In other words, two groupings separated by a rest of any length result in the same rule as if the notes occurred contiguously. Alice finds this logical since event notation includes rests implicitly rather than explicitly (i.e., rests occur as a result of different beginning and ending times). However, this approach means that new composition will ignore full rests, which may in fact be integral to the style of the work in progress or to the user's style as presented in the music in the database. To ensure that such rests occur in the output at a rate consistent with its input, Alice analyzes rests in terms of duration and timing and reinserts them in output separately from the composition process.

While Alice works automatically as a compositional tool, its interface offers many opportunities for user input and control. As previously mentioned, this includes setting the various pattern-matching controllers. What one composer may hear as a signature another may not. Users may also alter the various program and score variables and determine the extent and location of composition. Choice of databases further allows users to configure the type of music the program composes.

Ultimately, the most important decision in any algorithmic process falls to the user: determination of which works or fragments of works survive. The aesthetic choices made *after* machine composition are the most important. No other single decision made by either human or machine can rival this final arbitration. Thus, composers using programs such as Alice have ultimate control over the machine-composing processes.

■ OUTPUT

Figure 6.9a presents a brief melodic fragment created using the input window of the version of Alice on this book's CD-ROM. As an initial test of the analysis approaches taken by the program, I composed this small segment and called on Alice to extend it without the use of a database for rules. Alice thus created the extension shown in figure 6.9b using only the rules derived from the music in figure 6.9a. The program had to analyze the scale in use and avoid moving too far out of the range of the notes presented. Note how the machine-composed music in figure 6.9b provides a logical, if not musical, extension that fits the constraints presented by the user input.

Figure 6.9c presents a second attempt by Alice to extend the melody shown in figure 6.9a. One might imagine that Alice's extension would be more stepwise here, given the nature of the input music. The paucity of data and limited range in figure 6.9a would suggest a rather uncreative continuation. Alice, on the other hand, with its ability to infer, composes an imaginative and possibly even compelling variation.

Figure 6.9d provides a third attempt by Alice to extend the melody shown in figure 6.9a. This rather prosaic example introduces a simple back-and-forth motion that might prove eventually useful in a larger composition. Obviously, not all of Alice's potentially voluminous numbers of output will provide purposeful continuity, although

Figure 6.9   A simple melody (a) and three different Alice extensions (b–d).

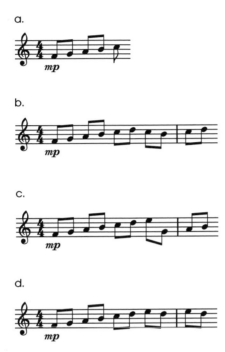

many may in fact present more interesting results than those shown here.

Figure 6.10a shows music of similar complexity to that of figure 6.9a but of deeper texture. I input this music, using the notation window of the version of Alice accompanying this book, to demonstrate how the program deals with tonal and triadic materials. Again, Alice was not given a database to use when composing. Figure 6.10b shows the results of Alice's first attempt at extending the music of figure 6.10a. Note how the output develops material from the input phrase in interesting and logical ways. In figures 6.10b–d, Alice provides smooth continuations of the triadic and tonal nature of the music in figure 6.10a and cadences appropriately.

I did not use Alice's pattern-matching program for either figure 6.9 or figure 6.10. Examples as short as these do not typically reveal significant earmarks or signatures. On the other hand, in the music generated in figures 6.11b–e, readers must imagine a small database and numerous preceding measures of composition since space limitations will not allow their reproduction here. The input music in figure 6.11a

Figure 6.10   A tonal chorale segment (a) and three examples of Alice extensions (b–d).

a.

b.

c.

Figure 6.10 Continued.

consists primarily of non-tonal parallel chromatic tenths. The continuation by Alice in figure 6.11b follows that same pattern, which represents a signature—the last four vertical pairs being a transposed version (seventh down) of the preceding four vertical pairs.

Figure 6.11c derives from repeating the last two vertical pairs of the input music and then moving to less obviously derived groupings. Figures 6.11d and e are more imaginative with sources not easily determined. In both cases, part of the horizontal interval content seems based on inversions of the original material. However, in all the cases in figures 6.11b–e, the extending material consistently continues the input music in terms of chromaticism, rhythm, vertical intervals, and melodic motives.

The examples presented in figures 6.9 to 6.11 represent initial attempts and thus do not take advantage of the weighting or *character* attributes of Alice. However, such personalizations of the program can typically be heard only by its user. I believe, however, that these attributes can be *indirectly* perceived by listeners and make for generally more convincing output. For more examples of Alice composition in a variety of different musical circumstances, see the Alice manual on this book's CD-ROM. The manual also includes tutorials and extended examples using the analysis and pattern-matching components of Alice.

To further demonstrate Alice's output, I have chosen a single and very short movement of *Mnemonics,* a seven-movement work for string quartet I composed interactively with my version of the program. The final draft of this work consists of roughly equal parts of composer- and program-created music.

Figure 6.11   A nontonal example (a) and four Alice extensions (b–e).

Figure 6.12 presents one movement of the score for *Mnemonics*. Signatures are outlined with rectangles and identified with an accompanying "S." In this particular case, I can verify that the signature here is present in one form or another in all the works used as a database (*Five Pieces for Flute, Bassoon, and Violin*, 1965; *Margins* for chamber ensemble, 1972; *Triplum* for flute and piano, 1973; *Arena,* for cello and tape, 1974; *Requiem for Bosque Redondo* for brass choir, 1974). The rectangle with an accompanying "E" indicates an earmark. As previously noted, my research indicates that earmarks portend critical junctures in a work's structure, such as ends of sections, ends of works, onset of recapitulations, and so on. In this example, the "E"-designated earmark signals the end of the movement. Completed compositions such as *Mnemonics* can be saved as standard MIDI files that may then be loaded into any commercially available sequencer or other MIDI program for performance, creating scores, and/or mixing with other media.

I should point out that determining exact sources of algorithmic composition can be a tedious and often impossible task, especially when works become longer than this simple movement from *Mnemonics*. This difficulty in locating origins results from the complicated manner in which the various mechanisms—rules composition, pattern matching in its various forms, and the previously mentioned statistical analyses—interact.

Most of Alice's code does not represent brilliant programming. In fact, I often use brute-force approaches. Thus, I must confess to a simple paradigm that I deliberately follow. I am interested almost exclusively in the quality of output and not very interested in the elegance or lack of elegance that leads to that output. My reasons for this are simple: I have seen too many programmers become infatuated with creating faster and more appealing widgets only to lose sight of the fact that, whatever the method employed, quality of output should be their primary objective. Thus, while Alice could be revised to run faster and cleaner, I would rather invest my time in more output-rewarding programming.

■ EVALUATING OUTPUT

I do not guarantee that Alice's output will fulfill any user's expectations of quality on any level. This lack of guarantee holds especially true for initial algorithmic composing efforts since neither the program nor the user will have had the opportunity to adapt to one another. However, I will admit to having more confidence as time pro-

Figure 6.12   One movement from *Mnemonics.*

Figure 6.12 Continued.

Figure 6.12   Continued.

Figure 6.12 Continued.

gresses, both in the program's ability to adapt to user preferences and in the ability of users to create better databases and to define the kinds of output they desire most.

Works composed with Alice may be performed using either a MIDI interface with an appropriate synthesizer or sampler or with QuickTime®, depending on the form of Alice chosen from the two available on this book's CD-ROM. Alice also offers music printing using the encapsulated postscript (EPS) format. Saving music in Alice as standard MIDI files further allows such music to be accessed by any commercially available MIDI-accessible application.

Users of Alice, and for that matter users of any other algorithmic or non-algorithmic composing program, must use their imaginations when they hear their music performed by synthesizers and samplers. No works played thusly will sound like they will sound when performed on acoustic instruments. MIDI-controlled performances of complex small ensemble works and especially large works for orchestra or similar forces can often leave composers with a sense of exasperation and frustration at best. At worst, such performances provoke composers to eliminate works or parts of works that otherwise might succeed if performed live. Repeated listenings and careful adjustments of the timbres in an output synthesizer or sampler can partially ameliorate this problem. I sometimes forgo MIDI performance entirely and make judgments completely on the basis of my interpretation of the notation and the sounds that result in my mind's ear.

Stephen Smoliar has argued that the output from many of my algorithmic composing programs has been successful primarily because of the performances by live performers that it has received. "Whether or not it was music when it came out of the computer, it was *certainly* music when it happened at the Santa Cruz Bach Festival. . . . The quality of performance often overrides whether what is being performed has come from a struggling genius, a commercial hack, chance decisions, or even a computer program" (Smoliar 1994). His thoughts mirror those of many critics of my work. This was one of the reasons (lack of performer interest being another) that led me to record the Experiments in Musical Intelligence program's first CD (Cope 1994) on a MIDI-controlled Disklavier without any performer interpretation—to demonstrate precisely what the program had composed.

On the other hand, Jason Vantomme questions the choice of such mechanical performances. "It is quite unfortunate that the examples on Bach by Design were not played by live performers . . . perhaps this was due to the lifeless sequencer playback that plagues the whole disc . . . suffered from the ill effects of sequencer playback . . . it was difficult to judge the success of this work's 'genuineness' because of the lack of human expression in the performance" (Vantomme 1995, pp. 66–68). It is not that Vantomme is unaware of my motive ("Perhaps Cope felt that this [live performance] would be cheating."), yet he chooses to level such criticism at almost every work on the Bach by Design disc (Cope 1994).

Thus, performance interpretation should be high on any wish list for output music of computer programs such as Alice. With this in mind, I offer a tutorial called *perform* on this book's CD-ROM. This performance program attempts to add to otherwise grossly quantized output some of the subtle and hopefully musical nuances we find in human performances, thus making the playing of such music more bearable. These nuances include non-simultaneous chords, gradations of dynamics according to logical schemes, and accelerandos and ritardandos following generally accepted performance principles.

Of course, the *perform* program does not begin to approach the subtleties of human performance, no less the details necessary for period performance practice. On balance, however, this small program occasionally warms cold performances and helps soften the often harsh edges of otherwise rhythmically regimented output. Ultimately, programs should have music input as real-time performances and then have the techniques of those performances applied to their output music.

Users of Alice may reject music for a variety of reasons other than poor performance or perceived lack of quality. For example, users may call for algorithmic extension of their works in progress simply for curiosity, for new ideas that they themselves would like to develop, or to experiment to hear how the program's ideas work, with no intention of actually using all or some of the resultant music. However, Alice adapts to rejected output by incrementally changing the values of certain variables—*character*—resulting in subtle changes in composing processes. Thus, continual rejection causes the program to create increasingly more significant changes, especially to the structural aspects of its output. Such changes reflect Alice's inherent objective: to offer users the most useful algorithmic composition possible.

In effect, when Alice composes music that the user rejects, the program reacts similarly to the BackTalk program when that program receives the equivalent of *no* as a response. Alice, however, has greater ability to control its output than BackTalk because Alice uses rules based on databases and analyzes large-scale structure, and because it uses pattern matching controllers. In the case of rules, when output is rejected, Alice weakens the weights in rules objects and/or lessens the effects caused by finding multiple versions of the same rule in the database. However, this imposed weakening is slight since voice motions are generally the least likely cause of rejection; after all, voice motions exist as user preferences in the database in the first place. In longer machine-composed extensions, user rejection causes Alice to actually create the form of the current piece rather than use a form from a work in the database. Alice may also change the values of the pattern-matching controllers when users reject output. Controllers are varied incrementally, as described in *Experiments in Musical Intelligence* (Cope 1996, chap. 7). Alice responds to positive as well as to negative input by users. Whereas negative decisions result in weakened weightings in rules, positive decisions produce stronger weightings. Such strengthening personalizes Alice's composing beyond that of simply providing one's own databases. The pattern-matching controllers also change, resulting in, it is hoped, a deeper understanding by Alice of the user's personal syntax. Continued positive feedback regarding certain kinds of output results in more output of that kind.

Output from Alice, as well as the Experiments in Musical Intelligence program and SARA, offers no guarantee of quality. Indeed, few *people* can agree about what, in fact, constitutes quality in music. On balance, I have found that the Experiments in Musical Intelligence program produces usable output at a ratio of between five and ten to one. Alice, on the other hand, is far less predictable since the choice of databases and the processes used can be so personal. In my own case, I use all or part of about one in seven Alice-composed additions to my in-progress scores. Some users may find my ratios too optimistic, while others may find them too pessimistic. Still others, my experience tells me, will find any ratio outrageous since their definitions of good music do not include music composed by computer programs.

A persisting general opinion, one that suggests that algorithmic composing programs produce output on a relatively even aesthetic plain, deserves being put to rest. Alice, like any other algorithmic composing program, produces output of widely varying quality. However, from time to time Alice can create memorable output, music worthy of saving, performing, and performing again. In this way, Alice resembles its human counterpart; capable of the routine as well as the inspirational. I am reminded of a line expressed by an early beta tester of a subset of the Experiments in Musical Intelligence program. He said, "The program only creates really good output about one time in ten." He then added that "to be successful, the program should at worst produce high quality one time in every four." My response, then as now, is that most composers throughout history would have been delighted with a 10 percent success rate and that to my knowledge few composers in history have ever created high-quality works for every four composed. Of course, greatness has little empirical meaning and is usually evoked more as a cultural phenomenon that can be fickle and highly personal.

Some critics exaggerate, I feel, the level of quality achieved by my programs. For example, Jason Vantomme places the Experiments in Musical Intelligence program in some rarefied company. "This middle movement presents itself as a work that might have been written by a more mature Mozart . . . the work did indeed provide a remarkable sense of having been written by Mozart" (Vantomme 1994, p. 67). I do not agree with these comments. I feel that all of my programs' works are flawed. In fact, most of these less-than-elegant computer creations simply make me appreciate the works of the composers being emulated more deeply than I had before.

Alice is a very complex program. Entered music must be analyzed for rules, patterns, scales, formal structures on a variety of levels, and so on, and composed music must adhere stringently to the constraints imposed by the results of these processes. As well, the rules derived from the program's analyses can contradict one another and lead to complex negotiations that further require detailed hierarchies on which decisions ultimately rest. And yet, even with these many layers of intricate, integrated, and interrelated processes, Alice cannot begin to compete with the composing prowess of humans. As Alice's programmer, I find that my admiration for the mental and intuitive abilities of human composers continues to flourish unabated. No matter how good the quality of Alice's output may occasionally be, it continually pales in comparison to the quality that its human counterpart contributes to the resulting lopsided collaboration.

The perceived quality of Alice's output can also depend on a number of important factors. For example, a skeptical or biased hearing can impair evaluation of even the best composition that an algorithmic composing program can offer. Other factors include choosing appropriate tempos, dynamics, timbres, and fidelity during playback. Even a Bach fugue played too fast, too loud, with poor timbres, or through second-rate speakers can cause negative reactions. Ensuring that hardware creates proper output, including the appropriate timbres, tempo, and dynamics, will help verify that aesthetic response justly relates to the music itself and not to superficial or extraneous conditions.

Obviously, personal taste represents the foremost benchmark for determining the quality and usability of Alice output. However, I have found that many apparently unsuccessful Alice extensions of my work have *some* element worth saving or ultimately influence the manner in which I subsequently compose. I have used machine-composed material as small as a measure and as large as half a movement. I have used contours or abstracted harmonic progressions from an otherwise rejected Alice-composed extended passage. Even when a machine-composed example fails miserably it tells me, at least, what *not* to do, which sometimes implicitly tells me what *to* do. The benefits of the collaboration between user and machine program are difficult to calibrate but certainly do not depend solely on the rate of acceptance.

Interestingly, unsuccessful output often provides *more* useful information than successful output. For example, the Experiments in Musical Intelligence program's initial failures taught me about the importance of signatures and eventually earmarks. Early trials and tribulations when programming rules for analyzing and composing functional tonal harmony provided me with insight into the use of ATNs and rule inheritance. Even the worst imaginable output from Alice may serve as renewed inspiration for the human collaborator or as a vehicle for more intelligent settings of the variables necessary for more successful algorithmic composition.

Ultimately, Alice's output may succeed only in inspiring the user of the program. Such inspiration can take many forms. Partially successful algorithmic music may inspire users to develop their ideas in certain directions not unlike those composed by the program. Users may appreciate the formal aspects of computer-composed music. Still other users may simply be encouraged to succeed by virtue of the program's failure. In general, however, Alice often succeeds even when it fails.

SEVEN

The Future

■ REMAINING PROBLEMS

Many computational problems remain unsolved in Alice (ALgorithmically Integrated Composing Environment). For example, in Alice's music, as in most algorithmic composition, we can hear the software in the output. Few programs are immune. Using the same procedures over time creates recognizable imprints. Works by Experiments in Musical Intelligence, as mentioned previously, tend toward duple meters, extremely sectionalized forms, high levels of sequence by fifth, and so on. The program has also developed signatures of its own resulting not from pattern matching music in its databases but from the manner in which the program operates. I sometimes recognize an Experiments in Musical Intelligence work less by its stylistic inaccuracies than by the software personality that belies its origins. However, algorithmic composition programs that produce complete works, such as Experiments in Musical Intelligence and SARA (Simple Analytic Recombinant Algorithm), exhibit this trait more than collaborative programs. For example, Alice's output interweaves with the music created by its user in sometimes intricate ways. Alice also offers users enough variables to personalize their work in ways that help disguise such recognizable imprints.

Alice also suffers, as does any computer application, from built-in biases despite my efforts to avoid them. The interface, for example, presupposes that users want to express their musical ideas by using traditional Western notation. Many composers would prefer graphical or numerical input. For example, Iannis Xenakis's UPIC uses a graphical interface linked to a highly flexible computer-based composing and sound synthesis system (Xenakis 1998). Programs such as MAX (Puckette 1991) utilize graphical interfaces to allow composers to describe and connect digitally represented synthesizer and sampler components. Many composers use improvisation as a primary form of compositional technique, evolving their music through more tactile and intuitive processes.

I could argue that Western notation has effectively served thousands of composers for hundreds of years and that the analytical approaches I have used in Alice represent standard paradigms agreed on by theorists and analysts. However, to do so would belie the real issue here. Alice, as with all software, consists of programs designed for specific ends and as such represents the conscious and subconscious biases of its programmer. I hope that admitting such biases openly will make users more aware of their presence and more likely to creatively negotiate their way through and around them.

Interactive delays also constitute serious problems for programs such as Alice. Many composers prefer to work with computers in what they refer to as *real time* rather than having to wait for programs to react to their input. For them, what real-time algorithmic composition may lack in terms of sophistication it gains in immediacy to the composing process. Since Alice requires thousands and even hundreds of thousands of individual computations, real-time composition is currently neither practical nor possible. My own compositional style does not suffer from waiting for output. In fact, time thus spent is usually time well spent. However, some composers feel their experience less vital when encountering collaborative delays with programs such as Alice.

Faster processors and better programs will no doubt make real-time composition possible in the future. Such real-time composition will create potential for improvisatory dialogues between human and machine and possibly produce quite arresting music, especially when users can foretell to some extent the general nature of machine responses and thus achieve musical conversations in live performance. Unfortunately, humans, unlike computers, are not noticeably improving their computational speeds. For most composers, quality still results from trial and error, which requires its own time, real or not.

Alice also relies on MIDI for performance. While MIDI synthesizers, samplers, and playback systems continue to improve in quality, control over the few parameters that MIDI allows does not typically produce elegant or often even acceptable performances of computer-composed music. In *Experiments in Musical Intelligence* (1996), I describe an approach that extends event notation (pp. 234–37) by including important information such as articulation, pitch bends, microtonal tuning, and so on. I then transcribe these additions into traditional notation using a variety of processes. Mostly I transcribe these by hand, a tedious and unfortunate task. I speak to an alternative to this and MIDI in general in the next section.

Another serious problem, a far less easy problem to correct, involves listener bias, an issue I examine at length in almost all my writings on algorithmic music. Unfortunately, one important issue often remains undiscussed. Many listeners have an aversion to treating individual machine compositions as unique. Since these listeners perceive algorithmic programs as capable of producing limitless quantities of music, treating one in a special way seems antithetical. In contrast, I believe that a good work is simply that: a good work. Some computer-composed music is routine, some bad, and some special. Each new work deserves its own aesthetic distinction, and appreciation should not wane with the awareness that millions of other yet unheard works exist. Vast numbers should not obscure the beauty of the one.

Alice's lack of true intelligence constitutes another unresolved problem. In chapter 2, I speak optimistically about computers attaining intelligent-like behavior. However, I feel that there is one attribute of intelligence that subjugates all others. While in and of itself it does not constitute intelligence, it makes intelligence possible. That attribute is *life:* the ability to procreate, to interrelate with one's environment, and to pass on information from one generation to another. Most other attributes of intelligence pale in comparison to life even though they may be essential to the very survival of that life. This means any life, not just human life. Until such time that our programs have the equivalence of life, they will produce only at our initiation and only in imitation. Hans Morovec, in reference to computers, states that "we are in the process of creating a new kind of life" (Morovec 1992, p. 3). This will have to be true, I feel, if we are going to create a true intelligence beyond ourselves.

I need not remind my critics that Experiments in Musical Intelligence is not alive, nor are SARA or Alice. Thus, these programs may appear to act intelligently, but they are not truly intelligent (Kurzweil 1990). Occasionally, output of these programs may be deeply moving to some, including me, but clearly in this case the emotion occurs in the beholder, without being intended by the source. John Cage remarks on his perception of the role that listeners play in the musical experience.

> Most people think that when they hear a piece of music, they're not
> doing anything but that something is being done to them. Now this is not

true, and we must arrange our music, we must arrange our art, we must arrange everything, I believe, so that people realize that they themselves are doing it, and not that something is being done to them. (Nyman 1974, p. 21)

The debate over machine-created art and music centers in part on whether machines can—or will ever be able to—express themselves in ways that humans perceive they themselves do (Boden 1977; Minsky 1968; Rose 1976). At issue here is the very nature of creativity and perception (Aiello 1994). I personally have put these matters to rest without resolution. I have no idea whether the emotions I hear in certain works are there by virtue of compositional intent, there because I want to hear them, there by means of all I know about the life of the composer and circumstances of composition, or not there at all. Certainly music is an imprecise tool for communication. Not only do its elements have vague meanings, if they have meanings at all, but our aesthetics blur what few meanings they may have.

Interestingly, I am not discouraged by Alice's lack of intelligence or emotion. To the contrary, I am delighted that Alice depends on me and other users for its "life." I have opted to embed in it an ability to inherit vague aspects of intelligence from data rather than attempting to imbue it with an intelligence of its own. As such, Alice works complementarily with its users. Ultimately, I believe, it will be programs such as Alice, although far more advanced and sophisticated than Alice, that will help make the transition to Morovec's new life form possible. Harold Cohen, creator of the painting robot called Aaron, describes his progeny: "Aaron is not a human being, and it's not intended to be. My goal is to allow Aaron to develop its own personality" (Boden 1996, p. 113). Some of Alice's personality derives from its databases that survive the program's compositional processes. After all, the databases Alice uses for composition stand only one generation removed from its output.

BackTalk and Alice achieve only minimal success using association nets. Apparently, adaptation to new situations requires more than a re-application of previous solutions to similar but not equivalent situations. This was apparent in the first chess match between Gary Kasparov and IBM's Deep Blue in 1996. The computer program, fixed with moves from thousands of games by previous masters for comparison, was confused by unique situations:

Even though it is a computer, it had its own psychology. For instance, it played complicated positions much better than simple ones. I tried to remove the image of a machine or some silicon monster sitting somewhere. It was a legitimate opponent, a very strong opponent, and before each game I tried to make an opening or strategy for the game based on my knowledge of this opponent, and I knew that I could learn much better because my opponent would need more time to learn and to come back with really sophisticated counter strategy. (Kasparov 1996)

The situation changed in 1997 when Deep Blue's developers increased its abilities to deal with the unexpected and to invent new strategies. In 1996, the six-game match had gone 4 to 2 in favor of Kasparov. One year later the computer scored a 3.5-to-2.5 win over the world champion.

While some heralded the news of Deep Blue's victory as a sign that in yet another domain machines had finally superseded humans, I viewed the news as a milestone in *human* achievement. After all, Deep Blue itself was created by humans, Deep Blue's software was developed by humans, and, most important, all the games on which Deep Blue based its strategies were originally played by humans. The same is musically true of Alice. While some view Deep Blue's victory as machine over mind, I view it as simply an extraordinary next step in human evolution.

■ EXTENDING ALICE

As mentioned in the previous section, even in the best of circumstances MIDI performance disappoints. MIDI lacks a sense of reality. For me, at least, composing incorporates physical processes as much as it does the right notes. For example, I believe that listeners have a sense of transference when hearing music. This transference ranges from expectations of breath, bowing, range, and dynamic limitations to the nuances of rhythm and phrasing. Music composed by programs lacking the ability to associate with the physical nature of their output and with the advantages and limitations that such physical association brings, lacks the sensitivity and grace that humans intuitively invest in their music. Even programs that attempt to inherit such capacity from their databases, as do Experiments in Musical Intelligence and Alice, fail to produce convincing output partly because of this shortcoming.

Thus, I have extended the version of Alice that I use to include both a software synthesizer and a performance module. The software synthesizer allows me to construct and manipulate, using either Fourier additive processes or frequency modulation, an almost unlimited variety of timbres. These timbres are accessed through a sublist located in the fourth position of events (i.e., in place of the channel number). The first element of each sublist is a symbol representing a defined timbre. All such timbres are stored in objects with slots that control their general constitution as well as a slot for the weighting of user preference. The second element of each list consists of a sublist that contains elements of the timbre's overall envelope described with as many amplitude characteristics as required. The composition portion of Alice then accesses this software synthesizer in much the same way as it accesses the inference program.

The performance module determines variables such as the overall tempo, timing subtitles, and dynamic shadings. This module may be controlled by users or by Alice itself using objects with built-in slots for preference weighting. The program and the user typically work in tandem, as the human setting of individual parameters for performance requires enormous time, while concomitantly the program rarely performs in a fully satisfactory manner even when properly influenced by user preferences.

With so many variables in the composing, synthesis, and performance subprograms in my version of Alice, adjusting appropriate weights from rejected music is impossible. Thus, this version of Alice incorporates a series of choices at the conclusion of each composing/performing run that indicates more accurately for Alice which parts of the program failed to meet the criteria of the user. These choices include differentiations between, for example, tempo and dynamics in the performing subprogram and envelope and timbre in the synthesis subprogram.

My version of Alice extends its BackTalk-like association net to the timbre and performance objects just described. This means that the program attempts to include timbre and performance in the composing process. While at present this inclusion remains primitive, future implementations of this version of Alice will incorporate more elaborate associations and produce more stylistically sensitive results. I hope that including timbre and performance in this way will make the program more intrinsically musical.

The version of Alice that I use saves user-prescribed timbres and performance settings so that, as collaboration proceeds, Alice can pattern match these elements just as the composing program matches intervals and durations. Timbral and performance signatures as well as earmarks can thus contribute to the overall creative process just as they do during the previously described inference composition.

I have also included an option for recombinant composition (see Cope 1996) in my version of Alice. Inference processes do not often produce good stylistic simulations of music that incorporate certain types of formalisms, such as those used in contrapuntal forms (e.g., canons and fugues), serialism, and repetitious musical styles, such as those typical of many minimalist composers. These musical paradigms simply transfer better using recombinance. The recombinance subprogram incorporates a series of algorithms that structure output according to the constraints required of the particular formalism desired.

Users of the version of Alice appearing on this book's CD-ROM may wonder how the previously described components can possibly fit into an already elaborate interface. To alleviate any confusion between the various subprograms, I have built three different but integrated environments that users approach through different menus. For example, the synthesis and performance subprograms remain invisible from the composing module until users want to access them. At that point, a single selection from the composing menu replaces the composing/analysis menu items with selections appropriate to the synthesizer or the performance subprogram. In this way, the various aspects of Alice remain separate and distinct while maintaining their integration through the overall software design.

The version of Alice that I use represents more of the type of program that I imagine will accompany many composers in the twenty-first century, although I am not presumptuous enough to assume that Alice will be the actual model these future composers will emulate. Certainly, however, such programs will involve many of the intrinsic elements of this version of Alice and provide what Charles Ives refers to in his seminal piece *Music and Its Future:* "The future of music may not lie entirely with music itself, but rather in the way it encourages and extends, rather than limits" (Ives 1965, p. 14).

■ PERSONALIZING ALICE

In the first volume of this trilogy, I wrote, "But the hand of the composer is not absent . . . even purely machine-composed music is born of programs created by human inspiration" (Cope 1991b, p. 236).

The future of programs such as Alice rests, at least partially, in their ability to successfully imitate the style of the composer using the program. In effect, the output of Alice must be unique to each composer thus personalizing the program. This uniqueness depends primarily on the user's implementation of the database. A well-defined and carefully selected group of works or parts of works for a database can personalize Alice's output to the degree that listeners should be unaware of the program's collaboration in the composing process. Less successful databases allow Alice's imprint to be heard and detract from the program's attempts at stylistic integrity. In effect, properly used, Alice should be as much the product of any other composer as the program is of me.

It is extremely important that users of Alice understand that once they have chosen their databases wisely, Alice does nothing that they themselves could not do given an enormous amount of time and assuming comparable accuracy. Thus, Alice represents a tool or an assistant rather than a separate or distinct composer in its own right. For me, the same is true of the Experiments in Musical Intelligence program: having programmed all the processes that the program uses, I feel that I could have composed every single work that Experiments in Musical Intelligence has produced and even created better—and in some cases far better—results myself. Thus, I have no qualms about assigning credit to myself for these works any more than composers using Alice should hesitate to call collaborative works composed with Alice their own. In fact, I see no reason to even assign partial credit to the program: Alice processes a composer's database in specific and known ways, acting only as a specialized calculator and assistant.

However, it certainly seems unlikely that Alice's output inherits any of that elusive property we call, for want of a better word, soul. At the same time it is equally hard to imagine that Alice or, for that matter, Experiments in Musical Intelligence and SARA can produce so many new works based on human-created databases and not inherit some aspect of the database composer's persona. Granted that many primary elements of the original (e.g., its deep underlying structure) cannot easily transfer to a new work, to assume that nothing survives the process underrates both the power of the original music and the ability of rules inheritance to logically forge successful new instances of previous music. In short, only the most naive could imagine that successful works by these programs do not depend in some part on the limited transfer of, if you will, the musical souls of the compositions in their databases.

Alice's *character* attribute also contributes to its personalization. Whenever possible, users of Alice should save this variable before closing the application (it reloads on subsequent use of the program). This saving and reloading ensures that the process of forming a true link between composer and program continues to develop from composing session to composing session rather than having to begin anew each time the program boots. As previously mentioned, the version of Alice on this book's CD-ROM takes a rather simplistic view of developing its weightings by incrementing or decrementing its weighting slots without regard to context. Future public versions of the program will have a much more elaborate form of weighting that more accurately reflects the personality of the user in the composing process.

Alice's play, score, and composing variables also help ensure that subsequent composition and performance follow personal rather than generic directions. The pattern-matching variables contribute further to unique interpretations of the music in the database and thus more personal output. The variety of settings that the thirty or so primary variables allow help produce significantly different output even when using the same database. Users should be aware of all their options as they compose to take full advantage of these aspects of Alice's operation.

■ MULTI-COMPOSER DATABASES

As random access memory (RAM) becomes less expensive, limitations on the size and number of different databases used with Alice and, for that matter, the Experiments in Musical Intelligence program and SARA, will relax. It will then be possible to create true multi-composer databases and produce a more worldly composing program that has immediate access to many different kinds and styles of music just as living composers do. One section of the database, the composer's own, will undoubtedly remain the principal source of local patterns or unifications. However, music in other sections of the database, while less influential, will also play a role in the composing process. This role includes signature selection, structural inheritance, and the use of occasional fragments as quotation. This compositional influence process differs from style mixes, as described in *Computers and Musical Style* (Cope 1991b), where two styles slowly morph, one into the other.

The use of multi-composer databases can provide a source of materials not unlike sources available to human composers whose works, although dominated by their own sensibilities and by inheritance from their previous work, demonstrate the influences of many other works that subtly affect their style. It is hard to imagine a program supposedly exhibiting intelligent-like behavior not having access to the wealth of musical materials made available by multi-composer databases.

While Alice can use smaller-version multi-composer databases in its current incarnation, the program cannot easily differentiate between the various works present. Composers using Alice may determine the relative importance of each database composer's style by restricting the size of the various sections of a database. However, users cannot prevent the program from honing in on a smaller section and using it for structural inheritance, pattern matching, and so on, except by eliminating all output that focuses too much on unwanted material. Future implementations of Alice will have more refined approaches to the use of multi-composer databases. Such refinements might include using one database exclusively for one parameter and not for others. For example, structure could be strictly inherited from one source while signatures and rules are derived from another source. This process could produce novel and possibly useful interpolations of rules and materials. Such experimentation seems natural for algorithmic programs such as Alice.

Multi-composer compositional processes and, for that matter, any compositional process used to create style-sensitive algorithmic compositions can be usefully reversed to derive the influences of new music. In Alice, such analysis can be enhanced by keeping records of the various decisions made by the program during composition—something that Alice, Experiments in Musical Intelligence, and SARA do to a certain extent anyway (Cope 1996). Certainly, tracking the composition history of Alice output, through the *history* variable, can help users better understand their music.

It does not then take such a great leap of faith to imagine that programs using multi-composer databases could also analyze other, non-machine-composed works for their influences. For example, it might be useful to analyze a work by Mozart using Haydn and Bach databases to discover what an objective pattern comparison could demonstrate about the work's influences (for my previous comments regarding such analysis, see Cope 1996, chap. 1). While it is doubtful that entire works could be reconstructed from their possible roots on a phrase-by-phrase basis, as the Experiments in Musical Intelligence program did with a Beethoven passage in figure 1.12 of Cope (1996), important quotation and paraphrasing would no doubt be revealed.

The use of multi-composer databases also helps computer programs such as Alice extend beyond the isolated world of experimentation into a more natural world of diverse musical experiences. Use of multi-composer databases for algorithmic music only seems unusual because we can explicitly document the contributing musical styles in a work written by one composer.

As mentioned previously, I discuss a method of melding more than one style in *Computers and Musical Style* (Cope 1991b, chap. 5) in the creation of *Mozart in Bali*—an orchestrated version of which has now been recorded (Cope 1997b). For the most part, this work and others (such as *For Keith* [1991b]) exemplify a kind of brute-force method of combining styles in which each style retains its individuality. Using rules in place of recombinancy allows for two or more styles to genuinely interlace without the dichotomy noted in these earlier works.

Figure 7.1 shows an example of this latter kind of algorithmic composition in the style of Beethoven. The databases for this composition consisted of the second movement of Beethoven's Moonlight sonata and Bach's first prelude from his Well-Tempered Clavier, thus constituting a multi-composer database. The resemblance to Beethoven's sonata movement in this example is obvious when compared to the original shown in figure 7.2. However, the chord progression results from Bach's prelude, as shown in figure 7.3. The

Figure 7.1   The beginning of a slow movement in the style of Beethoven composed by SARA.

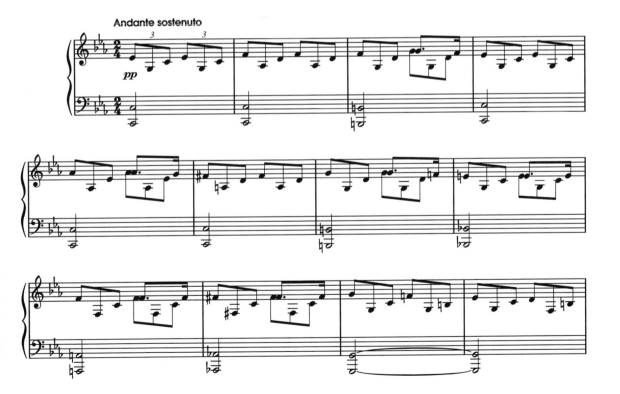

Figure 7.2 The beginning of Beethoven's *Sonata* Op. 27, No. 2.

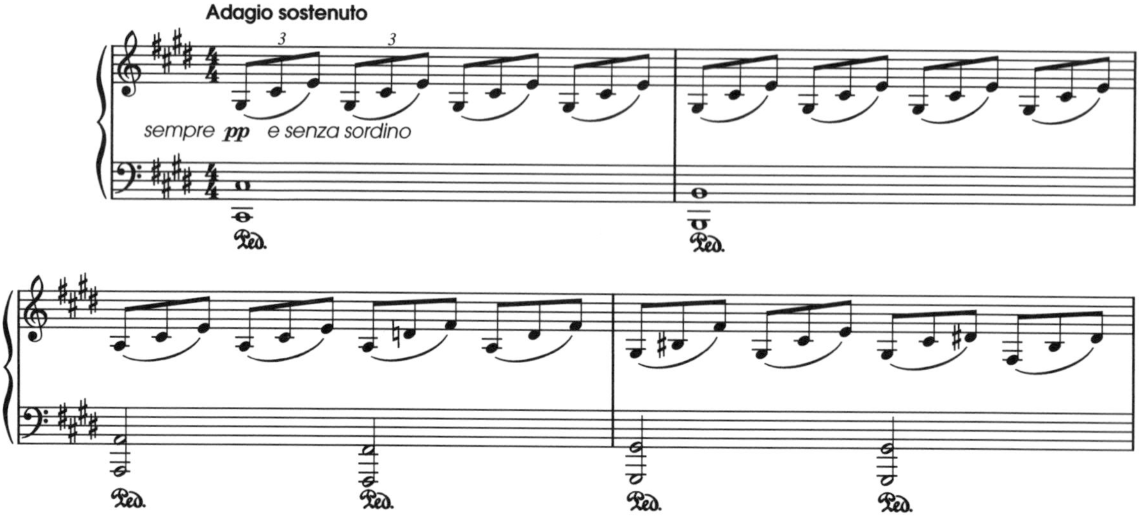

new music of figure 7.1, while derivative, nonetheless has a life characteristically its own. This form of style combination melds some of the parameters of one composer in a database with different parameters of another composer in the same database. One might further imagine the dynamics of Mahler combined with the rhythm of Debussy, the rules of Brahms, and so on. Future implementations of Alice will include opportunities for this form of style combination.

One of the more famous examples of such quotational grammar occurs in the music of Haydn, Beethoven, and Mahler. Figure 7.4a shows a trumpet passage from the middle of the fourth movement of Haydn's Military Symphony (No. 100), well known to both Beethoven and Mahler. This passage represents one possible origin of the now famous opening of Beethoven's fifth symphony (shown in figure 7.4b). Mahler, then, quotes Haydn at the beginning of his own fifth symphony and in so doing references both Haydn and Beethoven (see figure 7.4c). These references (and others, including the Wedding March from Mendelssohn's Midsummer Night's Dream) provide clues for the educated listener to help understand Mahler's work. With just a few notes, Mahler has pointed our ears toward the music of many composers and their resultant contexts. While the Experiments in

Figure 7.3   The beginning of the first prelude of Bach's *Well-Tempered Clavier.*

Figure 7.4   Melodic fragments (a) by Haydn in his *Military Symphony*, mvt. 2, mm. 153–156; (b) referenced by Beethoven, *Symphony No. 5* beginning and (c) Mahler, *Symphony No. 5* beginning.

Musical Intelligence program and Alice do not possess the necessary code to even approach this level of referencing, Alice can, by virtue of its capacity for positive reinforcement, produce at least shallow examples of the same type. The user, then, provides the context, while the program generates the surprising and possibly fortuitous juxtapositions.

I have recently created a number of composing programs that run independently but concurrently. Each of these programs began with a unique multi-composer database and algorithm but with identical interfaces. Each of these interfaces plays new compositions and requests user evaluation. This evaluation includes opinions about the just-heard work and which elements pleased or displeased the most. These elements include aspects of harmony, rhythm, dynamics, and so on. Each time listeners enter reactions to the hearing of a new work, the program alters relevant variables that then affect the way the program composes. Variables become incremented with successful works and decremented with unsuccessful works. In other words, these programs attempt to please their listeners as much as possible.

Successful works get downloaded, translated to notation, and attributed to the appropriate virtual composer. Many of these successful works are subsequently performed and some even recorded. All the resulting works are treated as if the virtual composer were a human composer. Each of these virtual composing programs has a human-like name. I have avoided revealing the machine-composed nature of the works of these virtual composers because I want their music performed and subsequently judged fairly, without the predisposition that knowledge of their origins typically engenders. It is my hope that one or more of these virtual composers may one day become important enough to enlist the kind of praise we reserve for human composers. My purpose is not to dilute contemporary music with impostors or prove that human composers are passé, which some of my critics have suggested is my intention, but to demonstrate that beauty and meaning can be found anywhere. If we but realize this, then our musical, artistic, and even our everyday lives can be elevated beyond the pedestrian to the remarkable.

Figure 7.5 shows the beginning of an early work by one of these virtual composers. In this simple chorale we see an almost childlike block-chord vocabulary. The music here is a far cry from the program's later attempts, one of which is shown in figure 7.6. While not precisely suited to my taste, this latter piece, written for string orchestra, demonstrates a more sophisticated rhythmic development and use of dissonance than that of figure 7.5. The association net that these virtual composers use to create musical works not

Figure 7.5 A first attempt by a virtual composer.

Figure 7.6 The beginning of a later work by the same virtual composer of figure 7.5.

only attempts to please, but also attempts to branch out and find new patterns and develop these patterns within the limitations imposed by the listener's aesthetic preferences.

■ PRELUDE TO THE FUTURE

I have been an avid amateur astronomer since my early childhood. I remember studying the pre-telescope astronomers and found my way through the sky much as they did, using the maze of mythologically named constellations. I had the advantage of using a simple Newtonian reflecting telescope on an equatorial mount to augment my eyes as I viewed the night skies. I have been astonished at the changes in astronomy since my nascent travails. Computer-driven telescopes, digital imaging, and radio astronomy have all added enormously to the arsenal of technology with which astronomers now study the heavens.

A few years ago I spoke with a well-known astronomer who researches certain types of globular clusters, specializing in one such cluster in a particular part of the sky. During our conversation I asked him in what constellation this cluster was located. He responded without hesitation or remorse that he had no idea. The parallel between his growing dependence on technology and mine seemed obvious to me. He did not mourn the loss of what had become rather useless information in the process of gaining more insights and control over his central subject.

Today, technology not only aides astronomers in their quest to learn more about the universe, but the instrumentation often actually makes the discoveries. A notable example is the Search for Extraterrestrial Intelligence (SETI). In one particular SETI project, receivers search over two million separate channels automatically, simultaneously, and continuously, for patterns that might signify the reception of a possibly deliberate signal. It is unlikely that a human could maintain the patience to monitor and detect patterns on a single channel for very long, no less two million. Of course, the ultimate determination of possible intelligence is made by humans, but the detail work falls to computers.

As of this writing, most composers already use some type of computer program for notation and/or performance prototyping. Such uses were almost unheard of a mere twenty years ago. As composers become more familiar with various computational tools, what previously was considered extraordinary will become routine. I believe that algorithmic composition will enjoy, in the twenty-first century, a similar routinization. After all, what rational composer would refuse to listen to an algorithmic attempt to solve a problem or prefer not to hear an extension of a just-composed passage of their music. Such composers can always make the ultimate decision as to whether to include algorithmic additions to their music. Even if these algorithmic attempts fail to please at *any* occasion, they might still inspire, if only by their failure to persuade.

Music composition means far more to me than notating quarter notes; it means designing and sculpting music at levels above the detail to which we so often bind ourselves. Of course, if you have read this trilogy or even just this current volume, then I am probably preaching to the converted. However, as we proceed into the new millennium, there will be many who doubt the propriety or even the ethics of algorithmic composition. These individuals will recite the canons of great composers of the past who worked with little but their quills and parchment. They will proclaim the weaknesses of those who must turn to technology for inspiration. Many, however, will understand that curiosity and experimentation are the wellsprings of inspiration and not its crutch.

Experiments in Musical Intelligence, SARA, and Alice pose challenges to our definitions of music, human versus machine creativity, and how we listen to music. Such challenges, it seems to me, are healthy and useful. Interestingly, a great many non-Western cultures do not share Western culture's conflicts over human versus machine expression. Indeed, animist cultures—those believing that all things have souls—find Western culture's preoccupation with human-centrist notions quite dumbfounding. I have performed Experiments in Musical Intelligence's works in Bali in Indonesia and on American Indian reservations in the United States and found the usual controversy that surrounds such performances completely lacking. For many of these people, curiosity and respect for all things, living and nonliving, far outweighs any antagonism toward machine creativity that one finds so often with Western sensibilities.

Programs such as Experiments in Musical Intelligence, SARA, and Alice also hold intriguing promise for solving difficult to resolve controversies. For example, authenticity, often determined without empirical evidence, can be revealed using computer programs with Alice-like analytical algorithms. Numbers and types of signatures, presence and placement of earmarks, repetitions of unifications, and so on, along with more standard forms of computational analysis, can help determine best guesses for composers of questionably attributed works. In some cases, it may even be possible to roughly date compositions, at least as far as general period of a composer's life, when other methods produce inconclusive results. Signatures can be especially useful in such research since signatures often show indications of evolution over time, as shown in figure 5.1 and related text in chapter 5.

Such approaches to corroborating attributions are not unique. The so-called Morelli method of identifying painters from their painting styles follows closely the analysis of signatures as a representation of musical style. Carlos Ginzburg, an Italian historian, writes of this approach:

> Museums, Morelli said, are full of wrongly-attributed paintings—indeed assigning them correctly is often very difficult, since often they are unsigned, or painted over, or in poor repair. So distinguishing copies from originals (though essential) is very hard. To do it, said Morelli, one should abandon the convention of concentrating on the most obvious characteristics of the paintings, for these could most easily be imitated—Perugino's central figures with eyes characteristically raised to heaven, or the smile of Leonardo's women, to take a couple of examples. Instead one should concentrate on minor details, especially those least significant in the style typical of the painter's own school: earlobes, fingernails, shapes of fingers and toes. So Morelli identified the ear (or whatever) peculiar to such masters as Botticelli and Cosmé Tura, such as would be found in originals but not in copies. Then, using this method, he made dozens of new attributions in some of the principal galleries of Europe. Some of them were sensational: the gallery in Dresden held a painting of a recumbent Venus believed to be a copy of Sassoferrato of a lost work by Titian, but Morelli identified it as one of the very few works definitely attributable to Giorgione. (Ginzburg 1980, p. 7)

Ginzburg also cites Freud, who writes,

> Long before I had any opportunity of hearing about psychoanalysis, I learnt that a Russian art-connoisseur, Ivan Lermolieff, had caused a revolution in the art galleries of Europe by questioning the authorship of many pictures, showing how to distinguish copies from originals with certainty, and constructing hypothetical artists for those works of art whose former authorship had been discredited. He achieved this by insisting that attention should be diverted from the general impression and main features of a picture, and by laying stress on the significance of minor details of things like the drawing of the fingernails, of the lobe of an ear, of halos and such unconsidered trifles which the copyist neglects to imitate and yet which every artist executes in his own characteristic way. . . . It seems to me that his method of inquiry is closely related to the technique of psychoanalysis. It, too, is accustomed to divine secret and concealed things from despised or unnoticed features, from the rubbish-heap, as it were, of our observations. (Ginzburg 1980, pp. 9–10)

As with authenticity, Alice-like programs may find use as arbiters of disputes involving plagiarism. Note or interval counting and text comparisons are often inconclusive in such matters. On the other hand, hierarchical pattern matching may corroborate sources in situations in which other tests prove inconclusive. Such matching can reveal fundamental patterns that otherwise may remain hidden or merely suspect as a result of aural recognition. Plagiarism may reach a whole new level of meaning, both colloquial and legal.

Much research still remains to be accomplished. First, signatures and earmarks are not the only attributes of musical style that pattern matching can reveal. For example, we have all had the sensation, when hearing a work for the first time, that the end is imminent. Discovery of what engenders that feeling, and the many other feelings that intuitively inspire composers and thus listeners, can greatly affect our analytical processes and ultimately our fundamental understanding of music. Second, programs such as Experiments in Musical Intelligence and Alice can, by using multiple-style databases, create entirely new musical styles. By virtue of their ability to produce a large number of works in a relatively short time, these programs can further establish full musical languages, even whole musical "cultures," that can inform us more concretely about the cultures we already have. Third, as computer programs such as Alice become more attuned to the tactile aspects of music, they should provide us with important revelations about the balance between the intellectual and physical in music that we appreciate. Ultimately, we should be able, with the aid of computer programs, to finesse more of the essence from the musical experience and, it is hoped, gain immeasurably from the conclusions that thus reveal themselves.

Now that we have reduced so many works to numbers, we should also be able to discover important facts about these works not known prior to the advent of computers. Alice's analysis program represents only one of many possible approaches that can reveal significant details about music. For example, proportions, figured in terms of a work's duration, ranges, textures, dynamics, and so on, should provide many useful facts to help our understanding. Semiotic analysis (Nattiez 1990), applications of set theory (Lewin 1987; Morris 1987), Rétian analysis (Réti 1962), and generative theories (Lerdahl and Jackendoff 1983), among others, should prosper using computer programs.

Alice and other Experiments in Musical Intelligence programs may extend even beyond musical boundaries. Researchers in the areas of architecture, economics, and stock market prediction have begun experimenting with Experiments in Musical Intelligence–like recombinative and signature-recognition techniques. Whether these non-musical disciplines will ultimately benefit from the use of these techniques is far from clear. However, the mere fact that such diverse areas of study have attempted to apply these techniques to their own fields suggests that both recombinancy and pattern matching for signatures have potential beyond the realm of algorithmic music composition. The process of abstraction and generalization of data into rules as utilized in Alice offers, I feel, further and possibly more interesting cross-disciplinary use. Rules are less data dependent and thus, by nature, more apt to have applications beyond a single discipline.

I believe that the computer programs I have described in this book and in the two previous books of this trilogy imitate, at least in part, many of the techniques that living composers use when creating. Recombinance, rules inheritance, signatures, earmarks, and so on, especially when used in various combinations, all have real-world parallels. Some ascribe human creativity to inspiration that they feel is beyond definition. I believe that such rhetoric represents a lack of logical thinking. Certainly it is no insult to humans, certainly not to me as a human, to imagine that human composers can find great delight in the complex and thoughtful interplay between themselves and the techniques used by Alice.

As discussed in chapter 1, most composers already use algorithms when composing, whether they use computers or not. These algorithms have ranged over the centuries from the isorhythms of medieval motets to the highly structured combinatorial constraints of the twentieth century. Achieving musical quality while adhering to the rigors of stylistic rules has long been the benchmark against which compositional worth is measured. Computer programs simply extend this model one step further. Unfortunately, many composers who work algorithmically suffer a fool's criticism for perceived inabilities to compose on their own. The future, I believe, will see algorithmic composers in a different light.

Many of these future composers will have been seduced into programming. For some this will seem initially distracting and apparently discontinuous with their creative processes. For me, however, programming has *become* composing, and I no longer think of the two as separate processes but rather as parts of a unified whole. I do not think that this experience is unique.

I recently received the following note: "I first became aware of you because of all of your work with the music generation software and your recording of that music. I found all that to be intriguing, but I do not generally deal with computer music so I was quite interested in your *normal* (that is, non-computer-generated) compositions." As wonderfully complimentary as this note is, it demonstrates a fundamental misunderstanding of the fact that my work with computers cannot be separated from my work as a non-computer composer; the two are synonymous.

As, I hope, it has been seen, collaborative computer programs such as Alice complement human composition. Humans intuit and recognize cultural symbols and contexts far beyond the current abilities of computer programs. Computers, on the other hand, can calculate, manipulate, and analyze raw data accurately at speeds far superior to humans. By sharing responsibilities, the best attributes of both humans and machines combine for what I believe will become the most inviting future that composers can imagine.

Ultimately, however, only time will reveal whether programs such as Experiments in Musical Intelligence, SARA, or Alice represent forerunners or will be doomed to obscurity. It seems a shame, however, if such obscurity were to result simply from a biased lack of appreciation of their output due to non-human origins. After all, we appreciate the beauty of many other non-human-created wonders, such as those found in nature. How tragic, for example, if the beauty of a rainbow, the grace of a sunset, or the wonder of the night-sky stars were ignored simply because they do not originate with human hands, because there are too many of them, or because they do not speak to the human condition. "What if a computer possessed the vision to develop, say, a new type of music or painting? To reject the innovation solely because it was produced by a computer would be to dismiss a host of intriguing and beautiful artifacts. We'd be the losers" (Boden 1996, p. 113).

In the three books of this trilogy, I have tried to show some of the ways in which we understand musical style, how the emulation of musical style often derives from recombining elements of former compositions, and how composers often work according to sets of prescribed rules or algorithms. I have been cautious in my estimation of the innovative worth of my ideas, preferring to believe that newness is often merely the embellishment of older, possibly less understood ideas. In all my work, there is a strong thread of reliance on extant music rather than the development of new formulas. Often this extant music consists of venerable old masterworks. Signatures, earmarks, unifications, and so on, while possibly newly applied terms to music, have existed in these traditional works long before my research began. Thus, while I appreciate whatever importance readers may ascribe to my ideas and code, I direct their attention specifically to the output—to the music created by Experiments in Musical Intelligence, SARA, and Alice—for it is in the understanding of that music, composed by a mix of human and machine, that there will come any true enlightenment that my work has to offer.

Ultimately, of course, my aim in these three volumes and in my ongoing research is to attempt to understand at least a part of what constitutes musical intelligence. For it is with that understanding that I hope to create more insightful and engaging music in league with my composing partner, Alice.

I believe that collaborative composition between humans and machine programs during the next millennium will become more personal and more personally meaningful. Ultimately, the differences between human and machine that so many feel so acutely will disappear, and the two will seem as one.

Bibliography

Agawu, V. Kofi. 1991. *Playing with Signs.* Princeton, N.J.: Princeton University Press.

Aiello, Rita, ed. 1994. *Musical Perceptions.* New York: Oxford University Press.

Ames, Charles. 1987. "Automated Composition in Retrospect: 1956–1986." *Leonardo* 20, no. 2: 169–85.

———. 1989. "The Markov Process as a Compositional Model: A Survey and Tutorial." *Leonardo* 22, no. 2: 175–87.

Anderson, Alan Ross, ed. 1964. *Minds and Machines.* Englewood Cliffs, N.J.: Prentice-Hall.

Anderson, John. 1973. *Human Associative Memory.* New York: John Wiley & Sons.

———. 1983. *The Architecture of Cognition.* Cambridge, Mass.: Harvard University Press.

Babbitt, Milton. 1961. "Set Structure as a Compositional Determinant." *Journal of Music Theory* 5, no. 2 (April): 72–94.

Bach, J. S. 1941. *371 Harmonized Chorales and 69 Chorale Melodies with Figured Bass.* Edited by Albert Riemenschneider. New York: G. Schirmer.

Bates, Madeleine. 1978. "The Theory and Practice of ATN Grammars." In *Natural Language Communication with Computers,* edited by Leonard Bolc. Berlin: Springer-Verlag, pp. 191–259.

Bel, Bernard. 1998. *Bol Processor.* ftp://ftp.hawaii.edu/mirrors/info-mac/gst/midi/.

Boden, Margaret. 1977. *Artificial Intelligence and Natural Man.* New York: Basic Books.

———. 1991. *The Creative Mind: Myths and Mechanisms.* New York: Basic Books.

———. 1996. "Artificial Genius." *Discover* 17, no. 10: 104–13.

Buxton, William. 1978. *Design Issues in the Foundation of a Computer-Based Tool for Music Composition.* Toronto: Computer Systems Research Group.

Cage, John. 1973. *Silence.* Middletown, Conn.: Wesleyan University Press.

Castine, Peter, Alexander Brinkman, and Craig Harris. 1990. "Contemporary Music Analysis Package (CMAP) for Macintosh." In *Proceedings of the International Computer Music Conference.* San Francisco: Computer Music Association, pp. 150–52.

Charniak, Eugene, and Drew McDermott. 1985. *Introduction to Artificial Intelligence.* Reading, Mass.: Addison-Wesley.

Cherubini, Luigi. 1837. *A Course of Counterpoint and Fugue.* Translated by J. A. Hamilton. London: R. Cocks and Company.

Common Music. 1998. http://ccrma-www.stanford.edu/CCRMA/Software/cm/cm.html.

Cooke, Deryck. 1959. *The Language of Music.* New York: Oxford University Press.

Cooper, Benjamin. 1978. *Some Mathematical Aspects of Music.* N.p.

Cope, David. 1987a. "Experiments in Music Intelligence." In *Proceedings of the International Computer Music Conference.* San Francisco: Computer Music Association, pp. 174–81.

———. 1987b. "An Expert System for Computer-Assisted Music Composition." *Computer Music Journal* 11, no. 4 (winter): 30–46.

———. 1988. "Music: The Universal Language." *Proceedings of the First Workshop on Artificial Intelligence and Music.* Minneapolis: AAAI-88, pp. 87–98.

———. 1990. "Pattern Matching as an Engine for the Computer Simulation of Musical Style." In *Proceedings of the International Computer Music Conference.* San Francisco: Computer Music Association, pp. 288–91.

———. 1991a. "Recombinant Music." *Computer* 24, no. 7 (July): 22–28.

———. 1991b. *Computers and Musical Style.* Madison, Wis.: A-R Editions.

———. 1992a. "Computer Modeling of Musical Intelligence in EMI." *Computer Music Journal* 16, no. 2 (summer): 69–83.

———. 1992b. "Algorithmic Composition [re]Defined." In *Proceedings of the International Computer Music Conference.* San Francisco: Computer Music Association: pp. 23–25.

———. 1994. *Bach by Design.* (recording) Baton Rouge, La.: Centaur Records.

———. 1996. *Experiments in Musical Intelligence.* Madison, Wis.: A-R Editions.

———. 1997a. "The Composer's Underscoring Environment: CUE." *Computer Music Journal* 21, no. 3 (fall): 20–37.

———. 1997b. *Classical Music Composed by Computer.* (recording) Baton Rouge, La.: Centaur Records.

———. 1997c. *Techniques of the Contemporary Composer.* New York: Schirmer Books.

Cope, David, and Galen Wilson. 1969. "An Interview with Pierre Boulez." *The Composer* 1, no. 2: 78–85.

Crumb, George. 1969. *Madrigals.* New York: Peters.

Dorian, Frederick. 1947. *The Musical Workshop.* New York: Harper and Brothers.

Dreyfus, Herbert. 1992. *What Computers Still Can't Do.* Cambridge: MIT Press.

Fodor, Jerry. 1983. *The Modularity of Mind.* Cambridge: MIT Press.

Forkel, Johann Nikolaus. [1802] 1920. *On Johann Sebastian Bach's Life, Genius and Works.* Translated by Charles Sanford Terry. Reprint, London: Constable.

Forte, Allen. 1973. *The Structure of Atonal Music.* New Haven, Conn.: Yale University Press.

Fux, Johann Joseph. 1943. *Steps to Parnassus: The Study of Counterpoint.* Translated and edited by Alfred Mann. New York: W. W. Norton.

Gjerdingen, Robert. 1988. *A Classic Turn of Phrase.* Philadelphia: University of Pennsylvania Press.

Ginzburg, Carlo. 1980. "Morelli, Freud and Sherlock Holmes: Clues and Scientific Method." *History Workshop* 9 (spring): 5–36.

Griesinger, Georg August. 1810. *Biographische Notizen ueber Joseph Haydn.* Leipzig: Breitkopf and Härtel.

Haugeland, John, ed. 1981. *Mind Design: Philosophy, Psychology, and Artificial Intelligence.* Cambridge: MIT Press.

Hindemith, Paul. 1942. *The Craft of Musical Composition.* Book 1. Translated by Arthur Mendel. New York: Associated Music Publishers.

Hofstadter, Douglas. 1979. *Gödel, Escher, Bach: an Eternal Golden Braid.* New York: Basic Books.

———. 1985. *Metamagical Themas: Questing for the Essence of Mind and Pattern.* New York: Basic Books.

———. 1995. *Fluid Concepts and Creative Analogies.* New York: Basic Books.

Hoppin, Richard H., ed. 1978. *Anthology of Medieval Music.* New York: W. W. Norton.

Ince, D. C., ed. 1992. *Collected Works of A. M. Turing.* Amsterdam: North-Holland.

Ives, Charles. 1965. *Symphony No. 4.* New York: Associated Music Publishers.

Jackendoff, Ray. 1992. *Languages of the Mind.* Cambridge: MIT Press.

Jefferson, G. 1949. "The Mind of Mechanical Man." *British Medical Journal* i:1105–1121.

Kasparov, Gary. 1996. "Kasparov Speaks." www.ibm.com.

Keene, Sonya. 1989. *Object-Oriented Programming in Common Lisp: A Programmer's Guide to CLOS.* New York: Addison-Wesley.

Kohonen, Teuvo. 1984. *Self-Organization and Associative Memory.* Berlin: Springer-Verlag.

Kurzweil, Raymond. 1990. *The Age of Intelligent Machines.* Cambridge: MIT Press.

Lerdahl, Fred, and Ray Jackendoff. 1983. *A Generative Theory of Tonal Music.* Cambridge: MIT Press.

Lester, Joel. 1989. *Analytic Approaches to Twentieth-Century Music.* New York: W. W. Norton.

———. 1993. "Composition Made Easy: Bontempi's *Nova methodus* of 1660." *Theoria* 7: 87–102.

Lewin, David. 1987. *Generalized Musical Intervals and Transformations*. New Haven, Conn.: Yale University Press.

Loy, Gareth. 1989. "Composing with Computers—a Survey of Some Compositional Formalisms and Music Programming Languages." In *Current Directions in Computer Music Research,* ed. Max Mathews and John Pierce. Cambridge: MIT Press, pp. 291–396.

Loy, Gareth, and Peter Todd. 1991. *Music and Connectionism*. Cambridge: MIT Press.

McCorduck, Pamela. 1979. *Machines Who Think*. San Francisco: Morgan Kaufmann.

MacKay, Donald. 1970. *Information, Mechanism and Meaning*. Cambridge: MIT Press.

Mackintosh, Nicholas. 1983. *Conditioning and Associative Learning*. New York: Oxford University Press.

Michalski, Ryszard. 1986. *Machine Learning: An Artificial Intelligence Approach*. San Francisco: Morgan Kaufmann.

Minsky, Marvin. 1968. "Why People Think Computers Can't." *AI Magazine,* fall, pp. 3–15.

Morovec, Hans. 1992. "Letter from Moravec to Penrose." In *Thinking Robots, an Aware Internet, and Cyberpunk Librarians,* edited by R. Bruce Miller and Milton T. Wolf. Chicago: Library and Information Technology Association.

Morris, Robert. 1987. *Composition with Pitch Classes: A Theory of Compositional Design*. New Haven, Conn.: Yale University Press.

Mozart, W. A. 1822. *Fundamente des General-Basses*. Edited by J. G. Siegmeyer. Berlin: Schneppelsche Buchhandlung.

———. 1978. *Piano Concertos: Nos. 17–22 in Full Score with Mozart's Cadenzas for Nos. 17–19*. New York: Dover Publications.

Nattiez, Jean–Jacques. 1990. *Music and Discourse: Toward a Semiology of Music*. Princeton, N.J.: Princeton University Press.

Newell, Allen. 1990. *Unified Theories of Cognition*. Cambridge, Mass.: Harvard University Press.

Nottebohm, Gustav. 1873. *Beethovens Studien*. Vol. 1. Leipzig: Rieter-Biedermann.

Nyman, Michael. 1974. *Experimental Music: Cage and Beyond.* New York: Schirmer Books.

Patchwork. 1998. http://www.ircam.fr/produits-real/logiciels/patchwork-e.html.

Perle, George. 1962. *Serial Composition and Atonality.* Berkeley: University of California Press.

Puckette, Millard. 1991. "Combining Event and Signal Processing in the MAX Graphical Programming Environment." *Computer Music Journal* 15, no. 3: 68–77.

Rahn, John. 1980. *Basic Atonal Theory.* New York: Longman.

Réti, Rudolph. 1962. *The Thematic Process in Music.* New York: Macmillan.

Rose, Steven. 1976. *The Conscious Brain.* New York: Vintage Books.

Rosen, Charles. 1971. *The Classical Style: Haydn, Mozart, Beethoven.* New York: Viking Press.

Rosen, Kenneth. 1988. *Elementary Number Theory and Its Applications.* 2nd ed. Reading, Mass.: Addison-Wesley.

Rowe, Robert. 1993. *Interactive Music Systems: Machine Listening and Composing.* Cambridge: MIT Press.

Schenker, Heinrich. 1933. *Five Analyses in Sketchform.* New York: David Mannes School of Music.

Sebeok, Thomas. 1977. *A Profusion of Signs.* Bloomington: Indiana University Press.

Sedgewick, Robert. 1983. *Algorithms.* Reading, Mass.: Addison-Wesley.

Smoliar, Stephen. 1994. "Computers Compose Music, But Do We Listen?" *Music Theory Online* 0/6.

Songworks. 1998. www.ars-nova.com.

Spitta, Philipp. 1899. *Johann Sebastian Bach.* Translated by Clara Bell and J. A. Fuller. London: Novello.

Steele, Guy L., Jr. 1990. *Common LISP: The Language.* 2nd ed. Cambridge, Mass.: Digital Equipment Corporation.

Straus, Joseph. 1990. *Introduction to Post-Tonal Theory.* Englewood Cliffs, N.J.: Prentice-Hall.

Stravinsky, Igor. 1960. *Poetics of Music in the Form of Six Lessons.* New York: Vintage Books.

Strunk, Oliver. 1998. *Source Readings in Music History.* Rev. ed. Edited by Robert P. Morgan. New York: W. W. Norton.

Symbolic Composer. 1997. http://www.xs4all.nl/~psto/.

Taube, Heinrich. 1991. "Common Music: A Music Composition Language in Common Lisp and CLOS." *Computer Music Journal* 15, no. 2: 21–32.

Turing, Alan M. 1950. "Computing Machinery and Intelligence." *Mind* 59, no. 236. Reprinted in *Mechanical Intelligence.* 1992. Edited by D. C. Ince. New York: North Holland, pp. 133–60.

Vantomme, Jason D. 1995. "David Cope: Bach by Design—Experiments in Musical Intelligence." *Computer Music Journal* 19, no. 3 (fall): 66–68.

Webern, Anton. 1928. *Symphony for Chamber Orchestra Op. 21.* Vienna: Universal.

Webster, Daniel. 1984. *Webster's New World Dictionary.* New York: Warner Books.

———. 1991. *Webster's College Dictionary.* New York: Random House.

Weizenbaum, Joseph. 1976. *Computer Power and Human Reason.* San Francisco: W. H. Freeman.

Winsor, Phil. 1987. *Computer-Assisted Music Composition.* Princeton, N.J.: Petrocelli Books.

Xenakis, Iannis. 1998. *Les Ateliers UPIC.* http://mitpress.mit.edu/e-journals/Computer-Music-Journal/Documents/UPIC.html.

Yavelow, Christopher. 1992. *Macworld Music and Sound Bible.* Foster City, Calif.: IDG Books.

———. 1997. *Music Is the Message.* http://www.xs4all.nl/~yavelow/docs/Media.html#MIM.

Appendix: The CD-ROM

■ GENERAL REQUIREMENTS

The programs on the CD-ROM accompanying this book require a Macintosh 680xx series computer or Power Macintosh with at least 32 megabytes of RAM (64 preferred) and a hard disk drive with at least 16 megabytes of free space. These programs also require Macintosh Common LISP (MCL) 4.x available from http://www.digitool. com. MCL must have a memory configuration (set in the Get-Info window of the application) of at least 20,000 kilobytes (20 megabytes). These programs were developed using System version 7.5, and while updates should pose no problem, this cannot be guaranteed.

■ MELODY PREDICTOR

The Melody Predictor is a small program that, when given the first three notes of a melodic line, predicts the next note. When correct, the program continues to predict on the basis of its answer. When wrong, the program retracts the incorrect note, accepts the correct note, and then predicts the next note and so on. Melody Predictor is discussed in chapter 1.

■ COMPOSE

Compose is a simple composing program which follows the concepts presented in chapter 1 for creating Bach-like chorales.

■ FUN

Fun is a simple application that provides its users with a colorful palette of mouse-controllable visual images. Users may select from a wide variety of drawing styles, including an algorithmic drawing program. Fun is discussed in chapter 2.

■ DÉJÀ VU

The *déjà vu* program recognizes images drawn in its input window. Users draw shapes using the computer's mouse. Déjà vu then analyzes and stores these figures in memory with a random name. When subsequent images resemble one already stored in memory, the program identifies the original image by name. Once one or more different figures have been stored in memory, déjà vu can create new images that have aspects of the originals recombined in what the program determines as logical sequences. Discussion regarding the déjà vu program can be found in chapter 2.

■ BACKTALK

BackTalk uses language (any language, including artificial languages) for its interface and attempts to respond appropriately to queries and statements by incorporating an association net in its algorithm. BackTalk is discussed in chapter 2.

■ TUTORIALS

The tutorials are small programs that, in combination with the relevant text, provide examples of particular aspects of Alice's operation. The tutorials include Inference Creativity, New Rules, Generalize Functions, Hierarchical Pattern Match, Density, Perform, and Loop.

■ ALICE

Alice (ALgorithmically Integrated Composing Environment) is an interactive computer program modeled on the Experiments in Musical Intelligence algorithm. Alice composes in the style of the music stored in its database while developing the musical materials of the work currently being composed. Alice can compose as much relevant music as desired either as connective material or as extensions.

Alice uses MidiShare, a free MIDI program available from GRAME in Lyon, France, and downloadable from http://www.grame.fr/english/Research/MidiShare.html. MidiShare is a real-time multi-tasking MIDI operating system especially designed for the development of musical applications. Alice also reads and writes MIDI-compatible files.

Alice also uses QuickTime™ which offers users the opportunity to perform music via the Macintosh speaker(s) using fifty or so different timbres. While substantially less effective than using a MIDI interface and associated equipment, QuickTime™ does not require additional software or hardware. Alice requires QuickTime™ version 4.0 or later. QuickTime™ is available from http://www. apple.com.

■ USING ALICE

The first window that appears after booting Alice asks users to decide whether to include the success/failure ratio of algorithmically composed music in its decision-making process. Most users select Yes from this window. Users wanting to test certain aspects of

Alice and/or to ignore the opportunities that collaboration presents can select No or Cancel.

Alice appears visually in two distinctly different regions. The desktop provides access to most of Alice's notation tools. The notation module, loading, editing, playback, and so on can be accessed from this palette. The menu provides Alice's analysis and composition-related programs.

The notation window that appears on selecting Notate from the main palette allows selection of pitches, durations, and dynamics. Pitches are entered by clicking directly on the piano keyboard that appears above the event scrolling table. Durations are selected by holding down various combinations of function keys while selecting pitches with an explanation of these combinations printed above the piano keyboard. Dynamic choices range from 0 (silence) to 100 (*fortissimo*). Various other buttons produce rests, opportunities for revision, and potential for playing the entered music whenever desired. Selecting Score produces a notated version of the music created in the notation window.

The Score palette appears to the right of the screen automatically whenever a Score page appears. The Score palette allows users to activate score-related activities, such as saving, playing, and printing.

The menu choices, as previously mentioned, provide access to the analysis and composition components of Alice. The Analysis menu item allows users to view the current work in a variety of formats. Most views provide information only (Graphs, Patterns, Maps, and Form). Some views—patterns—will affect composition. Signatures, once discovered from the Patterns selection, will be protected from recomposition by the algorithmic composing program.

Choosing Graphs from the Analysis menu item offers users the opportunity to view statistical analyses of their music that include pitch percentage (pie chart), scale (column chart), entrances (line graph), texture (dot chart), pitch/duration intersections (scatter chart), and channel use (bar chart). Note that clicking on any of the graphs creates an enlarged version of that graph for closer examination.

The Patterns menu item offers users the opportunity to view the results of pattern matching. Controllers allow users to determine the values of seven different variables during pattern matching. The Number Off scroll indicates how many notes will be allowed to diverge from a match. Amount Off indicates the amount, in half steps, of any error. The two limiters, High and Low, indicate the range of acceptable numbers of matches to create a signature. The Threshold scroll indicates the low limit of matches that must occur in each matched phrase.

The Map window allows users to visualize data in various manners, including SPEAC analyses of their music, a piano roll notation view, and a rules window. The Structure window provides a structural analyses view of chosen music.

The Variables windows allow users to change various performance attributes, such as tempo, key, and loudness, and to change the way in which the score appears on screen. The Compose menu item allows users to algorithmically extend new music by user-prescribed amounts.

The Listener window provides direct access to Alice's basic functions. The function find-it returns the location of a function's definition. Tracing the function as in (trace x) and then running the program shows the function in action. Volumes 1 and 2 of this trilogy (Cope 1991b, 1996) provide further information about LISP.

For a more complete description of Alice's menus, buttons, and windows, see the manual on the CD-ROM accompanying this book.

■ EXAMPLES FROM THE BOOK

These examples include recorded performances of many of the works presented in the text as well as MIDI performances of most of the music in the figures.

Index

Comprehensive Index

of

Computers and Musical Style (C)
Experiments in Musical Intelligence (E)
and The Algorithmic Composer (A)